Spectacle and Society in Livy's *History*

Spectacle and Society in Livy's *History*

Andrew Feldherr

UNIVERSITY OF CALIFORNIA PRESS

Berkeley / Los Angeles / London

University of California Press
Berkeley and Los Angeles, California
University of California Press, Ltd.
London, England

Library of Congress Cataloging-in-Publication Data
Feldherr, Andrew, 1963–.
Spectacle and society in Livy's history / Andrew Feldherr.
p. cm.
Includes bibliographical references and index.
ISBN 0-520-21026-3 (cloth: alk. paper).—ISBN 0-520-21027-1
(pbk.: alk paper)
1. Livy, Ab urbe condita. 2. Livy—Criticism and interpretation.
3. Rome—History. 4. Rome—Historiography. I. Title.
DG207.L583F45 1998
937—dc21 97-36872
CIP

Manufactured in the United States of America

9 8 7 6 5 4 3 2 1

The paper used in this publication meets the minimum requirements of American National Standard for Information Sciences—Permanence of Paper for Printed Library Materials, ANSI Z39.48-1984.

For Deborah

o mutis quoque piscibus
donatura cycni, si libeat, sonum . . .

Contents

Preface and Acknowledgments

In his own preface Livy professed not to care whether his personal fame remained "in darkness" provided that his work helped preserve the "memory of the deeds of the world's preeminent nation." Both aspects of his statement have proven prophetic in ways that not even the historian could have imagined. Because of the accidents of transmission, our knowledge of Roman history owes more to Livy than to any other single author. Although only a fraction of his work remains, 35 out of an original 142 books, his narrative is to the Early and Middle Roman Republic what Herodotus and Thucydides combined are to Fifth-Century Greece. Yet the quantity of irreplaceable historical data Livy provides has inevitably determined how his work has been read. The information he gives us is so valuable, and so tantalizing, that it has tended to overshadow, not only Livy's reputation as a historian, but also the very narrative through which it reaches us. We want to know where he gets his material, whether it is accurate, whether the image he creates of the Roman past matches the "facts." As often as not, Livy's own work has seemed to impede rather than facilitate a process of investigation that necessarily strives to move beyond it, to use the text as a means of recovering lost sources, and ultimately to gain access to the historical reality that all these texts describe. This book forms part of a now growing tradition of scholarship that aims to redress the balance by illuminating, if not Livy himself, then what he calls the "monument" he has produced.

For this reason, I start from a number of premises that may frustrate those whose interest in Livy is primarily as a "source." Above all, I resist imposing a dichotomy between the historical content of Livy's work and its literary form, treating the former as "raw material" and restricting the scope of literary investigation to the "shape" Livy gives what the preexisting historical tradition provided him with. I do this not because I deny that Livy's choices as a writer were in many ways conditioned by his source material and by the expectation that what a historian reports is in some senses true—although in what senses and within what limits is an issue that Livy, like any historian, will have to negotiate with his reader. Rather, given my goal of developing and exploring the significance of scenes and episodes in the context of Livy's narrative, questions of sources and of the historian's originality become less relevant than tracing connections that give his choices meaning within this larger whole. For my purposes, even if the "content" of Livy's narrative of an episode, even some of the language itself, derives from an earlier source, the task of interpreting its significance in Livy's text still remains.

If this effort to view Livy's text synchronically, rather than as but one stage in the development of the story of Rome's past, risks isolating his narrative from its historical context, my focus on the themes of vision and spectacle will locate the historian's work squarely within the political and cultural discourses of his own place and time. An interest in producing a vivid visual impression of the climactic moments of his narrative has always figured among the most striking features of Livy's style. But the use of visual display as a medium of persuasion and civic communication, both by the figures Livy describes and by the artists and political leaders of Augustan Rome, opens up broader possibilities for interpreting what might otherwise be regarded as a purely stylistic choice. By applying techniques and theories developed to analyze the social functions of political spectacle to the close reading of specific episodes, I offer here a new way of understanding the relationship between Livy's *History* as a literary work and the historical processes it describes. This in turn leads to a new awareness of how his representation of Rome's past could have acted upon the Augustan present. Ultimately, I hope to demonstrate that Livy's narrative claimed a much more dynamic role in shaping the civic and political life of his era than other models of literary reception might allow.

My selection of material requires one final caveat. Even the surviving portions of Livy's work are vast and were the product, quite possibly, of decades of labor. During this time, as David Levene has recently demonstrated, the historian's methods and indeed his conception of his task would necessarily have evolved. To treat all the visual elements even in a very restricted portion of Livy's narrative in the detail my project requires would exceed the scope of this book. Nor have I attempted to trace a chronological progression in Livy's use of such narrative devices. Rather, I have concentrated my analysis on a few episodes, mostly but not exclusively from the early books, that highlight processes of visual communication and their political impact. Among these scenes, however, are three whose placement in Livy's text, at the conclusion of his first book, first pentad, and first decade, marks them out as especially important: the rape of Lucretia and the expulsion of the Tarquins, Camillus's salvation of Rome after the Gallic invasion, and the defeat of the Samnites at the battle of Aquilonia. The significance and intrinsic interest of the passages I focus on will thus, I hope, compensate for the absence of a more comprehensive treatment.

• • •

The completion of what, measured in years if not in pages, has been a long project gives me at last the pleasure of thanking the many friends and scholars who have helped me along the way. Foremost among them are the three supervisors of the dissertation from which this book eventually grew, Erich Gruen, Tom Habinek, and Tom Rosenmeyer. Long after that dissertation was safely entombed in the archives of the University of California at Berkeley, their advice and encouragement have guided my labors, even as the examples of their own work reminded me how far I had to go. During the process of writing the book itself, drafts and the *disiecta membra* of drafts were generously read by T. J. Luce, Richard Saller, Chris Kraus, and Christian Wolff. Ann Vasaly and the anonymous reader for the University of California Press reviewed a preliminary version of this book with tremendous care and thoughtfulness, and their counsel has profoundly influenced its final form. I owe a special debt of gratitude to Jim Zetzel, who, in the middle of a busy semester, took the time to read the whole manuscript and offer decisive, yet tactful, recommendations for its improvement. It goes without saying that none of these scholars will approve everything that may meet their eyes in the following pages, but I hope that each will recognize ways in which his or her contributions have made this a better book than it would otherwise have been.

A fellowship from the American Academy at Rome provided the time and resources to develop the first stirrings of the ideas that led to this work. The process of converting these ideas into a dissertation was made much easier by a Lulu Blumberg Fellowship from the Classics Department at Berkeley. Mary Lamprech, Cindy Fulton, Peter Dreyer, and the University of California Press have helped me greatly in negotiating the final phases of converting manuscript to book.

Without the encouragement and tolerance of my wife, Deborah Steiner, this book would possibly never have been written; without her advice and editing, I am certain, it would never be read. The dedication expresses but a fraction of what I owe her.

Abbreviations

NOTE: The works of classical authors are cited using the abbreviations found in the *Oxford Classical Dictionary, 2d ed.*

AJP	*American Journal of Philology*
ANRW	*Aufstieg und Niedergang der römischen Welt* (Berlin, 1972–)
ARW	*Archiv für Religionswissenschaft*
ASNP	*Annali della Scuola normale superiore di Pisa, cl. di lettere e filosofia*
CA	*Classical Antiquity*
CB	*Classical Bulletin*
CISA	*Contributi dell'Istituto di storia antica dell'Università Cattolica del Sacro Cuore* (Milan: Casa editrice Vita e Pensiero)
CQ	*Classical Quarterly*
DK	*Die Fragmente der Vorsokratiker,* ed H. Diels and W. Kranz, 6th ed. (Dublin and Zurich, 1952), 3 vols.
FGrH	F. Jacoby, *Fragmente der griechischen Historiker* (1923–)
GIF	*Giornale italiano di filologia*
GR	*Greece and Rome*
GRBS	*Greek, Roman and Byzantine Studies*
HSCP	*Harvard Studies in Classical Philology*
ICS	*Illinois Classical Studies*
JRS	*Journal of Roman Studies*
LCM	*Liverpool Classical Monthly*
LEC	*Les Études classiques*

MAAR	*Memoirs of the American Academy in Rome*
MDAI (R)	*Mitteilungen des Deutschen Archäologischen Instituts (Römische Abteilung)*
MNIR	*Mededeelingen van het Nederlandsch historisch Instituut te Rome*
OLD	*Oxford Latin Dictionary,* ed P. G. W. Glare (Oxford, 1982)
PACA	*Proceedings of the African Classical Association*
PBSR	*Papers of the British School at Rome*
PCPS	*Proceeding of the Cambridge Philological Society*
PW	*Paulys Real-Encyclopädie der classischen Altertumswissenschaft,* ed. G. Wissowa et al. (Stuttgart, 1894–)
SPh	*Studies in Philology*
RA	*Revue archéologique*
REL	*Revue des études latines*
RhM	*Rheinisches Museum*
TAPA	*Transactions of the American Philological Association*

CHAPTER I

Vision and Authority in Livy's Narrative

In the preface to his *History of Rome,* Livy imagines his work as a visual artifact subject to the gaze of its readers:

hoc illud est praecipue in cognitione rerum salubre ac frugiferum, omnis te exempli documenta in inlustri posita monumento intueri; inde tibi tuaeque rei publicae quod imitere capias, inde foedum inceptu foedum exitu quod vites. [*praef.* 10]

This in particular is healthy and profitable in the knowledge of history, to behold specimens of every sort of example set forth in a conspicuous monument; thence you may choose which models to imitate for yourself and your *res publica,* and which, corrupt in their beginnings and corrupt in their outcomes, to avoid.

Livy here identifies the process of seeing as fundamental to the beneficial effects his narrative will exert upon his readers, both as individuals and as members of society.[1] The emphasis on visual communication resides not only in the concept of the monument itself, and in the verb *intueri,* "to look upon," but also in the adjective *inlustris,* both "transparent" and "luminous," which characterizes the *monumentum.* Besides serving as an object of contemplation, Livy's *monumentum* places itself at the center of a chain of visual images linking the past to the present and future; the conspicuous monument offers representations of past actions, which its viewers in turn reproduce through imitation—or obliterate from the public life of the state through avoidance.

1. For ancient theories of the utility of history and the rise of the concept of history as a source of patterns of behavior, see Fornara 1983: 104–20.

The visual language of the preface appears again in the brief introduction to the second pentad of the historian's narrative. In contrast to the subject matter of the first pentad, "things obscured by great age, as if seen from a distance" (6.1.2), the following books will present foreign and domestic events that are both "clearer and more certain" (6.1.3). Here Livy represents himself as literally exposing the events of the past to the gaze of the viewers (*exponentur*), and the intellectual process of learning about the past can be mapped directly onto the act of seeing. Things that are little known are "in the dark"; as information becomes more certain, events become "brighter." The metaphorical shift from temporal to spatial distance again reinforces the notion of the text itself as a monument.[2] As would be the case with a visual narrative, all past events coexist in the same space; it is simply that some are obscured because of the perspective from which they are viewed.[3] Finally, the references to vision are once more complemented by notions of civic renewal and by the imagery of agricultural fertility. The motion from darkness to light corresponds to the refoundation of the city after its destruction by the Gauls, an event through which the city is said to be "reborn from the roots, more prosperously [*laetius*] and more productively [*feracius*]." So, too, in the preface, the capacity it gives its audience to gaze on the events of the past is what makes history both health-giving (*salubre*) and fruitful (*frugiferum*).

What does it mean for the historian to define his work as something to be seen? How does the process of vision allow his text to accomplish the social aims that it sets out for itself? The desire to make the reader or

2. On this notion, see Kraus 1994b, esp. 269 f., and Jaeger 1993: 362–63. For this passage as an adaptation of Thuc. 1.1.3, see Kraus 1994a: 84 f.; for the importance of the device of presenting past events as a visible "landscape" in ancient technologies of memory, see Kraus (ibid.) and esp. Vasaly 1993: 100 ff.

3. The suggestion that the contents of the first pentad are not sufficiently clearly seen is itself somewhat problematic. Livy's account of the period down to the Gallic sack may not have achieved the gargantuan proportions reached either by the narratives of some of his predecessors (e.g., Cn. Gellius, who took 14 books to cover the same ground) or by Dionysius of Halicarnassus's. And in comparison to the scale of the later 137 books, the first 5, which describe the events of almost eight hundred years, may indeed seem cursory. Nevertheless, considering the general economy of Livy's narrative, especially his restraint in the composition of speeches, which make up so much of the bulk of Dionysius's work, his treatment of the period must be considered a comparatively full and detailed one, and the individual episodes of which the first pentad is composed are often represented in ways that make them fully accessible to the reader's gaze. For accounts of the growth of annalistic accounts of early Roman history in the second and first century B.C.E., see esp. Badian 1966: 11–36, Wiseman 1979: 16–26, 113–39, and Cornell 1986b.

hearer "see" the events described in a literary work appears to be above all a stylistic choice; and, as we shall consider, ancient rhetorical treatises discuss the effects of narrative in precisely these terms. But as Livy presents it in the preface, the importance of vision in the reception of his narrative relates particularly to his work's political function. By imitating the visual images that they behold in Livy's *monumentum,* his readers reproduce them in the conduct of their own public lives. This process offers one example of how vision provides the means through which the historian's literary representation of Rome's past becomes a part of the political life of the Republic in the present.[4] So, too, in portraying crucial events of the Roman past as spectacles, Livy assimilates the audience's experience of his text to their experience of the actual spectacles, such as sacrifices and public assemblies (*contiones*), through which so much of the political and religious life of the Roman state was conducted. By combining close readings of particular episodes with a consideration of the social functions of spectacle in Roman culture, this study aims to show how the narrative strategies that Livy adopts to engage the gaze of his audience allow his text to reproduce the political effects of the events described and thus to act upon the society of his own time.

The first section of this chapter discusses the literary background to Livy's description of his text as a visual image and shows how models of the political function of spectacle can enhance ancient conceptions of how a text "makes its audience see." The next task is to situate Livy's appropriation of the political potential of spectacle within the tradition of Roman historiography: among all the Latin literary genres, history particularly served as a means of communicating political influence, but, as his preface makes clear, Livy himself is unable to compete with other historians in terms of civic status. By making his narrative a visual image transparent to the cumulative power of the Roman past, therefore, Livy confers upon his text the social authority that he personally lacks. In addition to competing against other written histories, Livy's emphasis on vision as the medium through which his text communicates invites us to measure his work against other forms of public display that also presented a visible image of the Roman past. The third section of this chap-

4. For this purpose, I assume, with Kraus 1994a: 13–14, and Moles 1993: 152, that when Livy speaks of *tuae rei publicae* (*praef.* 10), he is using the second person rhetorically, to engage the reader and emphasize his involvement in the subject of the work. He is not imagining a hypothetical new republic to take the place of Rome after its final, inevitable collapse.

ter accordingly considers how Livy's interest in visual communication forms part of a larger discourse about the "power of images" in Augustan culture.

I. *Enargeia* and the Political Function of Spectacle

The visual language Livy uses to describe his work recurs with particular frequency in ancient estimations of the historian.[5] Quintilian, for example describes the "bright clarity" (*clarissimus candor* [*Inst.* 10.1.101]) of Livy's narrative, suggesting a style that is both revealing and brilliant. For Tacitus, Livy is "especially illustrious both for his style and his accuracy" (*eloquentiae ac fidei praeclarus in primis* [*Ann.* 4.34]).[6] While the similarity of these descriptions may suggest that Livy's ancient readers found visual terms especially applicable to the effect produced by his text, it also makes clear how deeply embedded visual imagery was in ancient conceptions of narrative style. Greek and Roman rhetorical treatises frequently described the aim of making an audience seem to see directly the events described in a literary work, a stylistic quality they designated as *enargeia* in Greek and in Latin as *demonstratio, illustratio, evidentia,* or *sub oculos subiectio* (placing beneath the eyes).[7] The author of the first century B.C.E. *Rhetorica ad Herrenium,* to take a Latin example, defines *demonstratio* as "the expression of things in words in such a way that an affair seems to be taking place and the subject to be present before the eyes."[8] The very adjective *inlustris,* which Livy uses to characterize the visual properties of his *monumentum,* appears as a technical term for a type of style that "sets events almost before the eyes" of its audience.[9] Indeed, Cicero had used a phrase very similar to Livy's concep-

5. The frequency with which Livy's work is described as bright or vivid was observed by A. D. Leeman (1961: 28; 1963: 192), who collects and discusses the examples.

6. The elder Seneca also employs the adjective *candidissimus* in describing Livy's moral judgment (*natura candidissimus omnium magnorum ingeniorum aestimator* [*Suas.* 6.22]).

7. Other Greek terms are ἔκφρασις and ὑποτύπωσις. For a history and definitions of the various terms, see Zanker 1981 and Vasaly 1993: 20 and 90, n. 4, with further bibliography.

8. *Rhet. ad Herr.* 4.68: *demonstratio est cum ita verbis res exprimitur ut geri negotium et res ante oculos esse videatur,*. Cf. also, e.g., Quint. *Inst.* 9.2.40, and Dion. Hal. *Lys.* 7.

9. Cic. *Part.* 20: *inlustris est autem oratio si et verba gravitate dilecta ponuntur et translata et supralata et ad nomen adiuncta et duplicata et idem significantia atque ab ipsa actione atque imitatione rerum non abhorrentia. est enim haec pars orationis quae rem constituat paene ante oculos.*

tion of an *inlustre monumentum* to describe the combination of pure Latinity and tasteful rhetorical ornamentation in Caesar's *Commentarii:* "It seems," he wrote, "as if he had placed a well-painted picture in a good light."[10]

As Cicero's comment suggests, the comparison of a literary narrative to a visual representation had a particular significance for historiography. In the next century, Plutarch would declare that the best historian is the one who makes his narrative an image, as though it were a painting.[11] Although Plutarch has Thucydides specifically in mind here, many very different historians share the aim of approximating the visual representation of events, and the particular contribution vision makes to the reception of a historical narrative could be understood in a variety of ways. Plutarch thinks primarily in terms of an emotional arousal of the readers that enables them to share in the experiences of those actually present at the events described, and also enhances their pleasure. For Polybius, by contrast, vision serves largely as a tool of intellectual investigation. His history presents the rise of Rome as a vast spectacle in which the entire network of causes governing human action stand revealed.[12] Finally, the issue of the credibility and accuracy of the historian's account of the past is also at stake in the conception of history as a "visible" reconstruction of events.[13] The ideal source of information was autopsy: Herodotus privileges seeing over hearing as a means of gathering data, and Thucydides promises to build his narrative from his own personal experiences and from the scrupulous investigation of the accounts of eyewitnesses.[14] In turn, he presents his own audience with a "clear vision" of both past and future.[15] This offer of a visual experience is all the more striking

10. Cic. *Brut.* 261: *tum videtur tamquam tabulas bene pictas collocare in bono lumine.*

11. Plut. *De glor. Ath.* 347A: καὶ τῶν ἱστορικῶν κράτιστος ὁ τὴν διήγησιν ὥσπερ γραφὴν πάθεσι καὶ προσώποις εἰδωλοποιήσας. For a fuller discussion of the aims of mimesis in historical writing, see Fornara 1983: 120–37, and Woodman 1988: 25–27.

12. For history as a spectacle, θεωρήμα, see 1.2.1. Thus universal history, like Polybius's, brings all the actions of fortune "under one and the same gaze" (1.4.1). By contrast, readers who think to gain an understanding of history from reading only accounts of particular events or places are likened to those who "beholding the scattered parts of a once living and beautiful body suppose they are sufficient witnesses of the energy and beauty of the living creature" (1.4.7). For the gaze in Polybius, see Davidson 1991.

13. See esp. the recent treatment of this subject by Miles 1995: 10 ff., to which this discussion is particularly indebted.

14. For Herodotus, cf. Candaules' comment on the reliability of the eyes (1.8); and see also 2.29, 2.99, 2.156, and 4.16, and Hartog 1988: 261 ff. For Thucydides, see 1.22.2, although in the next sentence he goes on to point out that even eyewitness accounts could be distorted by bias or faulty memory (on this topic, see Woodman 1988: 15–20).

15. 1.22.4: τῶν τε γενομένων τὸ σαφὲς σκοπεῖν καὶ τῶν μελλόντων.

since ancient texts were primarily intended to be heard rather than read.[16]

Thus Livy's description of his work as an *inlustre monumentum* not only reveals the influence of general rhetorical conceptions of style; it can also be read as a complex statement of purpose aligning his work with several strands of the historiographic tradition that employed vision as a model for the audience's reception of the historian's text. Like Polybius, who ties the intellectual value of his history to its inclusivity by promising to bring all aspects of Fortune's activity under the audience's gaze (ὑπὸ μίαν σύνοψιν, 1.4.1), Livy stresses the comprehensiveness of his *monumentum,* which not only covers the totality of Roman history, but contains every sort of *exemplum.* Livy's claim that his text constitutes a *monumentum* also serves to raise expectations about the accuracy of its depiction of the past, as Miles has recently shown. Earlier in the preface, Livy contrasts *monumenta,* which offer unmediated evidence about the past, with the oral transmission of information through "legends" (*fabulae*). The direct and reliable transmission of evidence through *monumenta* is associated with the genre of history itself, while *fabulae* are explicitly described as poetic.[17] Livy's presentation of his own text as a *monumentum,* therefore, not only locates his work squarely in the "accurate" tradition of historiography; it also seems to place the audience directly in the presence of those very pieces of visual evidence upon which his account is based. At first, Livy's suggestion of the transparency of his narrative seems comparable to Thucydides' use of vision to elide the levels of representation that separate his audience from the objective reality described and to place them in the position of the historian himself, evaluating the evidence before his own eyes.[18] There is, however, an important difference in Livy's statement, which diametrically reverses the Thucydidean model: it is not the events themselves that Livy sets before the eyes of his audience, but the visible traces that they have left behind. Since one of the meanings of *inlustris* is "transparent," a glimpse of actual events presumably does emerge from the *monumentum,* but the

16. A point emphasized in this context by Sacks 1981: 49 f., cited in Miles 1995: 10. As Woodman 1988: 26, notes, in Thucydides' case, "clear vision" contrasts with the merely auditory stimulations provided by "storytelling" (τὸ μυθῶδες).

17. See Miles 1995: 16–17, although he goes on to show how Livy continually undercuts the assertion that *monumenta* make possible objective knowledge about the past. For further implications of the opposition between history and *fabulae,* see ch. 5.

18. For another discussion of this passage as a Thucydidean allusion, see Moles 1993: 154.

intrusion of the *monumentum* shifts Livy's emphasis from the direct perception of the past to the tradition itself, the process of transmission through which the "vision" of the past is preserved.

When we turn from Livy's explicit reference to his work as a visible *monumentum* to his creation of visually explicit scenes in the narrative itself, the historian's use of "spectacular" effects has traditionally been attributed to a desire to stimulate the emotions of his audience. Far from enhancing the credibility of his narrative, elaborate set pieces like the account of the fall of Alba Longa (1.29) or of the scene in Rome following the announcement of Hannibal's victory at Lake Trasimene (21.7), in which Livy combines an attention to the precise sensory components of the scene, such as the dust cloud rising over Alba, with a description of the extreme emotions of those actually present, have suggested that Livy was drawn away from his historiographical duties by the "allure of dramatic techniques."[19] Since the pioneering treatment of Livy's narrative art by Erich Burck, this tendency in Livian narration has been derived from a movement, identified with certain Hellenistic historians, to claim for historiography the psychological effects that Aristotle associated with tragedy.[20] The key terms for characterizing these historians come from their rival Polybius, who insisted on a fundamental opposition between the purposes of tragedy and history: "Tragedy aims to astonish [ἐκπλῆξαι] and divert [ψυχαγωγῆσαι] its audience for the present through the most persuasive words; history to teach and persuade those who love wisdom for all time by means of true deeds and speeches" (Pol. 2.56.11).[21]

The very fact that Polybius's attempt to differentiate between tragedy and history occurs in an overtly polemical context actually points to the degree of similarity between the two genres (see ch. 5 below).[22] So, too, the deployment of vivid narrative to stimulate the emotions of the audience, which critics of the "tragic historians" define as mere sensationalism, is not incompatible with the evidentiary use of *enargeia* by Thucydides as a means of making the hearer a witness of events. Nor should we necessarily class vivid narration among the devices history uses to "delight" rather than "profit" its audience. The charge that a historian em-

19. The phrase is Walsh's (1961a: 170), although the sentiment does not do justice to his own nuanced and suggestive interpretation of Livy's use of such scenes.

20. Burck 1964b: 176–233.

21. See the discussion of this passage by Burck 1964b: 195.

22. This is the conclusion of Walbank's analysis of the relationship between history and tragedy (1960).

ploys narrative vividness meretriciously to enhance the immediate appeal of his own text rather than as a means of bringing his audience closer to the experience of real events seems, in the Hellenistic period at least, a commonplace of historical criticism. Thus Polybius compares Timaeus, whose knowledge of events derives exclusively from books, to a painter working only with "stuffed bags" and whose sketches therefore fail to convey the "vividness [ἐμφάσις] and actuality [ἐνεργεία] of real animals [τῶν ἀληθινῶν ζῴων]" (Pol. 12.25h.3). But Timaeus himself uses the same appeal to the reality of his own representations to differentiate his work from that of rhetoricians: "the difference between history and epideictic oratory is as great as the difference between real buildings and furniture and scene-painting" (Pol. 12.28a.1). In both cases, the production of mere images is contrasted with the ability to manifest the things themselves. The language of visual representation again forms a crucial part of history's claim to transcend the status of a secondhand reflection of reality. Nor is it impossible that some of the so-called tragic historians conceived of mimesis in these terms.[23] Even what might be regarded simply as an appeal to the audience's emotions can perhaps form a part of this process.[24] To return to Plutarch's account of Thucydidean ecphrases, the ability to reconstruct the emotional experience of the spectators is valued as a means of bridging the distance between present and past.

23. In the most explicit programmatic statement to survive from any of these writers (and again it is important not to assume that historians who are claimed to have used "tragic" effects constituted a school with shared aims), Duris of Samos seems to couple attention to "mimesis" with the desire to give pleasure, claiming that the historians Ephorus and Theopompus have an interest "neither in mimesis nor in pleasure in their narrative, but concern themselves only with the writing" (*FGrH* 76 F1). However, out of context, the statement is ambiguous and does not necessarily imply a connection between mimesis and pleasure as such. The point could be that they care neither for mimesis (i.e., the representation of "truth") nor for their readers' pleasure. In any case, Duris's essential criticism of these writers, that "they fall short of events" (τῶν γενομένων ἀπολείφθησαν) recalls the standard terms in which Timaeus and Polybius criticize their rivals. For an introduction to the scholarly controversies surrounding Duris, see Walbank 1960 and 1972: 34–38, and Fornara 1983: 124 ff., who offers a possibly overoptimistic reconstruction of Duris's theories of pleasure and historiography.

24. Cf., e.g., the link between *pathos* and "truth" in Diodorus Siculus's intriguing discussion of the separation between the actual experience of events and the mere imitation of them that a historical narrative can offer: "Whereas the experience (*pathos*) of events contains the truth, written history deprived of such an ability (viz. of representing disparate events simultaneously) merely imitates what happened and falls far short of the true arrangement" (Diod. 20.43.7). Although Diodorus explicitly denies the possibility that a narrative can ever bridge this gap, it is easy to imagine how the connection between truth and real experience could equally be used to justify a highly vivid style of writing that aims precisely to capture the *pathos* where truth resides.

This more positive evaluation of how the historian uses *enargeia*, not simply for "thrills and chills,"[25] but as part of a larger attempt to make his narrative approximate as nearly as possible the experience of "true" events has also been justly applied to Livy. Thus P. G. Walsh, for all that he regards Livy's vivid reconstruction of visual and emotional effects as "unscientific history," rightly interprets such descriptions as attempts "to communicate with the minds of the men of the past, to relive the mental and emotional experiences felt."[26] But consideration of a scene in which Livy himself comments on the power of visual communication suggests that in his case there is yet another dimension to *enargeia*'s capacity to make the past present. Within this passage, describing the *profectio* or ritual departure of the consul P. Licinius Crassus from Rome at the start of his campaign against Perseus of Macedon in 171 B.C.E., the process of vision plays a very precise role in communicating the social and political authority of the consul to the spectators and thus reinforcing the bond that links them to the collective power of the state:

It happened that during those days the consul P. Licinius, after offering vows on the Capitoline, set forth from the city in the costume of a general. This event is always [conducted] with great dignity and majesty, but it especially attracts eyes and minds when they follow a consul setting forth against a great enemy distinguished by his prowess or his fortune. For not only the performance of duty draws the crowd but also their enthusiasm for the spectacle, that they might see their leader, to whose power [*imperium*] and planning [*consilium*] they have entrusted the protection of the Republic itself. Then there enters their minds the reckoning of the contingencies of war, how uncertain is the outcome of fortune, and how impartial is Mars, what disasters have come about through the ignorance and rashness of the leaders, and yet what advantages have been the result of foresight and valor. What man knew which was the intellect and which the fortune of the consul they were sending to war? Would they soon see him in his triumph, ascend-

25. Walsh 1961a:170.

26. Ibid.:171. So, too, Burck stresses that Livy's "dramatization" of significant episodes has a functional, rather than purely aesthetic, motive, which Burck associates specifically with the historian's ethical aims. It provides a means both of highlighting moral and political themes and imparting them to the reader with the greatest possible power: "Die dramatische Form aber dient genau wie bei Vergil dazu, den Leser so stark als nur irgend möglich in den Kreis jenes psychischen Kräftespiels einzubeziehen und damit unter den Eindruck der grossen *virtutes* zu stellen, die Rom vorwärts gebracht haben und die er als lebendige Kräfte in seinem Volke wiedererwecken will" (Burck 1935 = 1967: 143). Cf. also the conclusion of Borzsák 1973: 66, that Livy uses the visualization of events as a means of emphasizing ethically significant moments in his narrative so that they stand out within the vast structure of his history.

ing the Capitolium with his victorious troops to the same gods from whom he was setting out, or would they offer this pleasure to their enemies?[27]

Livy's analysis of the spectators' reactions to the sight of their consul demonstrates how the act of watching modulates from the fulfillment of a "desire to see" (*studium spectaculi*) to a form of civic participation. The spectacle of the consul's *profectio* provides a representation of the Republic in microcosm; the consul's progress takes him from the physical and religious center of the city, the Capitolium, where he has just attempted through his prayers to engage the power of the gods on the state's behalf, to its periphery and the distant battlefield, where, if he has been successful, that power will manifest itself in Roman victory. The ability to cross these boundaries is not universally granted to all citizens; the consul's power to negotiate with the gods and to conduct battle both derive from his position as magistrate. The *profectio,* and its anticipated counterpart, the triumph, mark the moments when the bearer of this authority is present in the city itself. The citizens' glimpse of the consul provides their link to the totality of the state, the *summa res publica,* that he is entrusted to defend.

But the dimensions of the *summa res publica* are temporal as well as spatial. Together with providing a connection to the physical boundaries of the state and exposure to the divine sources of its collective power, the sight of the consul also brings the spectators into contact with Rome's past and future. The *profectio* prompts its audience to remember the entire series of past consuls who have marched off to war with the same ceremony, and to anticipate yet a further ceremony when the consul they now watch descending the Capitol will reascend it in his triumph. The prospect of past and future that emerges hardly constitutes a string of uninterrupted successes.[28] In both cases, the antithetical

27. 42.49.1–6: *Per hos forte dies P. Licinius consul, votis in Capitolio nuncupatis, paludatus ab urbe profectus est. Semper quidem ea res cum magna dignitate ac maiestate +quaeritur+; praecipue convertit oculos animosque cum ad magnum nobilemque aut virtute aut fortuna hostem euntem consulem prosequuntur. contrahit enim non officii modo cura, sed etiam studium spectaculi, ut videant ducem suum, cuius imperio consilioque summam rem publicam tuendam permiserunt. subit deinde cogitatio animos qui belli casus, quam incertus fortunae eventus communisque Mars belli sit; adversa secundaque, quae inscitia et temeritate ducum clades saepe acciderint, quae contra bona prudentia et virtus attulerit. quem scire mortalium utrius mentis utrius fortunae consulem ad bellum mittant? triumphantemne mox cum exercitu victore scandentem in Capitolium ad eosdem deos a quibus proficiscatur visuri, an hostibus eam praebituri laetitiam sint?*

28. Nor is Licinius Crassus himself an especially exemplary figure. Since he had once claimed as praetor that "he was prevented by solemn sacrifices from going to his province" (41.15.9), his acceptance of a proconsulship technically involves a violation of his vow (as his colleague and bitter rival, C. Cassius, points out [42.32.2–4]). Subsequently, he will be-

possibilities of victory and disaster are equally present. In fact, the sight of the consul opens up to the gaze of the citizens precisely the same vista that Livy's *monumentum* provides to the audience who gaze upon it, with its stark alternatives of *exempla* to be imitated and avoided. And as that *monumentum* provided for the reproduction of the *exempla* it contained, so the spectacle of the *profectio* situates itself precisely at the point where one of the past alternatives it recalls is on the verge of being actualized.

Livy's narrative of the *profectio* suggests that the actual civic spectacle produced by the consul provides both a parallel for and a complement to the historian's own task of representing the past. It is a parallel first in the sense that the spectators experience the *profectio* in terms that recall the readers' experience of Livy's history as constructed in the preface. But the expansion of the spectators' reflections to include the past and future generates a further sense of slippage between the two audiences. Livy's contemporary audience has a place in the same continuum of events recalled by the *profectio,* their own future and past can be mapped by the same series of victories and defeats—the very events that provide the annalistic structure of Livy's narrative. Both audiences therefore share an identical temporal perspective relative to the spectacle they observe, and this in turn further unites the experiences of reader and spectator.[29]

The complementary nature of the relationship between the historian and the consul mirrors the interaction between historical information and visual display within the narrative. It is the spectacle of the consul's appearance that serves as the cue for historical reflection. On the other hand, without the context provided by history, the spectacle itself would lose a good portion of its meaning. For the historian, the reproduction of the spectacle provides in the fullest sense the connection between past and present that I have suggested is a central function of the historian's use of *enargeia,* a chance to make his audience's experience approximate those of their ancestors. At the same time, the religious and political associations of the spectacle he describes enhance and amplify his own narrative; the historical content of the spectacle of the *profectio* provides a

---

have cruelly and illegally in the administration of Macedonia (*Per.* 43); see Levene 1993: 112–14. However, it is not Licinius's own conduct that is at issue here, but rather his capacity as consul to provide a visual link between the spectators and the gods, and concomitantly to recall by his actions the behavior of earlier magistrates.

29. For a more general discussion of how ecphrases in ancient historiography offer a "text within a text" and concomitantly generate a link between the internal spectator and the reader himself, see Walker 1993, esp. 361–63, who describes the device with the tools of modern narratology and shows that the idea is consistent with ancient literary theory.

model for how Livy's own representation of the past can be integrated into the center of the civic life of the actual state. But if the historian attempts to set his own representation of the past within the socially authoritative context of public spectacle, the passage simultaneously suggests that the significance of these spectacles depends in turn on just the kind of knowledge that his history provides.

Earlier in this section we noted a contrast between Thucydides' promise of "a clear view" of events and Livy's description of his work as an *inlustre monumentum.* Where the Greek historian suggests that his audience will be able to "see through" his text to the events it describes, in Livy's case the text itself, as a *monumentum,* also becomes an object of the audience's gaze. The analysis of Licinius Crassus's *profectio* helps clarify the significance of the distinction. The scene of the consul's departure forms part of the content of Livy's history; it is one of the *exempla* the monument contains, and indeed it possesses what the preface signals as a central characteristic of *exempla,* reproducibility. The regularity of the ritual pattern ensures that this scene will continue to be imitated. But at the same time, in its capacity to call to its audience's mind earlier events, it performs the function of a *monumentum.*[30] As this *exemplum* itself functions as a *monumentum,* so too Livy's *monumentum* itself can become an *exemplum.* The narrative takes its place in the sequence of public acts it records, eliding the boundaries between the representation and the event represented, and so becomes *inlustre* in a double sense: both "making the audience see," the rhetorical definition of an *inlustris* style, and brilliant or luminous in itself.[31]

• • •

If, as the previous analysis suggests, one effect of the visual element in Livy's narrative is to allow him to locate his representation of the past

30. On the basis of its etymology, Miles 1995: 17, defines *monumentum* as "something that makes one think." For the Romans, the fundamental task of a *monumentum* was to act as a prompt for memory, to remind; Varro defines the primary sense of *monimenta* (*sic*) as funeral markers or physical monuments, and from there extends the term to include "other things done or written for the sake of memory" (*cetera quae scripta aut facta memoriae causa* [*LL* 6.49, cited and discussed by Rouveret 1991: 3051–52]).

31. Cf. also the comments of Cizek 1992: 356, on this phenomenon: "Tite-Live attire son attention sur le fait que les bons et les mauvais exemples sont placés sur un monument illustre. . . . Il n'empêche que, à notre sens, ce monument est du même coup l'histoire de Rome et le récit qui en parle: l'ensemble des événements et le discours qui les concerne."

within the set of spectacles and performances through which the actual civic life of the state was conducted, then an examination of the role such spectacles played in Roman culture can in turn provide a new way of understanding the terms in which the historian's text communicated with its audience. By *spectacle* I refer not only to the shows of the circus and arena, the specialized definition of the Latin *spectaculum,* but to the external, visible component of all rituals and public acts. The English word *spectacle,* with its connotations of diversion and artificiality, and of the passivity of the spectator in the face of the production of the star or impresario, conveys neither the range of the phenomenon nor the reciprocity it involves. It was through seeing and being seen that the social relationships of watcher and watched were realized and the status of each defined.[32] The morning ritual of the Roman noble (*nobilis*) gives some sense of the omnipresence of spectacle as a way of articulating the structure of civic bonds in the Roman state. The senator's daily journey from his home to the Forum can be mapped as a series of spectacles before ever-widening audiences, each of which affirmed his place in a social hierarchy. Every morning, the *nobilis* would be greeted in the atrium of his home, whose decoration itself provided visible signs of his importance,[33] by his clients, dependents, and supporters, who could be distinguished among themselves by their costume and adornment. After the ritual greeting, this crowd would accompany its benefactor to the Forum; in the course of this journey, the number and status of these followers in turn provided an unmistakable marker of the extent of their patron's power and influence.[34]

As the importance of visual display as a mechanism for social communication at Rome has become the focus of increasing scholarly interest, new methodologies have challenged long standing assumptions about the political functions of spectacle. In his *Decline and Fall of the Roman Empire,* Edward Gibbon represented the difference in the quality of Roman political life under the tetrarchy from what it had been under Augustus by contrasting the relationship between power and public display under the two regimes:

Like the modesty affected by Augustus, the state maintained by Diocletian was a theatrical representation; but it must be confessed that of the two

32. The pervasiveness of spectacle and its importance as a medium of political participation in the Late Republic is thoroughly described by Nicolet 1980: 343–82, and also by Dupont 1985: 19–42.

33. See esp. Wallace-Hadrill 1994: 3–16.

34. For a fuller description of the *salutatio* and *adsectatio,* with testimonia, and a description of their political value, see Rouland 1979: 484–88.

comedies the former was of a much more liberal and manly character than the latter. It was the aim of the one to disguise, and the object of the other to display, the unbounded power which the emperors possessed over the Roman world.[35]

The notion that Augustus's public presentation of himself was crafted primarily to conceal the true nature of his power has a long heritage, going back ultimately to Tacitus's continual exposure of the incompatibility between the authoritarian nature of the principate and the Republican language in which it described itself. In the twentieth century, Sir Ronald Syme has treated Augustus's use of public display with a similar skepticism; triumphs and religious festivals are primarily instruments of propaganda, treated together with literature and the arts as a medium for "organizing public opinion."[36] This way of conceptualizing the function of visual display imposes a double separation between political power and its public manifestation. Not only do the visible signs produced by the emperor become a barrier between the public and the authority of its ruler, but spectacle itself is reduced to the status of an image, almost always opposed to the "realities" of power.

But it is also possible to assign a more important political role to spectacle than the dissemination of a prefabricated "public image." Clifford Geertz, for example, describes public displays where the ruler appears before his subjects as occasions on which political power is not so much "staged" as enacted. Geertz's formulation begins with the conception of charisma, developed by Weber and Shils, as the authority individuals acquire from their connection to "the active centers of the social order," the "loci of serious acts . . . where [a society's] leading ideas come together with its leading institutions to create an arena in which the events that most vitally affect its members' lives take place."[37] The public insignia adopted by the ruler, the visible manifestations of power that function to demarcate "the center as center," thus create rather than simply reflect his authority. As Geertz puts it, "the easy distinction between the trappings of rule and its substance become less sharp, even less real; what counts is the manner in which, a bit like mass and energy, they are transformed into each other."[38]

Geertz applied his model of the political efficacy of ceremony and ritual to the practices of a variety of societies in a variety of eras; the value

35. Gibbon, *Decline and Fall*, ch. 13. My attention was directed to this passage by its quotation in MacCormack 1981: 9.

36. Syme 1939: 459–75.

37. Geertz 1983: 122–23.

38. Ibid.: 124.

of such an approach for the interpretation of classical culture specifically was demonstrated by Price's treatment of the political role of imperial cult in Asia Minor. Price rejects attempts to use ritual as a tool for the recovery of the religious and political beliefs of its practitioners, a mere window to a set of opinions and dogma that make up the "realities" of ancient religion.[39] Rather, for Price, it is the observable and public dimensions of cult, "the processions and the temples, the sacrifices and the images," that constitute the primary aspect of ancient religious experience. Ritual becomes the space where "collective representations" of the power relations within a community are generated and expressed. "Ritual," as Price puts it, echoing a phrase of Geertz's, "is what there was."[40]

The spectacles surrounding the exercise of power in the Roman city itself, where political authority always possessed a strong religious component, particularly lend themselves to this kind of analysis. Not only were the political leaders of the state also in large measure responsible for the conduct of religious ceremonies, but the very person of the ruler possessed a capacity, very like the quality Geertz defines as charisma, to connect those who came in contact with them to the state's "active centers." Over fifty years ago, the Dutch scholar Hendrik Wagenvoort argued that the Romans conceptualized many kinds of power, from the might of the gods to the authority of a consul to the biological forces of reproduction, as physical substances transmitted through contact. While we need not accept Wagenvoort's reconstruction of a precise "physics of power" based on the literal translation of the terms in which the Romans describe authority[41]—much less his attempt to historicize the resulting set of beliefs by positing them as a primitive stratum of Roman religious thought—his work has immense value as a description of the language and rites through which authority was defined and as a demonstration of the symbolic importance of contact in Roman culture.

The ritual of the triumph provides a compelling demonstration of how Roman spectacles could create a context where power was at once recognized and manifested through the influence that the presence of the ruler exerted upon the community. The right of the returning commander to celebrate a triumph depended not only on the magnitude and importance of the victory but on the quality of the authority he possessed. A triumph could only be awarded to the person under whose *im-*

39. See Price 1984, esp. 7–11, 239–48.

40. Ibid.: 11.

41. See ibid.: 9, on the methodological issues involved in the "literal" approach to ritual.

perium and *auspicium* the victory had been won.[42] These two concepts, referring respectively to the ability to command citizens and to take the auspices, together define the power of the highest Roman magistrates. As a result of these criteria, every triumph necessarily becomes an affirmation, not just of the success won by a particular commander, but of the divine and human bases upon which supreme authority in the state rests.

The means by which the triumph expressed these meanings were primarily visual; the triumph was above all a spectacle. Polybius, in the earliest surviving description of triumphs, defines them for his Greek audience as ceremonies "through which the sight [*enargeia*] of the deeds that he has accomplished was set before the eyes of the citizens by the general."[43] A number of unmistakable visible markers distinguished the person of the general as he made his way from the *porta triumphalis,* a special gate opened only for the occasion of a triumph, to the temple of Jupiter on the Capitoline. He rode in a four-horse chariot, a laurel wreath on his head; his clothing, an embroidered tunic and purple toga, was of an opulence usually reserved for divine images. Most arrestingly, his face was painted a bright red, again a characteristic that made him resemble the statue of Jupiter Optimus Maximus toward which he was progressing.[44] But the visual distinctiveness of the triumphator had more than simply an honorific function. The similarities between the person of the triumphing general and the images of the gods suggest that the triumphator himself made immanent in his own person the divine power that underpinned his victory. Moreover, H. S. Versnel has argued that the triumphator's attributes, particularly his crown and the red color of his face, were particular signs of the magical qualities possessed by the triumphing general himself, and that the triumph as a whole provided the occasion on which the energy demonstrated by his victory, above all, his *felicitas,* was recirculated back into the state.[45]

42. This could, of course, be a controversial issue. Livy's own narrative, particularly of the period following the Second Punic War, is punctuated with accounts of debates about whether a commander who had petitioned for a triumph met the requisite criteria (see Phillips 1974). The various theories of modern scholars on the regulations for the awarding of a triumph are thoroughly analyzed by Versnel 1970: 164–95.

43. Pol. 6.15.8. Indeed, Polybius uses the same terms for the spectacular aspects of the procession that he elsewhere uses for the visual effects created by historical narratives; they, too, rely on *enargeia,* and set events before the eyes (ὑπὸ τὴν ὄψιν [1.4.1]) of the reader.

44. For a fuller discussion of the importance of the triumph as spectacle, see Nicolet 1980: 352–56.

45. See Versnel 1970, esp. 356–97. Versnel, whose work is heavily influenced by Wagenvoort's theory, argues that the influence exerted by the triumphator derives from his

This conception of the political function of spectacle at Rome has important implications for our understanding of the visual dimension of Livy's own work. In presenting a scene like the *profectio* of Licinius Crassus as a spectacle, where the responses of the contemporary spectators described in the narrative provide a model for the reader's experience of the event, and in the larger assertion in the preface that the entire history acts on its audience through being gazed upon, Livy not only draws a parallel between his text and the public spectacles of the state but makes his own narrative the medium through which these spectacles reach a new audience. If, far from being simple representations of political power, public spectacles were "what there was," in the sense that they provided the context where such power was constructed and actualized, then by linking his representation of the past to these visual manifestations of authority, Livy situates his work at the active center of Roman civic life.

But could a work of literature integrate itself so directly into the processes by which real political power was created? Two recent treatments of other Roman texts provide parallels for this phenomenon, and in both cases it is the technique of reproducing visual images through narrative that furnishes the link between the text and contemporary political discourse. Sabine MacCormack has argued that the increasing interest in ecphrasis among Late Roman panegyrists, at the expense of the catalogues of virtues prescribed by rhetoricians like Menander Rhetor, represents a convergence between the effects produced by oratory and by the visual elements of the ceremony in which it was performed. "Seen in this light, the panegyric will not merely reflect a visual and ceremonial setting . . . ; the panegyric will itself be seen to have drawn its cogency from the context in which it was delivered."[46] While MacCormack does not refer to Geertz, and her work predates Price's, she too describes the "splendid theatre" of Late Antique ceremonial not as simple propaganda but as providing the occasions where political concepts were articulated and negotiated.

But besides the distance in time, an important difference separates the practices of the panegyrists from that of Livy: the panegyrists' works were actually performed as a part of the vivid ceremonial whose visual component they attempt to appropriate; in the case of Livy's *History,* the "spectacles" with which he aligns his work are themselves the creations

own person and is not bestowed by the gods. But for our purposes the precise source of this influence is not an issue.

46. MacCormack 1981: 10.

of his narrative. The reader cannot necessarily raise his eyes from the text to find an immediate visual corollary for the scenes the historian describes. Ann Vasaly's study of Cicero's use of *enargeia* demonstrates how even purely literary representations of visual scenes can approximate the effect produced by direct visual contact.

Vasaly begins by analyzing the contribution setting or ambiance can make to the rhetorical effectiveness of a Ciceronian oration. By directing the gaze of his listeners to various aspects of the scene before them, Cicero uses the historical and cultural associations of these visual markers to influence and inspire his audience. Beyond furnishing another compelling example of the active role that visual contact played in Roman political life, Vasaly's analysis of Cicero's practice has a double relevance for an investigation of Livy's use of spectacle. First, she demonstrates that the "power of places" is as much made as found. The orator himself chooses among the various possible associations of a place or scene, and even generates new ones, to impose or construct the precise meaning he requires. In the same way, as we have already seen in the treatment of the *profectio,* Livy's narrative creates and shapes the significance of the scenes it describes, even as it uses them to enhance its own impact on its audience. Second, Vasaly shows that scenes and images produced solely through the orator's description of them can exercise the same rhetorical functions as the visual signs actually present before the audience's eyes. While the distinction between images produced by real objects and "empty appearances" was crucial in many ancient theories of perception, as Vasaly shows, the emotional effects of the two could be described in similar terms, especially by rhetoricians.[47] Indeed, Quintilian argues that the mind's ability to respond to the images of absent things as if they were present underlies the effectiveness of *enargeia,* "by which things seem not so much to be said as to be shown; and our emotions are aroused no differently than if we were actually present at an event."[48]

Like the festivals and performances of the Augustan regime, Livy's *History* too has been regarded as an epiphenomenon of Augustus's power. Syme treats Livy's work, together with those of Vergil and Horace, as propaganda for the new regime; it is described in the same terms, and in the same chapter, as the *princeps*'s use of public spectacles to organize

47. Vasaly 1993: 88–104.

48. Quint. *Inst.* 6.2.32: *quam non tam dicere videtur quam ostendere, et adfectus non aliter quam si rebus ipsis intersimus sequentur* (citation and translation in Vasaly 1993: 96).

public opinion.[49] Later, in a fuller treatment of the historian's attitudes, Syme conceded that Livy's support of the new regime was sincere and honestly come by, but still concludes by describing the historian as an "improving publicist."[50] Others have presented opposite opinions, some going so far as to describe Livy as a covert or indeed overt opponent of Augustus; but they still define the political dimension of Livy's history with reference to Augustus's power.[51] Augustus's authority in this view becomes the reality that Livy's text can only praise or blame, enhance or distort. More recently, scholars have emphasized the capacity of Livy's text to act autonomously.[52] As C. S. Kraus puts it, "the historian's project parallels/rivals Augustus' own building of a new Rome via (re)construction of its past. . . . But a shared project does not necessarily mean a lack of independence."[53] Livy's strategy of making his own work a "spectacle" provides a mechanism by which his text can participate directly in the political life of the state, not only through the meanings it conveys, but through the experience it makes available to its audience; it is thus that Livy's narrative generates its own *auctoritas*.

II. Political Authority and the Representation of the Past in the Latin Historiographic Tradition

In the preceding section, I argued that Livy treats the techniques of *enargeia* developed and described by Greek and Latin

49. Syme 1939: 459–75.

50. See Syme 1959, esp. 74–76.

51. As Deininger 1985: 265, puts it, "almost every theoretically conceivable position [sc. on the relationship between Livy and Augustus] seems to have found its advocates." Deininger himself offers a thorough survey of this range of views, from those who present Livy as an Augustan apologist to those for whom he is an arch-Republican (esp. Hoffmann 1954 and Petersen 1961). See also the survey in Phillips 1982: 1033 ff. Notable recent contributions to this debate are those of Badian 1993, who argues that Livy's lost account of Augustus's regime was far from flattering; Burck 1991, who defines Livy's relationship to the *princeps* as respectful and sympathetic, but distant, and Cizek 1992, who portrays Livy as a spirited Augustan polemicist, whose zeal for reform aimed at inspiring the *princeps* himself. See also the conclusions of Luce 1977: 290 ff., who recognizes a similarity in agenda between the historian and the *princeps,* but also points out significant differences between their outlooks. The positions of Kraus 1994a; Luce 1990, and Miles 1995 are discussed below.

52. Particularly important in this debate has been Luce's demonstration (1990) that Livy's narrative differs in many details from the *elogia* inscribed under the statues of great men in the Forum Augustum, a fact that makes it very difficult to claim that Livy's was somehow the official account of the Roman past.

53. Kraus 1994a: 8.

rhetoricians not as stylistic ends in themselves but as the means of integrating his work into the sequence of public acts it records. By reproducing the events of the past in a form that allows his audience to respond to them as spectators, the historian appropriates a crucial medium of political participation in Roman culture; in so doing, he makes his text not only "transparent" but "conspicuous," a monument to be gazed upon. This section seeks to show how Livy's use of vision to define the place of his text within the civic structures of the state relates to earlier Roman traditions governing the political functions of historical representations.

From its earliest introduction to Rome in the late third century B.C.E., writing history was a political activity. Many of the earliest Roman historians were important public figures in their own right. Fabius Pictor, the first Roman to practice the genre, belonged to one of the most ancient and distinguished families in the state, was the son and nephew of consuls, and himself served as a legate to the Delphic oracle during the Second Punic War.[54] M. Porcius Cato, whose *Origines* recounted the foundation legends of Rome and other Italian cities and gave an account of Roman history after 264, could not boast such ancestry, but his political career was among the most spectacular of his era. Indeed, of all the historians of the third and second century B.C.E., there is only one, L. Cassius Hemina, for whom we cannot attest senatorial status.[55] Not only did the historians themselves often occupy a high place in the political order, but their works too seem to have had largely political aims. In some cases, narratives of both early history and, particularly, recent events could provide a context for self-glorification and the denigration of rivals, which was also an important motive for the political activity of the Roman *nobilis*.[56] Nowhere is this aspect of early historiography glimpsed more clearly than in Cato's *Origines,* the last third of which describes recent

54. We know no other details about his political career. The fullest treatment of Fabius Pictor's role in the development of Roman historiography, together with complete biographical details is to be found in Frier 1979: 227–84. On Hemina, see Rawson 1976.

55. On the backgrounds of these historians, see especially the overviews of Badian 1966 and Frier 1979: 201–24, together with the fragments and testimonia in Peter 1914.

56. This aspect of early Latin historiography is, however, very controversial, as are most others, given the fragmentary nature of the evidence and the cumulative weight of scholarly interpretation it has had to bear. Badian 1966: 9, argues that Cato's *Origines* began a long tradition of using written history for personal political ends; Fornara 1983: 100–101, disagrees on the grounds that such strong expressions of bias would undermine the credibility of the authorial voice of the historian. Livy, in a passage that seems to refer specifically to the *Origines* seems to recognize a self-glorifying tendency when he refers to Cato as "someone who by no means takes anything away from his own praises" (*haud sane detrectator laudum suarum* [34.15.9]). (For the argument that the Catonian source Livy

events in which he himself played a major role and includes long excerpts from his often intensely partisan speeches.[57] On a somewhat higher level, the earliest extensive statement of purpose we possess by a Roman historian speaks explicitly of the value of history in terms of its ability to motivate political activity. Writing around the beginning of the first century B.C.E., Sempronius Asellio criticizes the genre of annalistic history on the grounds that mere records of events "can in no way inspire men to be readier to defend the *res publica* nor slower to act wrongly."[58]

The link between performing public actions and recording them emerges even more clearly if we broaden the focus of the discussion to include not only literary history but visual representations of *res gestae*.[59] As a means of preserving the memory of events—a *monumentum*—written history could be classed together with the paintings, statues, and dedications that created a visible record of a military victory or other

---

describes is in fact the *Origines* and not a speech *de consulatu suo,* see Astin 1978: 302–7.)

For some examples of how antiquarian scholarship was used to advance a contemporary political agenda among some of the early annalists, particularly in the Gracchan era, see Frier 1979, esp. 211–14.

57. Even the form of Cato's work can be related to his own political status as a *novus homo.* By emphasizing recent events at the expense of the early centuries of the republic, Cato not only increases his own role in his text but omits the series of ancestral accomplishments on which the status of many a noble rival might have depended. His unparalleled procedure of leaving out proper names of military leaders and referring to them only by the public office they held also contrasts strikingly with the idea that these offices served precisely to enhance the glory of one's clan. Astin 1978: 219, however, is skeptical about assigning a political motive to any of these features, given how little remains of the work. He also argues that Cato's omission, or compression, of the Early Republic resulted simply from a lack of information about this period in the second century and notes that Fabius's own treatment of the era was very brief (Dion. Hal. *Ant. Rom.* 1.6.2). For a full discussion of the evidence and a survey of scholarship on these issues, see Astin 1978: 211–39.

58. Semp. As. fr. 2 Peter: *Nam neque alacriores ad rem publicam defendundam neque segniores ad rem perperam faciundam annales libri commovere quicquam possent.* The influence of Polybian notions of the utility of history, which have been attributed to direct personal influence—we know that Asellio was military tribune at the siege of Numantia, where Polybius was also present—does not diminish the significance of the sentiment. For an interesting appraisal of Asellio as a historian who wrote "with the *auctoritas* of [a] statesm[a]n hoping to explain, anticipate, and forestall political disaster," see Fornara 1983: 69–70.

Speculation on the motives of Cato himself is hampered by the inconclusive nature of the fragments of the preface, but some have suggested an interest in fostering a sense of the development of the Roman state as the product of collective endeavor on the part of all its citizens, rather than the creation of a few outstanding individuals. For discussion of this theory and bibliography, see Astin 1978: 225–26.

59. Recent work on Livy and other Latin historians demonstrates a renewed interest in the relationship between written history and physical memorials. Wiseman 1986 has shown the importance of such monuments as a source of information for literary historians. Both Miles 1995: 9–74, and Jaeger 1993, with different emphases, have analyzed how Livy ultimately distinguishes his own work from these physical monuments and casts doubt on the

great deed.[60] The complementarity between these two kinds of *monumenta,* and their shared hortatory function, emerges especially in Pliny the Elder's idealized reconstruction of the home of the Republican noble:

In the atria of our ancestors, these were the things to be wondered at: not the statues of foreign craftsmen; not bronzes or marbles; wax models of faces were set out, each on its own stand, so that there might be likenesses [*imagines*] to accompany the funeral of members of the clan, and whenever anyone died, every member of the family [*totus familiae populus*] who had ever existed was at hand [*aderat*]. The genealogical connections between them were traced by lines that interconnected the painted images. The libraries were filled with books and the records of what they had done in their magistracies [*monumentis rerum in magistratu gestarum*]. Outside the house and around the threshold were other images of those great souls [*animorum ingentium imagines*]; mounted *spolia* taken from the enemy. These it was forbidden for any buyer to take down: The houses continued to triumph even when their owners had changed. This was a great incentive; since the houses every day would reproach an unwarlike owner that he had entered into the triumph of another. [*HN* 35.6–7]

In this passage, the written histories that record ancestral accomplishments function together with the funerary masks in the atrium and the *spolia* mounted on the façade of the house to form an integrated system of signs. The shared purpose of all these species of *monumenta* is to make manifest the "great spirits" of the home's previous noble inhabitants. The cumulative "presence" of these ancestors cannot but inspire anyone who enters into the physical space defined by this network of images[61] to emulate their conduct himself. This space in turn takes the form of a perpetual public spectacle, first a funeral, then a triumph, into which the observer is inevitably drawn. The alternative to equaling the achievements memorialized in the *domus* is to enter into someone else's triumph, presumably in the role of captive.

Like the memorials in the *domus,* the memorials erected in temples

---

veracity and value of the record they provide. Also very relevant to this topic are Kraus 1994b and Rouveret 1991's analysis of Tacitus's use of *monumenta.*

60. The point is made and emphasized by Wiseman 1986: 89, who cites in support Cato's description of the rewards that came to Leonidas after Thermopylae (*propter eius virtutes omnis Graecia gloriam atque gratiam praecipuam claritudinis inclitissimae decoravere monumentis: signis, statuis, elogiis, historiis, aliisque rebus* [Cato *Orig.* fr. 83 Peter]) and Festus's definition of *monumentum* (*quicquid ob memoriam alicuius factum est, ut fana, porticus, scripta et carmina* [Festus 123L]).

61. For *imagines* as a physical presence, see Dupont 1989.

and public spaces throughout the city also reveal the functional interdependence between performing great acts and recording them. In the very process of preserving the memory of *res gestae,* these memorials themselves influenced the course of public life in ways similar to the effects produced by written history. Such *monumenta* were by no means the anonymously bestowed gifts of a grateful nation; on the contrary, as the means by which accomplishments were converted into status, the creation and preservation of memorials belonged to the men whose deeds they celebrated. The personal connection of the performer of an action to the artifacts that recorded or, in the case of historical painting, represented it was stressed in a number of ways.[62] Most dramatically, after the fall of Carthage in 146 B.C.E., L. Hostilius Mancinus put on display in the Forum a painted map of the captured city containing depictions of the final battles, in which he himself was prominently shown as the first to break through the enemy defenses. What is more, Mancinus personally stood beside the painting to explain and describe his role in events, thus earning the enmity of the commanding general, Scipio Aemilianus, but winning himself a consulate.[63]

The continuities between act and commemoration also emerge from the dedicatory inscriptions that accompanied these memorials, which record not only the victory but the erection of the *monumentum* itself. In 174 B.C.E., the consul Ti. Sempronius Gracchus, after earning a triumph for his campaigns in Sardinia, erected a map of that island in the temple of Mater Matuta, on which were painted representations of his battles. The following inscription appeared with the map:

62. The first Roman painter that Pliny records was Fabius Pictor, "the Painter," both a member of the high nobility and a direct ancestor of that other Fabius Pictor who was the first Roman to produce written history. We do not know the subjects of his paintings, which decorated the temple of Salus erected in 311 B.C.E.; nor do we know of any particular accomplishment of Fabius himself worthy of such commemoration—the most likely subject is perhaps the battle of Bovianum at which the temple was vowed by the consul C. Junius Bubulcus, who later as dictator dedicated the temple itself. Even if this painting did not record his own deeds, Fabius advertised his connection with the work by signing his name to it. As Rouveret 1987–89: 107, argues, it is mistaken to regard Pictor's interest in painting merely as an eccentric pastime, much less as a source of scandal (so also Gruen 1992: 92). Valerius Maximus (8.14.6) may use the episode to exemplify the pursuit of glory by unworthy means, but nothing in his account suggests that it was so viewed at the time. On the contrary, Pliny suggests precisely that when it was first introduced at Rome, painting was regarded as an honorable activity (*HN* 35.19). For more on Fabius, see Frier 1979: 227–28. An attempt to establish a closer connection between the works of the two Fabii Pictores is made by Mazzarino 1966: 2.102–4.

63. Pliny *HN* 35.23. For the political importance of such displays, see esp. Hölscher 1980 and Rouveret 1986–9.

Under the *imperium* and *auspicium* of Tiberius Sempronius Gracchus, consul, the legion and army of the Roman people subdued Sardinia. In this province, over eighty thousand of the enemy were killed or captured. When the public business was successfully [*felicissime*] conducted, the [allies] freed, and the tributes restored, he brought back the army safe, intact, and full of booty. Triumphing for the second time, he entered the city of Rome. On account of this, he dedicated this map to Jupiter.[64]

While the final phrase was a customary way of closing such a dedication,[65] the self-referentiality of the inscription has a further significance. The creation of the artifact that places the successful campaign on display itself becomes a part of the action it records, the necessary final element in Sempronius's command. And indeed this narrative pattern is not just a feature of inscriptions; Livy himself often structures accounts of a military campaign in a similar way, concluding with the erection of the memorial or dedication of the *spolia* that record it.[66]

The larger political function of these *monumenta* was connected in turn with the public spectacles through which the artifacts themselves entered the civic space of the *res publica.* In Pliny's description of the *domus,* the hortatory power of *imagines* derived in great part from their ability to reproduce in the mind of the viewer the public ceremonies in which they were displayed, funerals and triumphs. And it is as visual components of these two rituals that most works of art were initially represented at Rome.[67] Not only maps and narrative tableaux, but *spolia,* which also constituted *monumenta,* and foreign works of art that came to Rome as booty formed a part of the spectacle of the triumph.

This triumphal context in turn allows us to define more precisely how

64. 41.28.8–10: *Ti. Semproni Gracchi imperio auspicioque legio exercitusque populi Romani Sardiniam subegit. In ea provincia hostium caesa aut capta supra octoginta milia. Re publica felicissime gesta atque liberatis[. . .]vectigalibus restitutis, exercitum salvum atque incolumem plenissimum praeda domum reportavit; iterum triumphans in urbem Romam rediit. cuius rei ergo hanc tabulam donum Iovi dedit.*

65. On the various kinds of significance conveyed by the public proclamation of the dedication itself, see Veyne 1983.

66. Cf., e.g., 6.29.8–9, 8.14.12, 10.46.7 (see ch. 2, sec. I), and 24.16.19 (see below, sec. III).

67. Cf. the comments of Rouveret 1986–89: 108: "Aux débuts de l'art pictural à Rome . . . on peut mettre en lumière un véritable système qui repose sur un va-et-vient entre les édifices publics, temples et forum, la *domus* aristocratique et le tombeau. La peinture y intervient à double titre, comme peinture historique et comme peinture des portraits, ces deux types de peinture ont leur pendant dans deux cérémonies complémentaires: le triomphe et les funérailles."

Even if it is not the case that every such artifact originally appeared in one of these rituals—the map displayed by Mancinus, for example, almost certainly did not form a part of Scipio Aemilanus's triumph—nevertheless it is fair to say, as the Pliny passage shows, that such visual *monumenta* acted upon the citizen body and to perceive that their civic function extended beyond the communication of information about distant events and even the simple glorification of the triumphator. Zinserling, whose treatment of the development of Roman historical painting especially emphasizes its connection to the triumph, argues from the connotations of *enargeia,* the word Polybius uses to describe the visual aspect of triumphs, that these representations themselves exerted a "dynamic" influence on the citizens who beheld them. The paintings presented in a triumph inspired their audiences not just through their informational content but through the exposure they offered to the authority and power of the triumphator.[68] This notion accords well with Versnel's later interpretation of the triumph as a whole as an opportunity for the city itself to reappropriate the good fortune (*felicitas*) manifested in the military success the triumphator had won. As we saw in the previous section, the other visual components of the triumph, the red face of the general and his distinctive attire, even as they made the person of the general more conspicuous, also served both to denote and to project the *imperium* and *auspicium* responsible for the successes that the triumph celebrated. Within this framework, the representation of the act celebrated by the triumph, through various forms of *monumenta,* comes to approximate as closely as possible the direct experience of the act itself;[69] both are effects of the power born by the triumphator.[70]

---

the triumph could provide an idealized context for such displays and established the semiotic framework through which they could be interpreted. On the effect of Mancinus's painting, see Zinserling 1960: 410.

68. Zinserling 1960: 414.

69. And the use of Hellenistic artistic devices in the Late Republic to enhance the capacity of such *monumenta* to convey a sense of the presence of the acts they represented offers a close parallel to Livy's deployment of *enargeia* as a technique of literary description. Hölscher 1980: 353–55, describes how the paintings displayed in triumphs acquired an increasingly sensational character during the early first century B.C.E. The representations focused on violent scenes of extreme emotion—for example, the death of Mithridates surrounded by maidens who had chosen to die with him (App. *Mith.* 117; see Zinserling 1960: 411). Hellenistic descriptive devices, like personification, allowed the artist to emphasize the physical circumstances in which actions took place, as in the painting of Mithridates besieged displayed in Pompey's triumph of 61 B.C.E., where both night and silence were personified. These applications of the language of Hellenistic narrative art—which Hölscher compares explicitly to the innovations of "tragic" historians—served to increase the Roman audience's emotional engagement in the scenes depicted. It was precisely the resulting sense that the scene was taking place before the eyes of the viewers that allowed these images, within the context of the triumph, to communicate the power and energy of the triumphator. Narrative forms and techniques borrowed from the Greeks operated within a distinctively Roman system of visual communication.

70. The notion that these representations must "become" the acts they represent is

• • •

This analysis of the functions of physical *monumenta* has demonstrated the extent to which placing *res gestae* on display itself constituted a component of political activity within the civic traditions of Rome. But if these visual monuments share with written accounts of the past the aim of intervening directly in public events, the terms in which the two forms of *monumenta* participated in political discourse were necessarily quite different. In the case of physical memorials, their very locations, in temples and public spaces and on the façades of the houses of the politically powerful, established their connections to the centers of civic life. Inscriptions recording the dedicator's name and office and the occasion of the dedication further enhanced both a monument's authenticity and its authority. But the links that bound literary records of the past to the realm of public acts were more varied and usually less direct. As we have seen, often they derived from the public status of the historian himself. Or the written text itself could approximate the form of an actual inscription. The genre of annalistic history, where the material was arranged by year and the presentation of each year's events began with a quasi-formulaic record of officeholders and religious prodigies, furnishes an example.[71] Although this way of organizing a historical narrative was in fact greatly influenced by Greek models of local history,[72] its success at Rome derived from its perceived connections to the *tabulae dealbatae,* the official records of events, which the Pontifex Maximus

---

also stressed by Zinserling 1960: 416: "Diese Identifizierung von bildlicher Darstellung und tatsächlichen Geschehen ist . . . nicht nur als äusserliche Gleichsetzung zu verstehen, sondern ist tiefer begründet, hat gewissermassen noch etwas vom magischen Identitätszauber längst vergangener Kulturepochen an sich." As in the case of Wagenvoort's work, the significance of Zinserling's observations does not depend upon his explanation of this phenomenon as the legacy of an earlier belief in sympathetic magic.

71. In what follows I do not mean to imply that historians chose the annalistic form as a way of compensating for their own lack of status. The earliest annalists, especially Piso (cos. 133), were among the most powerful men to write history at Rome, and Frier 1979: 278–79, has shown the extent to which the stylistic choices made by Fabius Pictor were designed to bolster further the authority of his narrative. Badian's (1966: 15, 18) assertion that in the early first century, *annales* became "socially degraded" by being taken up by men from outside the aristocracy has been called into question by Cornell 1986b: 78–79, who points out that there is no factual basis for the assumption that these annalists were not members of the Senate.

72. The extent of the early annalists' debt to Greek models is a controversial subject. Frier 1979: 206, who provides the crucial bibliography, describes the first local histories of Rome as "clearly the offshoot of Hellenistic local history." Fornara 1983: 27, stresses the indigenous elements of the genre but concedes that "Greek influence seems undeniable."

would present on whitewashed wooden boards affixed to his official residence.[73]

Perhaps it is no coincidence that their personal circumstances compelled both Livy and Sallust, whom later generations would regard as the classic pair of Latin historians to set against Herodotus and Thucydides, to define the political aspect of their historiographic work in particularly innovative ways. Sallust had, like many earlier historians, been a magistrate and a member of the Senate, a high degree of political success for someone whose origins were in the local aristocracy of an Italian municipium. But his public life had been marred by scandal; he was expelled from the Senate in 50 B.C.E. and later, after the restoration of his career by Caesar, prosecuted for extorting money from the African province he governed on a scale remarkable even by Late Republican standards. What is more, while charges of corruption and sexual excess formed an almost inescapable component of Roman political invective, they were particularly at odds with the emphasis on morality in Sallust's works.[74]

Faced with this discrepancy between his public reputation and the authorial persona he wished to adopt, Sallust chose in writing his histories neither to emphasize his actual status as a senator nor, perhaps more surprisingly, simply to remove himself from his narrative as completely as his model, Thucydides, had. On the contrary, in both the *Catiline* and the *Jugurtha,* Sallust draws attention to his withdrawal from politics and makes his abandonment of a political career itself a function of the larger decline of Roman public morality that his works chronicle: "As a young man, I, like many others, was at first borne by my zeal into public life; but many things were against me there. In place of modesty, restraint, and virtue, there flourished shamelessness, bribery, and greed" (*Cat.* 3.3).[75]

73. For the *tabula dealbata* and the process by which the belief in an official pontifical chronicle came into being at Rome, see Frier 1979, esp. 107–60, 161–78. On the patriotic connotations of the annalistic form, see Frier 1979: 201 ff., and Ginsburg 1981: 96–100.

74. Cf. the accusation made by his contemporary and fellow Sabine, Varro, and its elaboration by Aulus Gellius (*NA* 17.18): "*M. Varro, in litteris atque vita fide homo multa et gravis . . . C. Sallustium scriptorem seriae illius et severae orationis, in cuius historia notiones censorias fieri atque exerceri videmus, in adulterio deprehensum ab Annio Milone loris bene caesum dicit et, cum dedisset pecuniam, dimissum.*" For a full catalogue and discussion of the attacks made on Sallust's character, see Syme 1964: 274–79.

75. Cf. the more extensive rejection of a political career at *Iug.* 3.1. Sallust's comments have perhaps led scholars to overestimate the extent of his political debacle. He was, it must be remembered, not expelled from the Senate after the extortion charge, and, as Syme 1964: 39 points out, had gone about as far in politics as he was likely to. Thus Sallust seems deliberately to have overemphasized his lack of success.

Correspondingly, Sallust constructs a complex picture of the public aspect of his work as a historian by at once playing on and revising the traditional association between performing and recording *res gestae*. In the *Catiline*, Sallust presents the writing of history as an alternative means of accomplishing the aims that originally drove him into politics, the attainment of glory (even if less accrues to the historian than to the one whose deeds he narrates) and service to the *res publica*.[76] Indeed, he makes clear in the *Jugurtha* that given the current state of the Republic, the activities of the historian, even if they are regarded as a leisure activity, are the better way of benefiting the state.[77] Through a parallel inversion, Sallust sets the public utility of his own history against the system of preserving memory through *imagines* that was the prerogative of the nobility. It is the memory of deeds, such as the historian provides, not the wax image itself, that inspires.[78]

If Sallust attained high rank and then withdrew from it, the little we know of Livy's life suggests that his social status was largely that of an outsider; he certainly never held public office.[79] Like many other literary figures of his era, he was born not in Rome but in one of the large cities of northern Italy, in Livy's case, Padua. And, unlike Vergil, Livy seems to have maintained strong connections to his native city and to have died in the place where he was born.[80] Nor do we hear of a network of friends

76. On the praise and (unequal) glory that attends the historian, cf. *Cat.* 3.1: *et qui fecere et qui facta aliorum scripsere multi laudantur.*

77. *Iug.* 4.4: "If [those who accuse me of inactivity] will reflect on the times in which I gained office, and what sort of men were unable to attain this, and what species of men afterwards entered the Senate, they will surely consider that I changed my intentions rightly and not out of cowardice, and that more benefit will come to the Republic from what I do in my leisure [*otio*] than from the others' performance of their duty [*negotio*]."

78. *Iug.* 4.5–6.

79. For recent overviews of the evidence about Livy's life and the range of interpretations that has been applied to it, see Kraus 1994a: 1–9, and Badian 1993. The importance of Livy's ties to his native city are stressed by Leeman 1961 and especially Bonjour 1975b: 185, 249–50. Within the *History,* Paduan local traditions emerge particularly at 1.1 (see ch. 4), and also in the description of the failed Laconian expedition into Paduan territory at 10.2.4–15, commemorated both by the spoils displayed at Padua in the temple of Juno, and by the annual reenactment of a naval battle. More strikingly, in his account of the battle of Pharsalus, Livy includes a description of the prodigies that announced the battle at Padua, and were interpreted by a local augur, C. Cornelius, who was a relative of the historian's (Plut. *Caes.* 47). The consequences of Livy's status as an outsider for the aims and methods of his historical work are analyzed by Miles 1995: 47 ff. (see below, n. 88).

80. Jerome *a. A.* 2033. The extent of Livy's life that was spent in Rome has been a subject of debate. Walsh 1961a:4–5, suggests that he could only have worked in Rome and moved there before beginning his *History.* By contrast, Lundström, cited in Leeman 1961: 35–36, uses Livy's errors of geographical detail and failure to consult available public

in the capital of the sort that helped other Augustan literary figures to establish themselves. What *gloria* Livy possessed seems to have come exclusively from his literary accomplishments, as did his connection with the imperial family, which dated from relatively late in his career.[81]

Two pieces of anecdotal evidence further suggest how Livy's lack of status could affect the reception of his history. A passage in the *Suda*, an encyclopedic work of the Byzantine period, preserves an anecdote contrasting Livy's public readings with those of another historian, named Cornutus. Cornutus was both wealthy and without an heir; therefore his *recitationes* were always crowded. "Only a few men came to hear Livy; but they were those who found some profit in the beauty of his soul and in the eloquence of his teaching."[82] In this highly moralized tale, the imbalance of wealth that makes it impossible for Livy to win a wide audience is corrected by the workings of time, so that in the end it is Livy who possesses the "great name," while Cornutus is forgotten.[83] Another, better-known anecdote again shows how Livy's personal background could be used against his work. Asinius Pollio, himself a writer of history, who like Cato and several of the other early historians had also reached the highest political office, claimed to detect "a Paduan quality" (*patavinitas*) in Livy's work. What exactly Pollio meant by this "Paduanity" is uncertain.[84] The contexts in which the remark is reported

---

records as a sign that he visited the capital very rarely. This view has won the support both of Leeman and of Mensching 1986, but see Badian 1993: 31–32 n. 12.

81. Augustus's joking description of Livy as a *Pompeianus* (Tac. *Ann.* 4.34.3) was based on the historian's account of the civil wars, which he did not reach until bk. 109. Similarly, Livy's encouragement of the future emperor Claudius's historiographic activities (Suet. *Claud.* 41.1) dates from comparatively late in his career; Claudius was only born in 10 B.C.E. As Badian 1993: 14–16, points out, the language with which Livy reports Augustus's assertions about A. Cornelius Cossus (4.20.7) cannot be used to establish that there was any personal connection between the *princeps* and the historian in the early twenties B.C.E.

82. *τοῦ γε μὴν Λιβίου ὀλίγους*[sc. *ἀκούειν*]*ἀλλὰ ὧν τι ὄφελος ἦν καὶ ἐν κάλλει ψυχῆς καὶ ἐν εὐγλωττίᾳ παιδείας*, *Suda*, s.v. *Κορνοῦτος*.

83. For a full discussion of this passage and an attempt to identify the Cornutus referred to, see Cichorius 1922: 261–69. It seems difficult to use this passage as evidence of Livy's "initial success among the best people" (Badian 1993: 16), since the point of the anecdote is precisely Livy's failure to win a reputation immediately. The audience described here is unlikely to have included Augustus himself, as Cichorius suggests; rather, perhaps, we should think primarily of the leading rhetoricians with whom we know Livy to have been connected (see Kraus 1994a: 9 ff.).

84. Quint. *Inst.* 1.5.56, 8.1.3. The scholarship on the precise implications of this charge is vast. A recent survey will be found in Flobert 1981, who argues that the primary thrust of the term lies in its contrast not to *latinitas* but to *urbanitas* (so, in a different sense, Syme 1959: 76). For the significance of this anecdote and a further analysis of the kinds of pressures to which Livy's background may have subjected him, see Miles 1995: 51.

suggest that the reference is primarily to style and diction, but it is striking that Quintilian himself, our source for Pollio's criticism, cannot give any examples of irregularities and indeed seems somewhat surprised by the charge against a man whose eloquence he particularly admired.[85] Whatever its precise reference, the point of the comment is clearly to disparage Livy precisely on grounds of his origins.[86]

In a manner analogous to Sallust, although with very different aims, Livy deliberately raises the issue of his personal status in the preface of his history and uses it as a means of crafting the place his work will occupy in the *res publica*. In the second sentence, Livy implicitly draws attention to the fact that he is not a member of the nobility and at the same time rejects the traditional aristocratic motive of glory as the reward he expects for his labor:

However it turns out [i.e., whatever the ultimate success of his work], it will still be a pleasure that I myself, as befits a man [*pro virili parte*], took some thought for the memory of the deeds of the chief people of the earth, and if, in such a great crowd of writers, my fame will be in darkness, let me be consoled by the nobility and greatness of those who block out my name.[87]

Correspondingly, he adopts a posture of extreme diffidence in the face of the task he has set for himself. Not only does he not know whether his work will be worth the trouble of producing it; if he did know, he would not dare to say (*nec, si sciam, dicere ausim, praef.* 1).[88] But while emphasizing his personal lack of status and confidence in comparison to other historians, Livy simultaneously magnifies both the scope and the authoritative character of the work he intends to produce. In the first sentence, he defines his goal as "producing a complete record of the

85. Cf. Quint. *Inst.* 8.1.3: *et in Tito Livio, mirae facundiae viro, putat inesse Pollio Asinius quandam patavinitatem.*

86. Pollio was himself born outside of Rome, in the Abruzzi, and so is vulnerable to the same charge; cf. Syme 1959: 54: "No evidence survives of a retort from Patavium to Teate of the Marrucini."

87. *Praef.* 3.

88. Miles 1995: 52–53, interprets the attitude expressed here as one of deference to the social status of potential rivals, coupled with the suggestion that status alone will not make their historical works better than his. This accords with Miles's overall argument that what had been regarded as the historian's cavalier attitude to evidence in fact forms part of a larger historiographic strategy, which is in turn the product of Livy's particular social position (Miles 1995: 74): "In exposing the impossibility of wresting factual certainty from Roman tradition, it allows Livy to undercut attempts to monopolize the past without confronting directly the aristocracy whose position was served by that monopoly." Livy's attempt to make his *History* a *monumentum,* as I discuss below, is consistent with this view of the historian's aims and represents one other means by which Livy's work can compete with the historical productions of *nobiles* and the emperor himself.

deeds of the Roman people." The verb Livy uses here, *perscribere,* is also used of the written record that gave legitimacy to senatorial decrees.[89] Next, he proclaims that "it will be a pleasure . . . to have taken thought for the memory of the deeds of the chief people of the earth." "To take thought for," *consuluisse,* is the act of a senator, a magistrate, a *consul.* These opening sentences raise precisely the question of how it is possible for someone in Livy's position to act in this fashion.

The solution, I suggest, involves Livy's definition of his work as a *monumentum.* Livy's rejection of personal glory[90] has been regarded as disingenuous[91]—his eventual success would come to exemplify how much glory could in fact be won from literature[92]—but the modesty of his personal ambitions serves rather as a foil to the claims he makes for his work itself. The very phrase he uses for this history, *inlustre monumentum,* precisely answers the imagery of the earlier passage.[93] Livy's fame is in darkness, but his work is *inlustre,* not only in the light but also a source of light. His own *nomen,* as if on an inscription, is blocked out by those of others; his text, though, is not just an inscription but a whole *monumentum.* The effect of this strategy is to distinguish as much as possible the significance and public role of the work itself from his own personal status. The preface begins with a flurry of self-reference.[94] But as the text proceeds, the author himself progressively retreats from it, rarely

89. Cf., e.g., Caes. *BC* 4.1.6, Cic. *Cat.* 3.13, and, for the procedure, Mommsen 1889: 3.1003 ff. The verb helps define Livy's place in the historiographic tradition as well: Sempronius Asellio in his preface (fr. 1 Peter) contrasts authors of *historiae,* who attempt to narrate events thoroughly (*perscribere*) with the producers of *annales,* which merely recount "what was done and in what year it happened."

90. He will begin a later book with the claim that he "has achieved enough glory for himself and could cease to write, but his restless mind is nourished by work" (Pliny *HN, praef.* 16). Pliny approves his rejection of personal glory as a motive for writing, but suggests that he ought to have persevered for the sake of the glory of the Roman people rather than a desire for occupation.

91. So Cizek 1992: 361–62, who explains Livy's sentiments toward his fellow historians as motivated by a sort of "Judas complex" combining jealousy with timidity. Moles 1993: 145 f., also speaks of Livy's irony here, but then goes on to stress the "positive claims" made by the sentence.

92. Cf. the story told by Pliny the Younger (*Ep.* 2.3.8) about the man who, "inspired by Livy's name and *gloria,*" came all the way from Cadiz to Rome just to see the historian and, when he had seen him, immediately went back.

93. A similar opposition between the diffidence of the author and the "monumentality" of his endeavor is developed with different emphases by Wheeldon 1989: 55–59, who claims that the growth in confidence of the authorial voice and the shaping of a confused and daunting mass of material into a monument provide a model for the process that Livy's reader undergoes in approaching the work.

94. Wheeldon 1989: 56, notes that "of the fourteen instances of the first person verb [sc. in the preface], six come in the first sentence."

intruding his own persona into the narrative.[95] And it is precisely the visual qualities of the *monumentum* that facilitate this procedure—by deflecting the reader's gaze toward the monument of his work, he renders his own person invisible and increasingly irrelevant as the *monumentum* itself exerts its beneficial effects on the audience.

The implications of Livy's creation of his narrative as a *monumentum* can be clarified by contrasting it with the relationship Sallust establishes between his text and the visual monuments of the aristocracy in the *Jugurtha*. As we have seen, Sallust decouples the hortatory and mnemonic function of such images from the physical presence of the images themselves. It is memory that is important, not the wax statue; this distinction relates in turn to his exaltation of the soul, the image of which survives in the record of deeds, over the body, depicted by the physical *imago*. Far from linking his narrative to the power of visual images, therefore, Sallust suggests that his own history offers a superior way of preserving memory.[96] Livy's technique is the opposite. His text becomes the monument, providing at once a record of deeds and the visual sign through which memory is made present.

It was precisely the intrinsic connection between the representation of an act and the act itself, upon which a consul or dictator would rely for the effectiveness of his visual displays, that made it possible for Livy, who possessed no such authority in his own right, to produce his *inlustre monumentum*. Just as the visual image of a Roman victory displayed at a triumph could simulate for its audience the effect of being present at the battle itself, and thus expose them to the power and authority manifested in the triumphator's victory, so Livy's own representations of the past, whatever his personal position, gained authority from the very deeds and men they depict. His text summons up, like the visual signs Pliny describes in the homes of the *nobiles*, "images of great souls."

Two examples will demonstrate how Livy's narrative can approximate, and indeed substitute for, physical *monumenta* actually erected by victorious generals. The first involves the inscribed map of Sardinia erected by Ti. Sempronius Gracchus in 174 B.C.E. As I argued before, the inscription on the map portrays the erection of the dedication itself

95. In reference to this phenomenon, Henderson 1989: 77, describes Livy as "the Palinurus of the Augustan mission."

96. Correspondingly, perhaps, Sallust's link to the authority of the past comes not so much through the visual recreation of scenes—in which his work is notably poorer than that of Livy or Tacitus (although cf. *Cat.* 58–61, the account of Catiline's final battle, and *Hist.* 2 fr. 70)—as through his style, which emulates the language of the past, and above all that of Cato the Elder.

as a product of the consul's authority, extending and completing the act of conquest it records by placing it on display. This inscription is quoted directly in Livy's text (41.28.8–10)—and indeed only survives because Livy transmits it; Livy's narrative thus continues the same sequence of actions and provides the means by which the consul's representation of his victory reaches an even wider audience.

In the previous case, it was through the words of the inscription that Livy established the connection between the consul's *monumentum* and his narrative. Another example shows how he achieves the same effect through the vivid description of the scene depicted on the monument. In 214 B.C.E., another Ti. Sempronius Gracchus led an army consisting of slaves into battle against a Carthaginian force at Beneventum. Attempting to inspire his troops to fight bravely, he promised freedom to anyone who brought back the severed head of an enemy. The device almost caused disaster; the attack bogged down as the slaves labored to decapitate their victims and "heads took the place of swords" (24.15.5) in the hands of his bravest troops. Gracchus immediately ordered the soldiers to drop the heads they were carrying, and victory swiftly followed. The consul rewarded his troops for their valor by granting them liberty en masse, and the proclamation was celebrated by a feast at Beneventum:

> At the gates all the Beneventans had poured out in a crowd; they greeted the soldiers, congratulated them, and offered them hospitality. Preparations for banqueting were present in the forecourt of each home. They invited the soldiers to participate and begged Gracchus to allow the soldiers to feast with them. Gracchus agreed on condition that the feasts were held in public, outside the doors of the houses. Everything was carried outside. The former slaves celebrated clad in their caps of liberty or with their heads wreathed in white wool, some reclining, others standing, who both served and ate. The event was deemed significant enough that Gracchus, after he returned to Rome, ordered an image [*simulacrum*] of the festive day to be painted in the temple of Liberty. [24.16.16–19]

Livy's narrative here allows for the precise visual reconstruction of the scene; it clearly describes the setting, gestures, and sequence of actions. What is more, the few pictorial details included, the liberty caps and white fillets of the freed slaves, focus attention on the act of liberation that gave the event its political significance. Indeed, it has been suggested that Livy's account of the scene draws precisely on the painting in the temple of Liberty dedicated by the consul.[97]

97. This was suggested by Strong 1928: 1.58, cited by Zinserling 1960: 405, who raises the possibility that the painting might have shown not just the victory feast but the entire course of the battle.

It is possible that Livy did make use of the painting as a source for his account, but the text nowhere signals this dependence.[98] Rather, the juxtaposition of Livy's pictorialized account of the episode with the record of the consul's dedication suggests the equivalence of the two representations. Like the painting in the temple of Libertas, Livy's narrative constructs its own visual image of the scene at Beneventum, reproducing the sight of the victory celebration even for those who had never seen the consul's dedication. And, indeed, by so greatly expanding the audience to whom the image was made available, Livy's narrative provided an even more effective means of "broadcasting" the event than the painting.[99] The consul wished the celebratory banquets to be held in the open, outside the houses of the Beneventans. Yet the painting at Rome that publicized the scene was located inside the temple (*in aede Libertatis* vs. *ante . . . fores*). Livy's narrative exposes the painting itself.

Livy's attempt to make his narrative a *monumentum* by at once recording *res gestae* and providing a visual representation that makes them "present" shares its aim with two roughly contemporary historical productions, both of which approximated the actual forms of physical *monumenta* by adding a visual element even more directly to their text. M. Terentius Varro issued a collection of seven hundred portraits of great men both Greek and Roman, each accompanied by a verse epigram and a brief prose account of his achievements. In this way, Varro became, in the words of Pliny, "the inventor of a benefit to be envied by the gods, since he not only bestowed immortality, but extended it throughout the world, so that [the men depicted] might be able to be manifest [*praesentes*] everywhere like gods" (*HN* 35.11). While Pliny speaks of the service Varro rendered to his subjects, by the same device his book itself acquires importance as the medium through which the "presence" of these figures is transmitted. Cicero's friend Atticus also composed a work that becomes a graphic approximation of the *imagines* of men who "excelled the other Romans in greatness and the honor of their deeds" (Nep. *Att.* 18.5–6). Again, verse inscriptions recording deeds and offices accompany the visual representation of each figure in a form resembling the combination of portrait statue and inscription used in Roman public monuments.[100]

98. For the use of physical monuments as sources, see esp. Wiseman 1986.

99. Within the context of the episode, this celebratory scene also compensates for and supplants the grisly consequences of Gracchus's unfortunate first attempt to inspire his troops; cf. Livy's treatment of Tullus Hostilius's effort to convert the execution of Mettius Fufetius into a *documentum* (1.28) discussed in ch. 4, sec. V.

100. On this phenomenon, see Torelli 1982: 132–33.

But the activities of Augustus himself offer the most important and obvious parallel for Livy's historiographic project. Perhaps never before had the interdependence between political authority and the representation of *res gestae* been so manifest in Roman public life as it was to become during the reign of the first *princeps*. Velleius Paterculus would conclude his account of the blessings of Augustus's reign by stressing precisely the relationship between the exercise of *imperium* and instruction through *exempla*.[101] "The best *princeps* makes his citizens act rightly by acting, and though he is the greatest in power [*imperio*], he is greater still as an example."[102] The connection between this statement and the system of representation revealed by the *monumenta* of the Republic is clear. The leader's actions provide an image or pattern that benefits the Republic by providing a model for imitation, and this process in turn becomes a crucial component of how the emperor "acts," how his authority exerts itself on the *res publica*. Augustus himself highlights his role as producer of *exempla* in his own record of his accomplishments: "By carrying new laws, I have recalled many ancestral *exempla* that were falling into disuse, and I myself have handed down *exempla* of many things to be imitated by those who come later" (*Res gestae* 8). Here Augustus defines his role as producer of *exempla* in two ways; he both recovers and reproduces *exempla* from the past and offers new *exempla* himself. The similarities to Livy's own work, which also benefits the Republic by reproducing *exempla* for imitation and thus takes its place in the sequence of actions it records, are clear.

These similarities become even more striking when we realize that Augustus's claim to have produced *exempla* also forms part of his *monumentum:* his *res gestae* were inscribed on bronze columns erected in front of his mausoleum. It is above all in the visual monuments of Augustus's reign that the reciprocity between his *imperium* and his role of making the past present appears most distinctively. The *princeps*'s most explicit display of exemplary figures from the past was to be found in the Forum surrounding the temple of Mars Ultor, vowed after the defeat of Brutus and Cassius in 42 B.C.E. and finally completed forty years later.[103] Above the colonnade along the left side of the Forum, Augustus placed statues

101. For a thorough discussion of the role of such education in Augustus's self-representation, see Yavetz 1984, esp.14–20.

102. 2.126.4: *nam facere recte civis suos princeps optimus faciendo docet, cumque sit imperio maximus, exemplo maior est.*

103. This description and interpretation of the *Forum Augustum* is based primarily on Zanker 1988: 193–95, and 210–15. For the relationship between this monument and Livy's account of Roman history, see Luce 1990.

of all the men "who had made the power of the Roman people, from something very small, the greatest in the world," accompanied by inscriptions identifying each and summarizing his accomplishments.[104] The criterion for selection closely resembled the terms in which Livy describes the core subject matter of his own history: "I ask that each reader for himself direct his mind keenly to the following things: what were the customs, through which men, and by what arts at home and at war *imperium* was born and grew."[105] For Augustus, this display of *exempla,* however much it may have provided models of conduct to be emulated by future generations, served also to define and justify his own authority: in an edict, Augustus proclaimed that he had devised this program "so that against the [standard] of these men, as if an exemplar, both he himself while he lived and the *principes* of coming ages would be measured by the citizens."[106] But if these men provided the norms through which Augustus's own *imperium* was to be defined and measured, the program makes equally clear that it is only through Augustus's accomplishments that this inspiring display is made possible. Not only was the Forum explicitly built on Augustus's private land, but the entire complex functioned to commemorate his own acts, above all the victory at Philippi in which the killers of Julius Caesar were defeated.

So, too, in the case of Augustus's own *Res Gestae,* the inscription that records the emperor's accomplishments is set in an architectural context designed to provide visual manifestations of the magnitude of Augustus's *imperium.* As Nicolet has shown, the geographical detail of the central portions of the *Res Gestae* that define the parameters of Rome's power complements the elaborate cosmological symbolism of the physical monument of which it was a part.[107] Both the mausoleum of Augustus itself and the *Ara Pacis* were dominated by a gigantic sundial, which served to locate Augustus's accomplishments within a symbolic representation of

104. Suet. *Aug.* 31.5: *qui imperium populi Romani ex minimo maximum redidissent.*

105. *Praef.* 9: *ad illa mihi pro se quisque acriter intendat animos, quae vita, qui mores fuerint, per quos viros quibusque artibus domi militiaeque et partum et auctum imperium sit.* Livy goes on to draw attention to the subsequent decline of this *imperium,* and far from representing his own day as the culmination of a continuous process of growth, describes the moment at which he writes as past remedy. Again, I am not arguing that Livy shared the view of the past commemorated in the Forum—Luce 1990 points out discrepancies large and small between the two programs—but that the Forum can provide an analogy for the type of historical representation to which Livy's text aspires.

106. Suet. *Aug.* 31.5: *commentum id se ut ad illorum[. . .]velut ad exemplar, et ipse dum viveret et insequentium aetatium principes exigerentur a civibus.*

107. Nicolet 1991: 15–24.

the extent of the cosmos in space and time.[108] It is this elaborate complex that provides the *monumentum* for which the *res gestae* are the inscription; indeed, symbolically, it is the entire *imperium Romanum* that offers the defining visual corollary to Augustus's text. Augustus was therefore able to inscribe his text on an actual physical monument of enormous size and complexity, whose visual component manifested the magnitude of his own *auctoritas.* Livy's text must act as its own *monumentum,* but the scope of the visual signs that accompany his text bears comparison with the symbolic claims that would later be made by the *princeps* himself. All of Roman history provides the content of Livy's "unmeasurable opus" (*immensi operis, praef.* 4).

III. Avarice, Vision, and Restoration

In a Roman sacred grove, it was forbidden to cut away the deadwood. Paul Veyne imagines the visual impression that must have been produced by such a grove, where each decaying branch was festooned with the dedications erected by generation after generation: "One could see something almost unknown to us, a forest where the straight and living trees were less frequent than the twisted and fallen trunks and where the dead branches created an almost impenetrable undergrowth."[109] This image aptly conveys the spectacle the *monumenta* erected through the centuries of the Republic must have made of Rome before its Augustan reconstruction. Ancient shrines fallen into decay were crammed with moldering *spolia,* fading paintings, and unreadable inscriptions. Not only were the memorials of the past becoming obscure and unrecognizable, but huge tracts of the ancient city had been transformed by the potentates of the Late Republic, each of whom in succession attempted to devise a visual equivalent for the grandiosity of his accomplishments, and each of whom brought to the task the vast wealth obtained through conquest.[110] The magnificent gardens of Lucullus, which from their position on the height of the Pincian would have dominated the northern half of the city, stood in gaudy contrast to the most

108. For other discussions of cosmological significance in Augustus's building programs, see Bowersock 1990, Kellum 1990, Zanker 1988: 144, and Feldherr 1995.

109. Veyne 1983: 289.

110. See Zanker 1988: 22–24.

sacred public buildings on the Capitoline.[111] Each of these monuments in turn offered its own competing narrative of Roman history, culminating in the deeds of a Sulla, a Pompey, or a Caesar. The bewilderment of the Romans of the Late Republic in this forest of *monumenta* appears from the terms in which Cicero praises the antiquarian researches of Marcus Terentius Varro: "We were wandering about in our own city like strangers [*hospites*] and your books led us back home so that we might know at last who and where we were."[112]

Paul Zanker presents the creation of a coherent system of visual communication out of this disorder of competing signs as one of the major accomplishments, not just of Augustan art, but of the Augustan era. His book *The Power of Images in the Age of Augustus* traces the processes by which the reconstruction of decaying monuments, the modification of the Hellenistic visual idioms of the Late Republic, and the reconfiguration of the urban landscape all combined to create "a whole new method of visual communication,"[113] which in turn provided an effective medium for conveying and constructing a shared political ideology.[114] At the same time, Zanker emphatically rejects describing this transformation in visual media as mere propaganda, imposed from the top down. Rather, he insists on the "power of images" to shape and determine the way in which the regime itself was defined. Thus, while Zanker does not refer to Geertz's work, his approach dovetails well with the anthropologist's assertions about the interdependence between political power and its ceremonial attributes. Zanker's demonstration of the political centrality of visual communication in Augustan Rome also makes clear how Livy's own interest in vision not only reflected contemporary concerns but also allowed his text to participate in the civic regeneration of the state with particular efficacy.

Historical knowledge was doubly implicated in the creation of the urban landscape as a set of legible visual signs: it served as the "content"

111. On the scale and political significance of the *horti Lucullani,* see Coarelli 1983: 200 ff.

112. Cic. *Acad.* 1.9: *nam nos in nostra urbe perigrinantis errantisque tamquam hospites tui libri quasi domum reduxerunt.*

113. Zanker 1988: 3.

114. This aspect of Zanker's view of the reception of Augustan art, in particular his treatment of Augustan artistic productions as the bearers of precise ideological meanings, has been questioned by Elsner 1991: 51–52, who rightly emphasizes that such "meanings" were not the intrinsic properties of the images themselves but were determined by the viewers. He sees a visual monument such as the *Ara Pacis* as involving the viewer himself in "a cultural process," to which his responses will necessarily vary according to his background, perspective, and circumstances. On this issue, see ch. 4.

of the individual monuments, each of which recalled a particular event, and in turn imbued the monuments themselves with significance. Thus history, in the sense of an awareness of the past, was at once imperiled by the confusion of the system of visual communication at Rome and a crucial instrument in its restoration. It was ignorance of Roman history and traditions that stripped the ancient monuments of their significance and led to their neglect. For Varro, to recover knowledge about the ancestral religious practices of the Romans was tantamount to preserving the cults themselves from ruin.[115] Correspondingly, the decay and obliteration of the visual traces of antiquity meant the disappearance of the network of signs that ought to have preserved knowledge and memory. The process, of course, had a moral dimension as well. The invisibility of ancestral customs meant the loss of the influence they might have exerted on the present. So, too, in religious terms, the fading of traditional piety and the corresponding distance between contemporary Rome and the divine guarantors of its success found a visual corollary in the "images of the gods fouled by black smoke."[116] Viewed in this way, Augustus's interests in moral reform, the physical reconstruction of the city, and the representation of the past form not just complementary but inseparable facets of the same program.

A corresponding interdependence between producing a visual representation of the past and the moral renewal of the state underpins Livy's definition of his work as an *inlustre monumentum.* But not only does Livy explicitly connect the viewing of this monument with his history's capacity to benefit the state, his particular diagnosis of the causes of the decline of the *res publica* gives a special significance to the method he has chosen to "heal" it. The final paragraph of Livy's preface makes emphatically clear that the historian views the destructive forces endangering Rome as the products of wealth and the desires it brings:

Either my love for the task I have undertaken deceives me or no *res publica* has ever been greater, or more sacred, or richer in good examples; nor have avarice and luxury immigrated so late into any state; nor has there been a place where so much honor was awarded for so long to poverty and frugal-

115. "[Varro] feared lest [the gods] perish, not from an enemy attack but by the negligence of the citizens, and said that he had freed them from this negligence, as if from ruin, and reestablished them [*recondi*] in the memory of good men through his books and saved them with a more useful care than Metellus had saved the *sacra Vestalia* from fire or Aeneas the Penates from the destruction of Troy" (*Ant. rer. div.* fr. 2a Cardauns [= Augustine *De civ. D.* 6.2.6–13] cited by Zanker 1988: 103).

116. Horace *Carm.* 3.6.4.

ity. In addition, by how much there was a lack of substance, by so much was there less desire; recently riches have brought in avarice, and overflowing pleasures, and lust.[117]

The anxieties about the influence of wealth expressed here are by no means peculiar to Livy. The danger of riches forms a common topos in Latin literature.[118] So, too, the identification of avarice as an important factor in Rome's decline had a long tradition in Latin historiography, and, together with ambition, avarice figures prominently in Sallust's account of Rome's moral and political decay.[119] But as G. B. Miles has demonstrated, Livy's exclusive concentration on *avaritia* here, at the expense of both *ambitio* and that other traditional rationale for explaining the phenomenon, the absence of a significant foreign threat enforcing internal unity, would have appeared distinctive, especially in contrast to Sallust's position.[120] This focus on *avaritia* in turn serves to define and emphasize the social function of Livy's own history: for the danger of *avaritia* resides in its erosion, not only of the values and institutions of the Roman past, but of the very processes of historical communication by which the memory and influence of that past are perpetuated.

The *res publica* that *avaritia* "invaded"[121] already possessed its own kind of wealth, which distinguished it from all other states: no republic was richer in good examples (*bonis exemplis ditior* [*praef.* 11]). The particular currency of the old Republic therefore has a special connection to Livy's own history, which, as an *inlustre monumentum,* makes these *exempla* visible and so allows them to be reproduced again in the public conduct of its audience. *Avaritia* contaminates the state through an opposite but equivalent mimetic process. It is not greed that has drawn foreign riches to Rome but the presence of foreign wealth that has engen-

117. *Praef.* 11–12: *ceterum aut me amor negotii suscepti fallit aut nulla unquam res publica nec maior nec sanctior, nec bonis exemplis ditior fuit, nec in quam tam serae avaritia luxuriaque immigraverint; nec ubi tantus ac tam diu paupertati ac parsimoniae honos fuerit. adeo quanto rerum minus, tanto minus cupiditatis: nuper divitiae avaritiam et abundantes voluptates desiderium per luxum atque libidinem pereundi perdendique omnia invexere.*

118. See Edwards 1993: 176 ff., who explores the full cultural implications of Roman concerns about luxury and wealth.

119. Sall. *Cat.* 10.3: *primo pecuniae deinde imperi cupido crevit, ea quasi materies omnium malorum fuere.* The backgrounds to this idea are traced by Earl 1961: 44 ff., and Luce 1977: 271–75, to the view of Roman history developed by "Senatorial" historians of the second century. A full list of ancient and modern references will be found in Miles 1986: 3, n. 5.

120. Miles 1986: 3–4. See also Ogilvie 1965: 23–24.

121. For the depiction of *avaritia* as a foreign influence, infiltrating the Roman state, see Luce 1977: 273.

dered greed and luxuriousness.[122] The absence of wealth was the absence of *cupiditas,* a word used consistently of appetites for things that are inappropriate or illegal.[123] The resistance that *avaritia* offers to the reception of his own text was already hinted at earlier in the preface when Livy remarked that his audience was likely to be less interested in his account of the first phases of Roman history. These portions of his narrative, he says, will offer his readers less *voluptas,* one of the passions imported by foreign wealth, and they "will hasten to new things."[124] We shall often find this aversion to the old and pursuit of the new, sometimes coupled with the foreign, in Livy's condemnation of those figures whose disconnection from past traditions has imperiled the state.[125] Moreover, because of the ambiguity of the words *haec nova,* the eagerness of his audience for recent events becomes indistinguishable from the attraction of new or foreign things. And their haste in pursuit of the new means that their own reading of the history mimics the rush with which the Republic itself hurtles toward collapse.[126]

In Pliny's description of the ancient home of the *nobilis,* we have already seen an equivalent description of the effects of wealth and the threat that it poses to communication with the past. The ornamentation of the traditional *domus* consisted entirely of *monumenta,* works that recorded, indeed, made manifest, the ancestral deeds of the home's previous inhabitants. The "value" of these works derived from what they

122. *Praef.* 12: *nuper divitiae avaritiam et abundantes voluptates . . . invexere.*

123. For the negative connotations of *cupiditas,* see *OLD* s.v. §2–3. *Cupiditas,* or the cognate *cupido,* is presented by Sallust as the root of both the pervasive evils of the Late Republic: *avaritia* is glossed as *pecuniae cupido; ambitio* as *imperi cupido* (*Cat.* 10.3; see Earl 1961: 13). Within Livy's text, too, these words are often used to characterize a desire as improper or illegitimate; thus, for example, the Carthaginians accuse the Romans at the beginning of the Second Punic War of *cupido regni* (21.10.4). Cf. also the role of this and related phrases in the disputes between the Macedonian brothers Perseus and Demetrius (40.8.17, 40.10.1, 40.11.4, 40.11.7, 40.13.5) and between Romulus and Remus (1.6.4).

124. *Praef.* 5: *et legentium plerisque haud dubito quin primae origines proximaque originibus minus praebitura voluptatis sint, festinantibus ad haec nova quibus iam pridem praevalentis populi vires se ipsae conficiunt.*

125. For the representation of the new and the foreign as offering a challenge to traditional practices, especially religious practices, cf. the historian's comments at 8.11.1. Livy declares that he has not thought it irrelevant to record the exact procedure for the *devotio,* "although the memory of every human and religious practice has faded from the continual preferment of all things new and foreign [*etsi omnis divini humanique moris memoria abolevit nova peregrinaque omnia praeferendo*]." Again, notice that Livy presents it as the historian's task to resist the onslaught of the "new" by preserving the memory of the old. For a similar assertion of the gulf between the pious past and the negligent present, cf. Livy's aside at 10.40.10.

126. The implications of the reader's haste are also discussed by Moles 1993: 146–47.

represented, not from the material out of which they were made.[127] They had no price, and indeed provided continuity in the face of monetary exchange: even if the house were sold, these works could not be removed. As these ancestral images exert a strong moral influence on the viewer and thus serve to perpetuate the system of cultural values that they record, so the use of monetary value as the sole criterion for which works of art are esteemed introduces a corresponding cycle of corruption, which both results from and affects the visual arts. When portraits are valued only for their price, rather than for their capacity to depict both the bodies and the minds of specific individuals, they lack precisely the kind of inspiration offered by ancestral *imagines*. Because the owners of these portraits themselves will never accomplish any deed that will make their own features worth preserving, "laziness," as Pliny says, in turn "has destroyed the arts."[128]

Not only does the interference *avaritia* offers to the reception of Livy's *monumentum* mirror the dangers that wealth posed to actual physical monuments, but within Livy's text, the opposition between history and *avaritia* takes the form of a competition between two systems of visual signs, or two ways of reading the same signs. Indeed, Livy himself provides a passage that Zanker uses as evidence for an awareness of the tension between visible images that communicate the power of the state and merely superficial magnificence, a speech placed in the mouth of the Elder Cato and set in 195 B.C.E., just at the period when Rome's greatest victories in the east were beginning.[129] For our purposes, the passage is important not only because it reveals Livy's interest in larger anxieties about the visual effects of luxury but also because it does so in an explicitly programmatic context: as part of a debate about *avaritia* and *luxuria,* which, as T. J. Luce has shown, recalls precisely the language of Livy's preface:[130]

127. Cf. Pliny's criticism (*HN* 35.4) of those who decorate their homes with works of art chosen for their value as objects rather than for the people they represent, *ipsi honorem non nisi in pretio ducentes.*

128. *HN* 35.5: *artes desidia perdidit.*

129. See Zanker 1988: 23–24, where the passage is used to portray attitudes of the second century B.C.E., not of Livy's time. Briscoe 1981: 39, however, makes clear that the speech is in fact a Livian composition and not simply a reworking of an extant speech by Cato. No speech by Cato is known to have been delivered on this occasion, and elsewhere Livy explicitly avoids placing a speech in the mouth of Cato when the actual oration was preserved.

130. Luce 1977: 251–53. Briscoe 1981: 41, dissents from the view that the passage can be connected with Livy's own presentation of Rome's decline on the grounds that Cato is treated much less sympathetically than his opponent L. Valerius, who argues successfully for the repeal of the *lex Oppia*. But rarely in any set of paired speeches in Livy, or any other

As the fortune of the Republic grows better and more blessed every day—now we have already crossed into Greece and Asia and dragged back the treasures of kings stuffed with all the enticements of desire—so I fear all the more lest those things have taken us captive rather than we them. Trust me, those statues brought from Syracuse are perilous to the city. Already I have heard too many men praising and wondering at the ornaments of Corinth and Athens and laughing at the terracotta antefixes of the Roman gods. I prefer the latter, the propitious gods, and so I hope they will be if we leave them in their places. [34.4.3–4]

Here *avaritia* and *luxuria* take a concrete and visible form as royal treasures and Greek statues, which, as "enticements" (*libidinum illecebris*), set in motion a destructive cycle of desires.[131] The language in which Cato describes these foreign treasures correlates the march of *avaritia* with two other dangers. First, the statues themselves are the bearers of an inimical energy. They are perilous (*infesta*), and the images that they have displaced are specifically sacred images whose veneration is essential to maintain contact between the state and the gods. But at the same time as these *ornamenta* break the visual link between the Roman spectator and the sources of Rome's *imperium,* they also overturn the historical record of that *imperium.* The statues, brought to the city as *spolia,* are not just waging war on Rome, they have also reversed their commemorative function. No longer recording a Roman victory, they appear to have taken Rome captive. In these respects, the effect of the statues, as Cato describes it, contrasts precisely with that of such visual *monumenta* as the inscribed map erected by Ti. Sempronius Gracchus, with which, as I have suggested, Livy aligns his text. There, as we saw, the mnemonic function of the image, as a record of Roman victory, went together with a capacity to manifest the *imperium* and *auspicium* by which the victory had been won.

Cato suggests that the foreign images of the Greeks seem to have taken Rome captive. It is the one time in Rome's history when the city actually was taken captive, the Gallic invasion described in book 5, that

---

Roman historian, are only the arguments of the winning side valid. The fact that Cato is defeated, and even to a certain extent made fun of, by Valerius in no way makes him an inappropriate vehicle for representing the particular concerns of Livy's text. In fact the very unpopularity of Cato's speech has a special aptness for this purpose. Like the terracotta statues he describes, the historical outlook Cato manifests here is continually represented as uncongenial and lacking in superficial attractiveness.

131. 34.4.2. The origins of the very word Cato uses to describe these foreign treasures, *gazae,* recapitulate precisely the trajectory of the decline of great empires to which he alludes. It is a word Latin takes from Greek, but that the Greeks themselves took from the Persians.

provides Livy with his most extensive opportunity to depict the dangers of *avaritia* and the remedies that historical memory can offer. Book 5, at the end of the first published pentad, is perhaps the most elaborately patterned unit in the historian's work, and it can be read as a microcosm of the entire course of Roman history.[132] Rome's greatest foreign success to date, the conquest of Veii, led immediately to her greatest danger, the attack by the Gauls. The central issue in the book has sometimes been taken to be religious propriety, but as Miles has demonstrated, *avaritia* is at least as important a theme.[133] As in Cato's speech, it is the seductive power of wealth that motivates the Romans' neglect of their gods.[134] Camillus's dedication of one-tenth of the *spolia* of Veii to Apollo alienates the people and contributes to his banishment (5.23.8–11). Although the vow is fulfilled, the avarice of the Romans here appears as a force that hinders their performance of their duties to the gods and thus prepares for the loss of divine support that leads to the sack. The danger posed by the success at Veii again takes the form of a distracting visual image that threatens to draw the Romans away from the native traditions that secured their victory. The opulence of Veii—which, Livy emphasizes, is within sight of Rome—leads the Romans to contemplate abandoning their own city (5.24.5). As with the threat posed by the eastern *spolia,* the result of succumbing to this temptation would be to reverse the situations of conqueror and conquered.[135]

This threatened transposition of conqueror and conquered prepares for the victory of the Gauls, where, as Livy puts it, the superior Roman and the inferior Gaul seem to have changed places.[136] When the Gauls enter the abandoned city, their perceptions of it, or rather their failure to perceive the significance of the images they are exposed to, makes their experience comparable to that of the Roman who has lost the ability to read the monuments around him. In both cases, the breakdown in visual comprehension has the same cause, *avaritia.* The Gauls are only interested in plunder and therefore perceive each object only in terms of its material value, its superficial magnificence. Camillus will say of them ex-

132. For important recent discussion of the structure of bk. 5, with full bibliography, see esp. Luce 1971, Miles 1986, and Kraus, 1994b.

133. Ogilvie 1965: 626; and see also Luce 1971: 268.

134. Miles 1986: 5–13.

135. Thus the idea that, by occupying the site of the enemy city, the Romans will become *Veientes* recurs throughout Camillus's final speech; cf. 5.52.14, and 5.53.7.

136. A motif analyzed especially by Luce 1971: 269. Cf. in particular Livy's remark that at the battle of the Allia, there was among the defenders *nihil simile Romanis, non apud duces, non apud milites* (5.38.5).

plicitly that they have been rendered blind by avarice, *caeci avaritia* (5.51.10).

Since from the beginning of Livy's text, *avaritia* has been personified as a foreign immigrant that causes the Romans themselves to adopt the values of their defeated opponents, it is doubly appropriate that he should conjure up the effects of *avaritia* by making his own audience see the city through the eyes of foreigners. And of all foreign nations, the ethnographic tradition has made the Gauls particularly fitting representatives of the consequences of avarice.[137] Their well-known extravagance and love of pleasure become, in Caesar's *Commentarii,* one of the sources of their weakness; they are "softened" by the enticements of civilization.[138] The image of the individual Gaul as a creature of vast size ultimately undone by his own bulk is also not inapposite for the task of representing the danger of *avaritia,*[139] which derives from too much success and makes the Republic collapse under its own weight. Livy elsewhere characterizes the Gauls in terms of a similar failure to produce or interpret visual signs effectively, particularly in the pair of duels they fight against Roman champions in book 7 (analyzed in detail in ch. 4). The first Gaul sports a magnificent set of golden armor, which proves utterly ineffective against Manlius Torquatus's might (7.10). The next duel illustrates the corollary phenomenon: the Gauls' blindness to truly powerful signs. Here a sign from the gods, in the form of a persistent crow, literally blinds another Gaul by pecking at his eyes (7.26).

The Gauls' distinctly un-Roman response to visual signs appears especially clearly in their encounter with the aged senators who have agreed to remain in the unprotected city in order to preserve food for the fighting men in the citadel (5.41). The senators await the Gauls arrayed

137. For a sketch of Roman stereotypes of the Gaul, see Balsdon 1979: 65–66. The history of Greek and Roman ethnographic writings about Celts is traced by Momigliano 1971: 50–73. On Livy's portrayal of the Gauls as barbarians, and the use he makes of accounts of barbarians in bk. 5, see Kraus 1994b: 274–82.

138. Cf. his remark in the introduction that the *Belgae* are the bravest of Gauls, *quod . . . minime . . . ea quae ad effeminandos animos pertinent important* (*BGall.* 1.1.3). Livy begins his own account of the Gauls by recording a story that they were enticed into Italy by the physical pleasures it offered: "the sweetness of the fruits and especially wine" (5.33.2). Wine was something new for the Gauls, and the phrase Livy uses to describe its influence over them, *nova voluptate captam,* recalls the discussion of luxury in the preface. Especially interesting is the suggestion that even before the sack of Rome, the Gauls have already been "captured" by *voluptas.*

139. Cf. especially the descriptions of the Gallic challenger in the duel of T. Maulius Touquatus (Livy 7.10 and Claudius Quadrigarius [fr 10^b Peter]) and the contrast between the *Gallus velut moles* (7.10.9) and the deft maneuvers of the Roman.

in their insignia of office and seated on ivory stools in their atria. The Gauls are disconcerted by the sight and have a presentiment of the majesty of the senators' adornment that initially causes them to treat the old men like gods. But ultimately, as outsiders, the Gauls respond only to appearance; like the Romans Cato describes, they are enthralled by the visual splendor of what are really *infesta signa*. Indeed, the Gauls turn to the senators as if they were statues, *ad eos velut simulacra versi* (5.41.9). One Gaul continues to treat the old Senator M. Papirius as though he were merely an image by reaching out to stroke his beard, an act that elicits a rap from Papirius's ivory staff and thus precipitates the massacre of all the senators.

A Roman audience ought to read the senators' appearance very differently. The insignia in which they array themselves not only possess a memorializing function, recalling the magistracies the old men have held,[140] they are also precisely the visible signs through which authority is displayed in Roman public spectacles. In fact, Livy specifies that this is the same clothing as would be worn by a triumphator, or by someone conducting a religious procession.[141] What is more, the senators' appearance is also twice described as *augusta,* a word that is not only cognate with *auctoritas,* but that Wagenvoort has shown is particularly associated with the transfer of power through *contactus.*[142] Therefore, while the mere appearance of the old men does not, as the Gauls think, make them gods, their insignia do form a bridge to the collective power of the Roman gods, but only for those whose vision is historically informed.

The desolation that greets the Romans returning to their city contrasts utterly with the bewildering and enticing array of visual images encountered by the Gauls. For those whose perspective depends on surfaces, the landscape seems void of meaning or value, and the people again contemplate abandoning Rome for Veii. Camillus's second salvation of his *patria* consists in reeducating the vision of his fellow citizens

140. In this and other respects, the senators can be seen as recalling, not only their own previous service, but the entire tradition of Roman history as Livy has recorded it through the previous five books. Thus in the scene where the old men watch as the young defenders go to take their place in the citadel—itself perhaps a reversal of the triumphs they have celebrated—they are described as "entrusting to the young men, whatever fortune remained for a city victorious in all wars *through three hundred and sixty years*" (5.40.1).

141. 5.41.2: *quae augustissima vestis est tensas ducentibus triumphantibusve.* And indeed in donning this clothing again, it is as though the senators are preparing themselves for a complementary set of public spectacles—their own funerals.

142. For the religious significance of *augustus* and its cognates, see Wagenvoort 1947: 12 ff.

in order to restore the possibility of contact with the divine power that resides uniquely in Rome, even in the absence of the visible signs of this power. Camillus accomplishes this task of constructing an *evidens numen* (5.51.4) preeminently by showing the Romans their city. From the beginning of his great speech, he continually challenges his audience to look upon the city and perceive it as something more than "surfaces and roofing stones" (5.54.2). His speech is filled with literal and metaphorical references to vision and with commands to the audience to direct their gaze to certain aspects of the landscape.[143] In the last sentences of his peroration, the demonstrative adverb *hic,* "here," recurs at the beginning of three successive clauses.[144] This anaphora could be interpreted simply as an emphatic device used to stress the overall point of Camillus's argument: "Here at Rome [i.e., and not at Veii] is the Capitoline," and so on. At the same time, *hic* can be taken as strongly deictic, actually directing Camillus's listeners' eyes to the places he describes: the Capitoline, the temple of Vesta, and the like. This final coalescence of argument and demonstration perfectly captures the active role that visual display takes on in Camillus's oration: to show is to persuade.[145]

But Camillus's use of vision in this speech, as a way of restoring his audience's contact with the religious power latent in Rome's physical landscape, also involves the recollection of past events. Each *monumentum* becomes literally that: the reminder of an event or sign, such as the shields of Mars falling from the sky or the discovery of a human head on the Capitol. And it is the memory of these events that in turn generates the bond between his audience and the physical place itself.[146] Above all, Camillus employs a narrative of the recent past, the very events that Livy himself has just described in book 5, as an argument for maintaining continuity with both the site of the Roman city and the traditions that it records.[147]

Ultimately, just as in the passage of Livy's preface with which we began, Camillus treats the past itself, cast in an annalistic framework, as

143. *Intuemini* (5.51.5), *cernentes* (5.52.1), *videte* (5.52.8), *apparet* (5.53.1), *apparere* (5.53.2), *videte* (5.53.3), *oculis* (5.54.3).

144. 5.54.7: *hic Capitolium est ubi quondam capite humano invento responsum est eo loco caput rerum summamque imperii fore; hic cum augurato liberaretur Capitolium, Iuventas Terminusque maximo gaudio patrum vestrorum moveri se non passi; hic Vestae ignes, hic ancilia caelo demissa, hic omnes propitii manentibus vobis di.*

145. For the Ciceronian applications of this technique, see Vasaly 1993: 15–87.

146. For the importance of the emotional bond to place in this speech, see esp. Bonjour 1975b: 168–69, and also ch. 4.

147. Cf. 5.51.5, and the subsequent narration.

a landscape, which his audience is instructed to gaze upon, *intuemini horum deinceps annorum vel secundas res vel adversas* (5.51.5). Camillus's account of recent years draws out the significance of the historian's own narrative, highlighting the role of the divine in human affairs. Livy's text is itself thus revealed as a medium that facilitates contact between its audience and the powers responsible for Rome's success.[148] It is the existence of such a system of communication that here literally preserves the endangered city from abandonment and converts its landscape in turn into a repository of historical memory.

The relevance of the issues raised at the conclusion of the first pentad to the preoccupations of Rome in Livy's day hardly needs to be stressed. The position of Camillus's restoration of the city, both within Livy's narrative at the end of the first pentad, and within the course of the city's history, at the halfway point between Rome's original foundation in 753 B.C.E. and 27 B.C.E., when the *princeps* took on the title of Augustus, roughly the time when the first portion of the *History* was published,[149] makes the parallels between past and present almost inescapable.[150] The

148. For a somewhat different view of the relationship between Livy's text and the landscape of the city, according to which, in place of a symbiosis between history and the visual stimuli offered by the physical monuments of the city, the written record appears as the only trustworthy and truly meaningful "landscape," see Jaeger 1993.

149. Since we do not know the precise date when the first unit of Livy's history was made available, Camillus's restoration may not mark the exact chronological halfway point between the "now" of Livy's first readers and the foundation of the city, but by any calculation, it would come very close to it. Indications of date are, in fact, remarkably rare in the surviving portion of Livy's work and allow for many competing theories. The most explicit evidence is provided by Livy's comment at 1.19.23, that Caesar Augustus closed the doors of the temple of Janus after the battle of Actium. This would seem to permit the date of this passage to be fixed between 27 B.C.E., when Octavian became Augustus, and 25 B.C.E., when he closed the doors of the temple a second time. But following on a suggestion originally made by Bayet 1940: xvi–xxii, Luce 1965 has demonstrated, to my mind convincingly, that both this passage and the account of Augustus's "correction" of Livy's description of Cornelius Cossus (4.20.5–11), represent later additions to the narrative, and that the first pentad could have been complete by 27 B.C.E. Syme 1959: 42–50, is tempted to push the date of composition back toward the period of Actium, but he is rightly cautious about pinning too much on the pessimism of the preface and points out that such pessimism was possible even after Actium. For similar reasons, I cannot accept Woodman's arguments (1988: 131–34) that the ills described in the preface can only refer to civil war, and that therefore the preface must predate Actium. For an outline of the evidence and positions taken, see Walsh 1974: 6.

150. On the importance of this kind of cyclicality in Livy's ordering of his material, see Miles 1986, who also argues that the resulting link between the end of the first pentad and the historian's own day is enhanced by the appearance of what the historian signals as the critical issues of his time, above all *avaritia,* as consistent themes in the treatment of the sack of Rome.

necessity for the reconstruction of Rome, the narrow escape from the danger that Rome herself would be supplanted by a foreign capital—here, Veii; in the rhetoric of the 30's, Alexandria—and above all the insistence that the physical restoration of Rome is inextricably bound up with the restoration of her religious and moral traditions, all speak directly to contemporary concerns that Augustus had and would address in the years after Actium.[151] Indeed, Livy has often been assumed to have tailored his portrayal of Camillus to recall the *princeps* himself, whether as a means of celebrating Augustus's achievements, or of rousing him to action and proposing an *exemplum* upon which he, like the other readers of the *History,* might model his own behavior.[152] The titles Livy uses to describe Camillus, above all the term *conditor,*[153] which the historian also applies to Augustus,[154] particularly establish a parallel between this figure and the *princeps.*

But the attention directed to Camillus's perceived resemblances to Augustus has tended to overshadow his function as a model for Livy's own activity, which is at least equally important. In his discussion of the word *conditor* (founder), Miles points out that it could also be applied to a writer. For Miles, the historian's contributions to the refoundation of the city consist in "endorsing" Augustus's activities, creating support for them among his audience, and, most centrally, emphasizing the importance of adhering to tradition, even in so potentially radical an act as refounding Rome.[155] I suggest that Camillus's actions demonstrate how

151. Cf. the similar lists in Miles 1986: 30, and Burck 1991.

152. In addition to the works cited below, other important points of reference for the discussion of how the situation of Augustus may have influenced Livy's treatment of Camillus (or vice versa) are Burck 1964a, Hellegouarc'h 1970, Syme 1959: 55, and Mazza 1966: 186–91 (further citations in Miles 1986: 14–15, n. 30, and Phillips 1982: 1033 ff.) It should also be noted that Walsh 1961b and others, have doubted that a specific allusion to Augustus is intended, on the grounds that, given some of the details Livy includes about Camillus, such a comparison would not have been flattering.

153. Used of Camillus in the expression with which he is saluted as *triumphator: Romulus ac parens patriae conditorque alter urbis* (5.49.7). For the contemporary relevance of all these terms, see Miles 1988 and Burck 1991: 276–77.

154. See 4.20.7: *templorum omnium restitutorem ac conditorem.*

155. Miles 1988: 207–8. Cf. also Varro's use of the term *recondi* in the description of how his own books save the gods from neglect by establishing, or planting, them in the memory. He compares his actions to those of Aeneas himself, saving the *penates* during the sack of Troy (*Ant. rer. div.* fr. 2a Cardauns; see above, n. 115). Again the negligent citizens of Rome are likened to an invading foreign enemy, and the antiquarian takes on the role of preserving Roman religious institutions in much the same way that Camillus will at the end of bk. 5. The verb *recondere* recalls the events of the sack of Rome in another sense as well: the sacred objects of Vesta are literally buried (*condita*) to keep them from destruction (Liv. 5.40.8).

a historian can do even more. Camillus's great speech, with its many allusions to the program of Livy's own *History*, makes clear how putting the past on display itself constitutes a political act, which here effects the preservation of precisely the traditions it recalls. Indeed, it is Camillus's representation of the city that Livy's narrative highlights, not its physical rebuilding, which takes up only a few sentences (5.55.2–5). His use of vision as a means of restoring contact between his audience and the power of their religious and political institutions cannot be separated from the preservation of historical memory, nor, in a larger sense, from the perpetuation of Roman history as an ongoing sequence of actions.

CHAPTER 2

Historian and *Imperator*

In chapter 1, Livy's account of P. Licinius Crassus's *profectio* in 171 B.C.E. furnished an example of how the historian's representation of the past embeds itself in the system of spectacles that facilitated the exercise of political authority within the Roman state. The consul's procession from the temples on the Capitoline to the gates of the city provided a prompt for its spectators to reflect on the series of past magistrates who had made the same journey. But an interesting tension emerges between the substance of the spectators' reflections and the nature of the ceremony that provoked them. The rituals that the consul had just performed on the Capitol, according to the logic of Roman public religion, ought to influence the outcome of the consul's campaign. Yet in this case, when the spectators consider the factors that determine military success or failure, ritual propriety never enters their calculations.[1] Their concerns center on the uncertainty of fortune and the mental qualities of the commander:

Then there enters their minds the reckoning of the contingencies of war, how uncertain is the outcome of fortune, and how impartial is Mars, what disasters have come about through the ignorance and rashness of the leaders, and yet what advantages have been the result of foresight and valor. What man knew which was the intellect and which the fortune of the consul they were sending to war?[2]

1. Cf. the observation of Kajanto 1957: 78–79: "It is worth noting that though Livy describes a departure for war after all religious ceremonies have taken place, the people are not made to think the gods are responsible for success or failure."

2. 42.49.4–6: *subit deinde cogitatio animos qui belli casus, quam incertus fortunae eventus*

To be sure, this discrepancy can be explained in a number of ways. An insistence on the correct observance of religious practices before a military campaign is by no means inconsistent with a requirement that the commander himself possess experience, courage, and, indeed, good fortune (*felicitas*).[3] Nor, as many recent studies of ancient religion have stressed, does the pious participation in religious ritual necessitate "belief" in a particular mechanism of divine agency.[4] But the manner in which Livy has chosen to represent the crowd's reflections possesses a significance that goes beyond questions of skepticism and belief on the part of either the audience described or the historian. For besides the allusion to the positive and negative *exempla* his own history promises to present, Livy's description of the crowd's thoughts recalls precisely the terms in which Cicero says a historian ought to explain the causes of events: "When outcomes are described [the proper arrangement of material necessitates] that all the causes be explained, whether they derive from *chance,* or *wisdom,* or *rashness*"(*De or.* 2.63). Livy's emphasis on fortune is also important in this regard since the concept of fortune played an especially important role in the systems of causality that many influential Greek historians, preeminently Polybius, invoked in the claims they made for the value of their works.[5] Thus Livy's treatment of the *profectio* stresses his text's participation in two systems of representation, the civic spectacles through which the political and religious authority of the state are made visible to the citizens, and the traditions of literary history developed and described by his predecessors. This chap-

---

communisque Mars belli sit; adversa secundaque, quae inscitia et temeritate ducum clades saepe acciderint, quae contra bona prudentia et virtus attulerit. quem scire mortalium utrius mentis utrius fortunae consulem ad bellum mittant?.

3. Cf., e.g., Cicero's description (*De imp. Cn. Pomp.* 28) of the virtues demanded of a general in his speech for the Manilian law: *ego enim sic existimo, in summo imperatore quattuor has res inesse oportere, scientiam rei militaris, virtutem, auctoritatem, felicitatem.* Nor does this emphasis on human causes in the selection of a general inhibit Cicero from making a strong appeal to religion in his *peroratio* (*De imp. Cn. Pomp.* 70). Not only were multiple explanations of military success perfectly compatible, as we shall see more fully below, but the flexibility that such overdetermination allowed proved highly useful in the competitive atmosphere of Roman politics as a means of gaining credit for victory and avoiding blame for defeat. See Rosenstein 1990.

4. See, e.g. Price 1984: 7 ff., and Scheid 1985: 12 ff.

5. For the importance of fortune in Polybius, see Walbank 1972: 58–68: "*Tyche* and Polybius are shown as being in a sense complementary to each other: each is a creative artist in the relevant field, the one producing a unified *oecumene,* the other its counterpart in the unified work of history" (1972: 68). Within Polybius's text, see esp. 1.4. For the possible significance of fortune in Duris of Samos's conception of the function of history, see Fornara 1983: 126 ff.

ter explores how Livy constructs the relationship between these two systems.

Previously, I suggested that acts of representation played a fundamental role in the exercise of supreme magisterial authority at Rome. Not only could the person of a triumphing general, for example, function as a "light bulb," relaying the powers responsible for the Romans' success through his very appearance, but the visual depictions of victory produced by the triumphator possessed a similar dynamic potential. But this is not the unique respect in which an *imperator*'s power operated through the images and appearances he projected. Additionally, a consul or magistrate could act as an interpreter for his subjects, regulating their perceptions of the world around them and constructing an image of reality that came to count as real. The religious aspect of the magistrate's authority, his *auspicium*, demonstrates this facet of his power most clearly.[6] It was the magistrate who possessed the right to ask the gods for signs regarding the propriety of public endeavors and to relay those signs to the public. In the case of the ritualized consultation of the gods (*auguria impetrativa*), what counted was not the signs themselves but how they were reported to the magistrate.[7] So too signs sent unilaterally by the gods outside the context of formal consultations (*auguria oblativa*) only acquired validity when they were either seen by the magistrate or accepted by him.[8] We shall see that in practice this gave the consul or dictator a wide authority to disregard or invalidate unfavorable omens on technical grounds.[9] Most dramatically, the consul M. Claudius Marcellus used to ride into battle in a closed litter lest he observe any unfavorable lightning flashes that would require him to postpone the engagement.[10] Whether such signs actually occur is irrelevant; they only count as omens if Marcellus observes them. Provided he wins. A military defeat could act as a prodigy, pointing out some irregularity in the conduct of religious ritual on the part of the Romans or their commander.[11]

His *auspicium* thus gave the magistrate some discretion in representing the will of the gods, and victory in battle affirmed that his interpre-

6. For the definition of magisterial *auspicium,* cf. esp. Mommsen 1887: 1.89–90.

7. See Linderski 1993: 60: "The curious thing is that it did not matter whether the auspices were true or false; what mattered is that they had to be reported or accepted as true."

8. See Linderski 1986: 2195–96, and Mommsen 1887: 1.106–8. If an oblative sign was announced by an augur, however, it automatically counted as valid.

9. For a more general treatment of magisterial authority in the religious sphere, see Scheid 1985: 47–56.

10. Cic. *Div.* 2.77.

11. On the religious significance of military defeat, see Rosenstein 1990: 56 ff., with bibliography.

tation was legitimate. Other seemingly unrelated dimensions of a magistrate's command can be understood according to the same logic, particularly the pre-battle exhortation, which offers the historian a special opportunity to highlight the commander's capacities as leader. In cataloguing the forces that guarantee a Roman victory, the general puts forward a particular interpretation of the world around him. The Romans are brave and confident; the enemy, desperate and demoralized cowards. The gods are favorable to us; hostile to them. Often these arguments amount to a comprehensive representation of the universe and its history demonstrating how everything from the landscape of the battlefield, to the power of the gods, to the ancestral *virtus* of the state is working together on the Romans' behalf.[12] If the general's representation is persuasive, it can provide a powerful, often decisive, impetus for the army to fight bravely. But the general's speech also raises the stakes for the coming battle by putting this inspiring image of the world at risk. Victory affirms not just the propriety of the Romans' cause in this particular war but their claims about the power of the gods, the legitimacy of their political structure, and, not least, the continuing validity of the historical *exempla* the general invokes. Defeat calls these claims into question or at least suggests that for some reason the Romans have lost the ability properly to engage the forces that should aid them.

Although the power or *imperium* of a consul or dictator possessed a civil as well as military dimension, as Mommsen asserts, "military command formed the defining core of the power of the highest magistrates, and was formally inseparable from it."[13] And it is in the military sphere that the commander's ability to control appearances is best observed.

12. For the valor of the Roman troops as a topos, cf. 6.12.8, 21.41.10; on the weakness of the enemy, cf. 21.40.8–9, 36.17.5; for the gods as favorable to the Romans, cf. 6.12.9, 9.1.8–9 (there used against the Romans by the Samnite C. Pontius), 26.41.18; for the gods as hostile to the enemy, cf. 10.39.16, 21.40.11; for the advantages offered by the landscape of the battlefield, cf. 24.14.6, 36.17.4; for the hortatory use of previous Roman victories, cf. 7.32.8–9, 26.41.10–12.

13. Mommsen 1887: 1.116. This is not to argue that *imperium* was originally an exclusively military power. For a discussion of the various competing theories on the origin and definition of *imperium,* see esp. the discussions of Versnel 1970: 313–55, and Combès 1966: 2–49. A central distinction may be drawn between those who investigate *imperium* primarily as a constitutional phenomenon, and correspondingly try to define the range of powers it entitled its possessor to wield and how these powers developed over the course of time, and those who treat *imperium* as originally and fundamentally a magical or religious capacity possessed by the ruler. Among scholars in the latter category, Wagenvoort's definition (1947: 59–72) of *imperium* as "the chief's *mana,*" or the power of the commander to exert a quickening or life-giving influence on his troops, is especially noteworthy.

The success or failure of magisterial command receives an objective demonstration on the battlefield in the victory or defeat of the Romans. Indeed, it was military success that affirmed a commander's right to be called an *imperator*, a wielder of *imperium*.[14] Furthermore, battle also had an important heuristic function for the Romans. Each side mobilized various forces to guarantee the legitimacy of its claims. Every international treaty imposed a religious obligation on its adherents, and the gods who served as witnesses to a treaty were frequently called upon to punish its violators. Since these forces would not cooperate with those whose claims were false, every demonstration of military superiority necessarily also established the winning side's version of events. This interdependency between power and truth, something much more sophisticated than what we now mean by the adage "might makes right," has clear implications for the construction of Livy's narrative. If the battlefield was where competing interpretations of events were tested against one another, then the history that Livy reports is that which the cumulative victories of all Roman commanders had established as correct. And since the techniques the commander used to mobilize the resources of gods and men were those that had been established as valid by his predecessors' successes, whether we mean the ritual formulas to which the gods had always responded or the skillful use of *exempla* to inspire the troops on that day to emulate the courage of their ancestors, each success depended to some extent on the general's own ability to recreate the past.

I. The Battle of Aquilonia (10.38–41)

The battle of Aquilonia, one of a series of decisive engagements fought against the Samnites in the 290's, provides a particularly good opportunity to study the link between military success and the control over appearances. Both its position at the end of the first decade and the elaboration of Livy's account, which stretches for four long chapters, signal the special importance of this episode. The victory is

14. For the ceremony of the *apellatio imperatoris*, where the troops collectively addressed their victorious leader as *imperator*, see Combès 1966: 74–93. I agree with the interpretation of this rite as an affirmation of the commander as possessing the qualities that lead to victory, rather than as in some way bestowing *imperium* upon him, in Versnel 1970: 340–49.

made the first event of its year, and Livy recasts the conventional annalistic formula to highlight its significance.[15] "The next year there was a *consul insignis* [a distinguished or conspicuous consul (Papirius Cursor)], . . . a huge battle, and a victory over the Samnites such as no one, except the consul's father, had ever won before." The historian also singles out the visual splendor of the Samnite forces as one of the episode's distinguishing features.[16] The particular appearance of the Samnites in the battle results from an elaborately described initiation ritual, an ancient practice that had brought victory a hundred and thirty years before in the capture of Capua and was therefore resuscitated by one of the Samnite priests, who had discovered it in an old linen text.[17] Thus Livy's introductory comments already emphasize the role of appearances in the coming battle and treat the spectacle offered by the Samnites as guaranteed both by religious authority and historical precedent. The battle, however, will determine which historical tradition is to govern the meaning of the spectacle the Samnites produce. A Samnite victory would affirm the propriety of their conduct at Capua and the power of their gods, while Papirius's victory could be read as a repetition of his father's success, which was won, as Livy mentions, against Samnites whose appearance was the same (10.38.2).

But the appearance of the Samnite legion had more than symbolic value. It was the result of a ceremony that had itself used appearances (*apparatus* [10.38.8]) to generate fear. Each soldier was led individually into a linen enclosure, where he was confronted by the sight of slaughtered sacrificial victims and centurions menacingly drawing their swords. He was then told that if he would not swear an oath not to desert himself and to kill anyone he saw deserting, he would be killed immediately.[18] The appearance of the legion itself, which Livy describes with the same word, *apparatus,* operated on those exposed to it in a similar way to the sacrificial "apparatus" that confronted each Samnite soldier, inspiring fear in the enemy and enforcing solidarity within the legion. For the Romans, the soldiers' strange appearance would be

15. Cf. Lipovsky 1981: 164, n. 3.

16. 10.38.2: *eodem conatu apparatuque omni opulentia insignium armorum bellum adornaverunt.*

17. 10.38.6: *ibi ex libro vetere linteo lecto sacrificatum sacerdote Ovio Paccio quodam, homine magno natu, qui se id sacrum petere adfirmabat ex vetusta Samnitium religione, qua quondam usi maiores eorum fuissent, cum adimendae Etruscis Capuae clandestinum cepissent consilium.* For the Samnite conquest of Capua, see 4.37.1.

18. A fuller treatment of the Samnite sacrifice will be found in ch. 4.

disconcerting, and for the initiated Samnites, it would be a constant reminder of the fearsome consequences of desertion.[19] At the same time, their *insignia* also put Samnite history directly on display, since these troops were now visually identical to the victors at Capua. Indeed, if the manuscript reading *linteo lecto* in 10.38.6 is accepted,[20] then the name "linen" legion recalls at once the religious ritual of initiation in the linen enclosure and the "linen" of the historical text from which it had been recovered.

If the *apparatus* of the Samnite legion can be read as an attempt to translate religious and historical authority into a physical force, the Roman consul, Papirius Cursor, counters its influence by questioning the efficacy of mere ornaments in his pre-battle speech: "He said much about the present appearance of the enemy,[21] an empty façade without effect on the outcome: for crests do not make wounds, a Roman javelin passes through gilded and painted shields, and a battle line gleaming with brightness, when the work is done with iron, grows bloody" (10.39.11–13).

The Roman spear and the iron of battle become instruments for demonstrating the worthlessness of Samnite appearances. Papirius's attempt to reduce the Samnite battle array to "mere appearance" also involves reinterpreting the religious rituals that for the Samnites give their insignia meaning. The Roman pronounces these rituals unquestionably corrupt and emphasizes precisely that aspect of them most antithetical to correct sacrificial practice, the mixing of human and animal blood. The soldier initiated in such a ceremony is not set apart in the way the Samnites hope; rather, he is accursed, a *devotus,* whom the angry gods cannot help but punish. And far from binding the soldiery more closely, the fear produced by the ritual will dissolve all social bonds, so that the enemy soldier will "fear simultaneously the gods, his citizens, and the enemy."

Papirius complements his dismissal of Samnite ritual by juxtaposing a set of Roman rituals and spectacles that do have validity. Not only is the Samnite initiation ritual impious, but the Samnites have also violated their treaty with the Romans, thus ensuring that the gods who witnessed it will also be working against them. So too the Samnite finery, so use-

19. Cf. Livy's comment (10.40.12) that the equipment of the legion was *hostibus quoque magnificum spectaculum.*

20. Madvig's emendation of *lecto* to *tecto* would make the adjective linen apply to the enclosure rather than the book.

21. The word *praesens* ("present") used of the Samnite apparatus is also the correct term for the manifestation of a divinity.

less on the battlefield, will be given meaning when incorporated into the context of Roman spectacles:

Once a golden and silver Samnite army was slaughtered by his father, and those ornaments were more honorable as *spolia* for the conquering enemy than as arms for the Samnites themselves. Perhaps it has been granted to his name and his family to be leaders against the greatest efforts of the Samnites and to bring back spoils that will be conspicuous[22] even in the adornment of public places. [10.39.13–4]

The display of Samnite weapons in Roman public spaces, where they serve not to make Samnite warriors stand out in battle but to enhance the nobility of the Roman *gens* responsible for their defeat, also implies that it will be the Roman rather than the Samnite historical tradition that fixes the meaning of the weapons as signs. Rather than recalling the battle in which the Samnites defeated the Etruscans, for the Romans the Samnite *apparatus* refers only to the Roman victory won by the consul's father.

The consul's battle speech itself becomes a kind of *spectaculum,* which affects its audience in the way that the Samnites had hoped their initiation ceremony would, by creating a unifying and inspiring bond among its spectators.[23] In place of Samnite *terror, ardor* is the operative force among the Romans. The battle speech sets up a reciprocal transfer of *ardor* between soldiers and leader, which Livy emphasizes through chiasmus: *Dux militum, miles ducis ardorem spectabat* ("The leader gazed upon the soldiers' *ardor,* the soldiers the leader's" [10.40.3]). The very act of watching, *spectabat,* becomes a channel for this communication of energy. Livy describes how this *ardor* affects each type of man from highest to lowest. Thus as opposed to the corrupt ritual that isolates the Samnite soldiery both from their peers and from the gods,[24] the Roman *contio* creates a common link between the various levels in the Roman camp.[25]

22. The use of the word *insignia* here answers the Samnites employment of *insignia arma* to make the initiates conspicuous among their troops (10.38.12).

23. The contrast is made all the more pointed when Livy points out that Papirius received his information about the Samnite practices from deserters (10.40.1), again emphasizing the fragmentation resulting from the Samnite ceremony.

24. The Samnites are killed *deorum hominumque attonitos metu* (10.41.4).

25. Although the metaphorical usage of *ardor* to describe strong emotional excitement is at least as common as the original meaning of "flame," nevertheless its use here suggests a similarity between the effect of the consul's speech and a physical property that is kindled, or rather reflected back and forth, through the medium of visual contact. The idea of a flame passing from one man to another well represents the communication of a dynamic power. In fact, Wagenvoort cites a phrase used by Cicero of Marius that exemplifies a similar conception, *imperatorius ardor oculorum* (Cic. *Pro Balb.* 49; see Wagen-

The outcome of the battle itself turns out to depend very much on the consequences of the pre-battle spectacles orchestrated by the leaders on each side. As the fighting begins, the crucial difference between the two forces is the condition of their *animi*,[26] and the emotional state of each army results directly from the spectacles to which they have been exposed. Romans march into battle full of anger, confidence, and ardor, all of which Livy connects with the effect of the consul's pre-battle speech.[27] The Samnites on the other hand are kept in place only by the constraining fear resulting from the oath they have sworn. At the moment when the Samnite troops themselves are a *spectaculum*, they see only the terrifying scene of the sacrifice. And although this vision accomplishes its intended purpose—it keeps the Samnites from fleeing—nevertheless it has a paralyzing effect far different from the alacrity and zeal that result from the consul's exhortations. Livy describes the Samnites as bound by chains (10.41.3), a common but telling metaphor. But while the "unequal spirits" of the two sides already give a huge advantage to the Romans, the winning momentum of the enemy progressively reinforces the Samnites' despair. In the end, the Samnites do eventually break ranks and desert: "Then, already conquered by the force of gods and men, the linen cohorts were overwhelmed; sworn and unsworn desert equally, nor do they fear any one except the enemy" (10.41.10). Thus the Roman victory successfully obliterates the social effects of the Samnite spectacle; the mutual fear evaporates, and the distinctions that the Samnite ritual sought to impose are lost. Correspondingly, the Roman success ensures that the alternative spectacle anticipated by Papirius will actually come to pass: the Samnite weapons are indeed displayed in triumph and decorate the temples of the Romans and their allies.[28]

The Romans' victory thus results from the energizing power of the consul's speech, and at the same time, the victory itself provides the

---

voort 1947: 129). There, *ardor* is not only defined as a characteristic of the *imperator;* it also resides in the eyes.

26. 10.41.1: *Proelium comissum atrox, ceterum longe disparibus animis.*

27. For *spes,* cf. *spei pleni,* 10.40.1; for *ira,* cf. *infensos iam sua sponte,* ibid. Notice that in becoming *infensos,* the Roman soldiers come to resemble the gods (cf. 10.39.16).

28. And Livy's account of Papirius's triumph concentrates its emphasis on the visual aspects of the scene, particularly the distinguishing insignia of the troops: *Triumphavit in magistratu insigni, ut illorum temporum habitus erat, triumpho. Pedites equitesque insignes donis transiere ac transvecti sunt; multae civicae coronae vallaresque ac murales conspectae; inspectata spolia Samnitium et decore ac pulchritudine paternis spoliis, quae nota frequenti publicorum ornatu locorum erant, comparabantur; nobiles aliquot captivi, clari suis patrumque factis, ducti* (10.46.2–4).

"touchstone" Papirius required, which would affirm his own claims about the significance and validity of the Samnite spectacles. But what is the relationship between Livy's text, as a permanent record of the battle, and the consul's interpretation of the Samnite spectacle? Looking again at the historian's description of the Samnites' demoralization, we find many verbal echoes of Papirius's predictions: "In everyone's eyes was all the equipment for the occult rite, armed priests, the slaughter of animals mixed with that of men and the altars spattered with blood both holy and accursed."[29] The scene that appears before them is simply an expansion of the consul's brief account of the sacrifice: *qui nefando sacro mixta hominum pecudum caede respersus.* The pollution that results from the mixing of human and animal blood is the central image in both sentences, and the words *sacrum, nefandum, respersus,* and the phrase *hominum pecudumque* are repeated from the consul's description (10.39.16). Again, when the slaughtered Samnites are described as "dazed by fear of gods and men" (*deorum hominumque attonitos metu* [10.41.4]), Papirius's assertion that they would "fear gods, citizens, and enemies together" (*uno tempore deos, cives, hostes metuat* [10.39.17]) is verified.

Given what we know of Livy's working methods, we can safely assign priority to Livy himself, not the historical Papirius Cursor, in determining the details and interpretation of the battle as they are presented here. That is to say, Livy has composed or redeveloped the consul's speech to reinforce his own themes[30] rather than tailoring his narrative to reflect the emphases of some preexisting account of Papirius's speech, much less any actual speech delivered by the consul on that occasion.[31] How-

29. 10.41.3: *quippe in oculis erat omnis ille occulti paratus sacri et armati sacerdotes et promiscua hominum pecudumque strages et respersae fando nefandoque sanguine arae.*

30. The interest in Samnite impiety also makes clear how the Romans' victory at Aquilonia reverses their defeat at the battle of the Caudine Forks, where it was the Samnite leader, C. Pontius (9.1), who could claim that the Romans had alienated the goodwill of the gods by violating the treaties.

31. Regarding Livy's practice in composing and adapting speeches, Ullmann 1927: 18–19, concludes that the occasions on which Livy introduces speeches were generally taken over from his sources, but that the content and expression could be considerably reworked (although the only one of Livy's sources of whom enough survives to provide grounds for comparision is Polybius, and, as Ullmann points out, he may be a special case). He goes on to observe that since the earlier historians in turn would themselves have altered and transformed the orations they found in their sources, Livy's versions can provide no evidence of the actual content of any such speeches, nor that they were in fact delivered. Thus it would be extremely unlikely that any interpretations of the battle of Aquilonia offered by Papirius Cursor himself had an impact on later historians' descriptions of the battle (although perhaps some influence through the medium of the dedicated *spolia* is possible; see Wiseman 1986). On the extent to which Livy could reshape source material to fit his own thematic aims, see Luce 1977: 185–229, esp. 224 ff. on the early books.

ever, if we consider not the mechanisms by which the text was produced but the effect of Livy's presentation on the reader absorbed in the narrative, the relationship between the consul and historian is reversed. It is the figure of Papirius Cursor whose speech appears to impose a pattern and meaning on the events that follow, and the historian's narrative, in reproducing precisely the details the consul predicted, seems both to affirm Papirius's interpretation and consequently to be determined by it.

Papirius's response to the Samnites' battle array is not the only context in which the consul's powers as an interpreter and presenter of signs prove decisive. Within the same episode, Livy highlights two other consular acts, which, although they seem to belong to very different spheres, ultimately rely upon the same ability to regulate appearances. The first is a purely strategic maneuver orchestrated during the course of the battle. The consul orders that servants riding pack mules be interspersed with a cavalry squadron. As the squadron charges into sight, the servants drag brambles behind the mules to stir up dust and give the impression that Roman reinforcements have arrived: "In front, the weapons and standards shone through the turbid light; behind a thicker and higher dust cloud gave the appearance [*speciem*] of horsemen leading a body of troops and deceived not only the Samnites but the Romans themselves" (10.41.6). This false *species,* designed to fool both sides in the battle, thus provides a Roman parallel to the Samnites' use of appearances. And the Roman consul not only produces the spectacle; again he interprets it for the spectators: "The consul confirmed their mistaken impression, shouting among the first standards, so that his voice would reach even the enemy, that Cominium had fallen, and that this victorious colleague was coming" (10.41.7). Here, if anywhere, is a *vana species,* but such is the authority of the consul that even this mere appearance, unlike the Samnite *species,* has the power to affect the real outcome of the battle decisively. And although there are, of course, no reinforcements, the town of Cominium nevertheless does in fact fall to the Romans in a simultaneous engagement, so as to suggest a correlation between even the consul's false claims and the "real" course of events recorded by the historian.

More complex is Papirius's role as an interpreter of omens. So great is the eagerness for battle aroused by the consul's speech that when the sacred chickens refuse to eat, a very bad omen, one of their keepers lies to the consul and reports that the *auspicia* were favorable. Later, the consul's nephew, a "young man born before the learning that rejects the gods" (10.40.10), finds out about this deception and reports it to his uncle. Papirius, however, although praising his nephew's concern, dismisses his warning. "If the attendant present at the omens announces anything false, he takes the religious responsibility on his own head; to me it was announced that the "grain danced," an outstanding *auspicium* for the Roman people and army" (10.40.11). The consul then orders that the chicken keepers be placed in front of the standards. Before the battle proper begins, the guilty chicken keeper is struck by an errant javelin, which for the consul confirms that the gods are aiding the Romans.

Livy's explicit commendation of the young Papirius's behavior helps highlight the contrast between Roman piety and the illegitimate Samnite practices.[32] But the real emphasis of the episode is less on the power of the gods per se, or even on traditional piety, than on the role of the consul as the one who fixes and disseminates divine messages. Even if the omens were unfavorable, the mere fact that the consul apprehends them as favorable determines that they are favorable for the army. The consul is made *laetus,* a word often used of those inspired by exposure to divine or human authority, by the report and communicates his encouragement directly to the troops by announcing that they will fight with the gods as *auctores,* and giving the sign for battle.[33]

Despite what may seem an excessively pragmatic approach to the auspices, neither the historian nor the consul display any skepticism about the existence or efficacy of the gods. Papirius's attitude differs greatly from that of the infamous P. Claudius Pulcher, who, while commander of a Roman fleet, ordered the abstemious chickens to be drowned and consequently sailed into a disastrous defeat.[34] Nor in this episode are the gods regarded simply as useful fictions who behave exactly as the consul claims they do. On the contrary, the consul insists on the absolute propriety of his conduct,[35] and the quasi-legalistic formula with which he explains his decision to his nephew reinforces the impression that he is scrupulously adhering to the established procedures.[36] Again, the effect is to stress the interdependence between the power of the gods and the

32. So also Liebeschuetz 1967: 49, n. 56, and Linderski 1993: 61.

33. 10.40.5: *consul laetus auspicium egregium esse et deis auctoribus rem gesturos pronuntiat signumque pugnae proponit.* Linderski 1993: 60, notes that the word *laetus* "regularly appears in various sources to describe the state of mind after the report of a propitious omen." It should also be noted that many of the examples he provides for this usage come from Livy himself (ibid.: 68, n. 24).

34. Pol. 1.52.2–3; Cic. *Div.* 1.29; Cic. *Nat. D.* 2.7; Val. Max. 8.1.4. See also the discussions in Rosenstein 1990: 79, 84–85, and Linderski 1986: 2176–77.

35. As Linderski 1993: 60, points out, in rising "silently" (*silentio* [10.40.2]) in the middle of the night to summon the chicken keeper, Papirius is scrupulously maintaining the ritual prerequisites for the taking of auspices.

36. In fact, this statement is often read as expressing a fundamental tenet of augural practice. See Linderski 1986: 2207, n. 225.

authority of the consul who procures and interprets it on behalf of his troops. Livy's narrative seems calibrated to represent the congruence of human and divine power rather than to establish the priority of one over the other. The consul's success rests on his correct handling of religious matters; at the same time his victory provides the surest sign of divine action. This relationship is played out again just after the guilty chicken keeper is killed. The consul proclaims that this event is yet another favorable omen demonstrating the gods' support of the Romans. And his interpretation is immediately affirmed by yet another sign, the cry of a crow. Papirius, again made *laetus* by a new *augurium,* once more affirming the presence of the gods, orders that the sign for battle be given and the clamor be raised. Ultimately, the sign for battle sounded at the consul's command (*signa canere*) is made to seem like another reiteration, or even extension, of the miraculous voice of the crow (*corvus occinuit* [10.40.14]).

Livy's account of the battle of Aquilonia thus provides almost a catalogue of the techniques of a successful Roman commander, inspirational rhetoric, scrupulous piety, and clever strategy, and relates them all to an underlying capacity to construct credible and effective representations. These representations are the means Papirius uses to accomplish the "enlivening" of his troops that Wagenvoort gives as the fundamental function of *imperium.* In turn, the power unleashed by the consul against the enemy ultimately confirms his portrayal of the Samnite ritual as disastrous and impious, proves his own ability to manipulate images effectively, and justifies his handling of the auspices. But Papirius's role as a giver of empowering signs is not confined to the course of the battle; the Roman victory itself, as a manifestation of the collective power of the state, acquires its own significance and power to inspire. The news of the victory had "increased the *laetitia*" of another Roman army (10.44.1), a phrase that recalls the effect of the favorable omens on Papirius, and the reports of the consul and his colleague are heard with *laetitia* in the political assemblies at Rome (10.45.1). Papirius's triumph places the entire *populus* in contact with the visible signs of their success. Livy describes the triumph as *insignis,* the same term he had used in his initial account of Papirius's magistracy. The troops themselves are similarly *insignes* on account of their decorations; the military honors won by the troops are *conspectae,* and the Samnite *spolia,* which proved so worthless as *insignia* in the battlefield, are gazed upon (*inspectata*) by the Romans. Finally, as he had predicted, Papirius perpetuates the influence of the *spolia* by placing them on permanent display in the temple of Quirinus.

II. *Ad Deos Auctores: Imperium* and the "Existence" of the Gods

The preceding analysis of Livy's narrative of the battle of Aquilonia has made clear how the exercise of *imperium* by a Roman commander at once operated through the representation and interpretation of signs and events and offered a mechanism for establishing the validity of these interpretations. What is more, this truth-making function of *imperium* is inseparable from its political effectiveness. The representations produced by the *imperator*, whether we regard them simply as rhetorical and military strategies, or as offering a form of *contactus* with superhuman sources of power, function to inspire their audiences and thus are instrumental in securing victory. This success in turn establishes the legitimacy of the *imperator*'s actions and the "truth" of his interpretations. Assertions about divine agency are doubly involved in this system. To engage the support of the gods and to make that support evident to his troops was one of the chief tasks of the *imperator*. In return, the claims that the gods themselves have favored the Romans give the victory its significance and provide a superhuman affirmation of the privileged position of Rome's *imperium* in relation to that of her enemies.

The narrative of the battle of Aquilonia also showed the extent to which Livy's own presentation of the battle links itself to the representations produced by the *imperator*. The consul's pre-battle statements about the piety of the Romans and the impiety of the Samnites appear to fix the terms in which Livy frames the events of the battle and the interpretation he gives them. As the victory itself becomes another manifestation of Roman *imperium*, Livy's own account of it takes its place in the series of inspirational signs produced through the agency of the consul. Given the important role that claims about the gods play in Papirius's success, the relationship between the historian and the *imperator* would seem to motivate the way in which Livy himself portrays the supernatural in this episode. To treat the *imperator*'s pre-battle assertions about the gods or his manipulations of divine signs as mere ruses or fabrications would not only have distanced his own representation of the battle from that produced by Papirius; it would also have stripped the victory of much of its historical meaning.

But these were not the only constraints governing Livy's treatment of the supernatural. One of the characteristics that crucially distinguished history from other forms of narrative in Greek and Roman rhetorical theory was that it included only what was "true" and rigorously excluded the "fabulous" or "mythical."[37] Supernatural events as such lay outside the province of historian.[38] Livy's own awareness of this distinction is signaled in his preface, where he declares that the legends of Rome's founding are more appropriate for *fabulae* than for history. And here too the particular story that he singles out to demonstrate his point involves miraculous divine intervention in human affairs, Mars' fathering of Romulus.[39] For Livy to attribute events to superhuman causes, therefore, was to violate one of the historiographic norms that he explicitly calls attention to in his preface. Thus the historian's portrayal of divine action becomes an issue that brings into play two contrasting sets of expectations, one deriving from the conventions that defined history as a literary genre, the other from the representations of the Roman *imperatores* who also function as predecessors and "sources" for Livy's narrative. Yet I want to argue that Livy's treatment of the divine, variable though it is, by no means represents an incoherent response to two contradictory sets of narrative aims. On the contrary, precisely because of the potential contradictions they involve, such passages provide the historian with an opportunity to draw his audience's attention to the conflicting claims of both traditions of representation and correspondingly to differentiate his own treatment of the supernatural from that of his literary predecessors.

In the case of Papirius, Livy never calls into question the consul's interpretation of the gods' will. While the historian does not presume to

37. Cf. Quint. *Inst.* 2.4.2: *narrationum, excepta qua in causis utimur, tris accipimus species, fabulam, quae versatur in tragoediis atque carminibus, non a veritate modo sed etiam a forma veritatis remota, argumentum, quod falsum, sed vero simile comoediae fingunt, historiam, in qua est gestae rei expositio.* Similar tripartite divisions of types of narration will be found at *Rhet ad Her.* 1.12 f., Cic. *Inv.* 1.27, and Sext. Emp. *Adv. gramm.* 1.263 f. For the implications of these criteria in the development of historiography, see esp. Walbank 1960: 225 ff., and, with special reference to Thucydides, Woodman 1988: 24 ff.

Where precisely to draw the line between the "true" and the "fabulous" was a tricky question, and one that different historians would answer in different ways. For the difficulties, especially given the fact that many periods and events now regarded as mythical were considered to belong to the realm of history, see Walbank 1960, and for Roman distinctions between the mythical and historic periods in their own history, Poucet 1987.

38. Cf. Fornara 1983: 81: "After Thucydides . . . how wars began, how alignments were made and unmade, were the primary questions investigated by the historian. For these a variety of explanations could be pressed into service. Only one was excepted, the supernatural, for belief in divinity had become irrelevant to historical explanation."

39. *Praef.* 6–7. On the distinction between *fabulae* and history here, see Miles 1995: 16 f. This passage is discussed in greater detail later in this section.

represent the divinities directly, throughout the account of the battle, he never casts doubt on their reality or their support of the Romans. In fact, so eager is he to establish the independent existence of the gods that he appends a story to explain why they change the auspices. In the middle of the battle, Papirius vows to pour a libation to the gods before drinking wine himself. The gods are pleased by his vow and so come to favor his victory.[40] This implies that the gods' will, made manifest in the auspices, has an independent existence, and that the divinities have not become favorable simply because the consul proclaims them so. Such a treatment of the gods doubly reinforces the validity of the consul's claims: the gods do provide an absolute, superhuman reservoir of power, which justifies Rome's conduct, and the consul in turn offers a unique and reliable means of access to that power.

Yet Livy's acceptance of Papirius's pronouncements in this episode by no means exemplifies a consistent practice. In his account of the religious reforms of Numa Pompilius, he dismisses the king's story that the goddess Egeria directly instructed him about the proper ritual forms as a fabrication.[41] In book 26, Rome's future savior Scipio Africanus also bolsters his authority among the people through claims about the gods, which Livy again identifies as fictions:

> For Scipio was not only remarkable for his true virtues [*veris virtutibus*], but from his youth on, he was also disposed to put them on display [*in ostentationem earum compositus*] through a certain art, arguing many things among the multitude as warnings sent through nocturnal visions or put in his mind by divine intervention, either because he himself possessed a mind shackled by some superstition or in order that his own commands [*imperia*] and advice be followed without delay, as if sent by some oracle. [26.19.3–4]

An example of such deceptions occurs in Scipio's first speech to his troops:

> Recently the immortal gods, guardians of Roman *imperium,* on whose authority [*qui fuere auctores*] all the centuries ordered that *imperium* be given to me, these same gods have portended even through nocturnal visions that all things will be successful [*laeta*] and prosperous. [26.41.18]

However, Livy's exposure of the public statements of Numa and Scipio as false neither in any way discredits either figure nor diminishes the value of the actions endorsed by their fictive claims: Numa's reforms

40. 10.42.7: *id votum dis cordi fuit et auspicia in bonum verterunt.*

41. 1.19.5: *commento miraculi.*

established the religious institutions under which the Roman state achieved its empire, and Scipio's election provides the turning point in the Second Punic War.

The variations in Livy's treatment of the supernatural have prompted highly contrasting portrayals of Livy's own attitudes toward religion. Some have emphasized passages where Livy seems to introduce accounts of divine action into his narrative without qualification and so depicted Livy as possessing either a religious or a credulous cast of mind.[42] For others, Livy is primarily a rationalist following in the skeptical tradition of his historiographic predecessors.[43] The historian's insistence on the utility and validity of religious practices, coupled with his explicit presentation of the divine tales used to legitimize these practices as false, allows for another alternative. The idea that the statesman will use such deceptions for the greater good of his society has a long lineage in ancient philosophy, emerging most famously as Plato's "noble lie."[44] Livy's portrait of Numa using the gods as a source of fear to exert a check on the Romans' behavior has been connected with the theory, put forth in the *Sisyphus* of Kritias,[45] that the gods were originally invented by the first lawgiver for that purpose. (Livy does not go so far as to suggest that the gods themselves do not exist, however, and neither does their constraining influence work in the same way.)[46] This type of religious outlook, it has been argued, would have much to recommend it in the intellectual climate of Late Republican Rome, where a pragmatic and patriotic respect for traditional religious forms came into conflict with a new intellectual skepticism.[47]

A new and more sophisticated approach views Livy's treatment of the supernatural less as an expression of his own personal beliefs than as a literary device. David Levene has recently suggested that by explicitly

42. So, e.g. Stübler 1941 attempts to demonstrate Livy's sincere belief in the traditional gods of the state, while from the opposite perspective Rambaud 1955 portrays Livy's practice as a retreat from Cicero's rationalizing interpretation of the legends of early Rome.

43. See esp. Kajanto 1957. The evidence for both Livy's religiosity and his skepticism, with a fuller catalogue of earlier scholarship, may conveniently be found in Levene 1993: 16–29.

44. Plato *Rep.* 414B, cited by Ogilvie 1965: 95.

45. DK fr. 25. See Ogilvie 1965: 90.

46. Livy portrays the *metus deorum* as something that helps to maintain the discipline of an entire society, whereas Kritias adopts the perspective of the individual wrongdoer, who is made to fear that the gods are watching over him and will punish him for his actions.

47. Particularly Liebeschuetz 1967. Walsh 1958a and 1961a: 46–81, connects this attitude with the influence of stoicism.

questioning miraculous stories about the gods, Livy was demonstrating the kind of rational critical intellect expected of a historian.[48] Levene's assertion is particularly borne out by the frequency with which Livy ties statements about the supernatural to the question of what material appropriately belongs in a historical narrative. Numa's meeting with Egeria would be a *miraculum,* and therefore by its nature unsuitable for history. Similarly, Scipio's pretended visions are explicitly contrasted with his "true" virtues. So too one of Livy's most direct and intriguing statements about his own religious attitudes occurs in the context of defending his practice of recording prodigy lists:

> I am not unaware that because the portents of the gods are now commonly believed to be worthless, prodigies are no longer announced anymore, nor are they recorded in *annales.* Yet somehow, as I write about the past, my mind becomes old-fashioned, and a certain religious scruple prevents me from regarding the prodigies that those most provident men thought had to be acknowledged publicly as unworthy of including in my *annales.*[49]

This passage juxtaposes two attitudes toward prodigies. A skepticism directly associated with contemporary historical practices[50] contrasts with the perspective of the historical figures whom Livy describes. What is more, the historian presents his own anomalous decision to include this material as an effect of the influence that those figures exert upon him as he writes. The record he produces results directly from their recognition of the prodigies' validity. In consequence, his *annales* come to mirror the *annales* in which prodigies were officially collected. Again, Livy's treatment of religious material becomes a defining feature of his distinctive historical method, a method that reproduces and revives the practices of the religious authorities within his narrative.

Among Livy's predecessors, Polybius in particular made a skeptical attitude toward the gods a defining characteristic of his own historical

48. Levene 1993: 29–30.

49. 43.13.1–2: *non sum nescius ab eadem neglegentia qua nihil deos portendere vulgo nunc credant, neque nuntiari admodum ulla prodigia in publicum neque in annales referri. ceterum et mihi vetustas res scribenti nescio quo pacto antiquus fit animus et quaedam religio tenet, quae illi prudentissimi viri publice suscipienda censuerint, ea pro indignis habere, quae in meos annales referam.* For a fuller discussion of this passage and a review of previous interpretations, see Levene 1993: 22–24 and 115–16.

50. Levene 1993: 115 and n. 28, assumes that the passage refers to the "inclusion of contemporary prodigies in the works of the writers of his day," not their omission by one of Livy's sources. Livy's words seem designed specifically to recall the official practice of recording prodigies in the pontifical record. See Frier 1979: 274.

method and applied this approach decisively to the study of Roman traditions. Indeed, Livy's presentations of both Numa's religious innovations and Scipio's pretended visions reflect Polybian concerns, and the latter seems explicitly to allude to Polybius's treatment of the same event. Polybius's interpretation of Roman religious institutions strongly resembles the attitude Livy takes toward Numa's reforms: he praises the Romans for their handling of religious matters, but treats them from an entirely pragmatic and political perspective. Superstition has been carefully cultivated by the Romans as a check on illegal or seditious behavior.[51] Polybius, moreover, identifies this view of Roman religion as his own particular contribution and thus uses the discussion as an occasion to distinguish his work from that of his rivals. To others, the Roman emphasis on religious pageantry might seem inexplicable, but he can make sense of it.[52] With his remarks about Scipio, we can be certain that Livy is responding to Polybius, who makes a similar comment in the same context, and in this case too the Greek historian's interpretation has a polemical edge: Polybius criticizes earlier writers who accepted Scipio's tales of divine apparitions uncritically; he on the other hand regards them as proof of Scipio's political astuteness, a quality in his eyes more significant than divine favor.[53]

But if Livy's skeptical statements about Scipio and Numa's claims recall Polybian attitudes, he also employs these episodes to differentiate his own approach from his predecessor's. Alongside the inheritance from Hellenistic historiography, Livy draws attention to other forces that shape his narrative. In the cases of both Numa and Scipio, he links the publication of these stories about the gods, whose fictive nature he himself emphasizes, to the means by which each figure gains or exercises *imperium*. Furthermore, Livy reports both claims in contexts that encourage an identification between the voices of the king or consul and that of

51. Pol. 6.56.6–12. Since Polybius's argument deals with the political intentions of those who imposed Rome's religious institutions, it is completely appropriate that Livy would adapt it to his treatment of Numa, whom he makes particularly responsible for establishing Roman cult practices. Needless to say, I disagree with the view that Livy only came to know Polybius when he reached the middle of the third decade; see Luce 1977: 188 ff.

52. 6.56.8–9. The phrase μοι δοκεῖ provides the main clause for four of the six sentences in this section.

53. In 10.5.9, he contrasts his own proper esteem for Scipio's greatest attributes, his ἐπιδεξιότης and φιλοπονία from the "common opinion." Earlier, at 10.2.6, he refers to "others" who have depicted Scipio as particularly indebted to divine actions for his success rather than his own calculation.

the text's narrator. As in the treatment of Papirius Cursor at the battle of Aquilonia, the authority figures within the text provide a model for and confirmation of the historian's own representation of the past.

In Numa's case, the falsehood the king uses to justify his religious innovations detracts neither from their social effectiveness nor from the historian's own endorsement of their importance. The general purpose ascribed to the king's reforms, to prevent the "*animi* of the Romans, which fear of the enemy and military discipline had held in check, from growing lax [*luxuriarent*] through peace" (1.19.4), suggests that the religious program introduced by the king operates as a substitute for the inspirational displays of *imperium* we have seen on the battlefield. Livy encourages the comparison again in his final summary of Numa's reign: "So two kings in succession, each in their own way, one in war, one in peace, both increased the state [*auxerunt civitatem*]" (1.21.6). Here Romulus's conquests and Numa's institutions parallel one another in their effects, and the verb *auxerunt* connects both with the transmission of energy through *contactus*.[54] Thus Numa's whole religious program, which his false stories about the gods help to justify, becomes a central means by which he exercises *imperium*.

Despite the historian's reference to the "rude and unsophisticated multitude" of Numa's day, Livy's presentation of the king's reforms also emphasizes both explicitly and implicitly the continuing impact of his institutions, however distant in time, upon contemporary Rome. He reminds his audience that the doors of the temple of Janus were closed by Augustus after the battle of Actium for only the second time since Numa's reign.[55] But Augustus is not the only contemporary figure recalled in the account of Numa's religious reforms. The moral purpose Livy ascribes to the king's program, with its emphasis on *luxuria* and the dangers of decline through *otium*, echoes his own analysis of the ills that beset the Rome of his own day.[56] In Livy's preface, the progress of *luxu-*

54. Indeed, since Numa's reign begins with a full description of the ritual of *inauguratio* by which the king himself "received increase" (1.18.6 ff.), the phrase *civitatem auxerunt* establishes a compositional ring that frames Numa's entire reign with the imagery of *contactus*.

55. On the contemporary resonance that the emphases on peace would have had for Livy's audience, cf. Ogilvie 1965: 90, who elsewhere (ibid.: 94) suggests that the practice of closing the doors of the temple of Janus to signify peace was one that Augustus himself revived after a period of long neglect. For a demonstration of the techniques Livy uses to highlight the theme of peace in his account of Numa's reign, see Burck 1964b: 146–49.

56. Cf. the comments of Luce 1977: 290, on the analogies between the moral situation Numa attempts to remedy and that of the historian's own day.

ria and its attendant vice, *avaritia*, figures as an index of the nation's decline (*praef.* 11) and results specifically from the failure of *disciplina* (*praef.* 9). Alongside the similarity between the moral preoccupations of king and historian, the king's perception of Rome's dangers results from an understanding of the state's historical development that would have been very familiar to Livy's audience, the idea that the absence of an external enemy encourages internal dissolution. So too the means by which Numa exerts his influence resemble the efficacy of the historical text: the king becomes an *exemplum* "upon whose *mores* men molded themselves,"[57] just as Livy offers his own readers *exempla* for imitation.

Like Numa's, Scipio's claims about the gods also function directly in the exercise of his *imperium;*[58] indeed they are first reported in the narrative of the election in which that *imperium* is won. The context in which the consul makes these claims in his own voice, the first pre-battle speech of his command, also demonstrates with particular clarity the connection between the historian's narrative and the *imperator's* presentation of events. The length, occasion, and structural position of this speech within the third decade all mark it out as especially significant. In many respects, it signals the turning point not just of the Spanish campaign but of the entire Second Punic War. That war began five books before when the Carthaginian forces crossed the Ebro; now Scipio stands on the banks of the same river urging Roman troops to cross in the opposite direction as a prelude to the capture of a city named Carthage, Carthago Nova, the center of Punic power in Spain. The long oration that Livy has Scipio deliver goes far beyond the simple exhortation Polybius composes for him on this occasion.[59] The new consul offers nothing less than a résumé of the entire course of the war, in essence, a summary of Livy's narrative of it up to this point, to emphasize that they are at the decisive moment of the conflict. "This lot has been given us by some fate, that in all great wars we conquer when we ourselves have been conquered."[60] Scipio's observation, in addition to inspiring the troops who go on to actualize the predicted reversal, simultaneously illuminates a pattern in Livy's own account of the war, and one that in turn clarifies

57. 1.21.2: *ipsi se homines in regis velut unici exempli mores formarent.*

58. Livy leaves open the question of whether Scipio actually believed the stories he told or simply made them up for political purposes. But the historian represents them as false in any case.

59. Pol. 10.6. In many other respects, Livy's account of the campaign follows Polybius's almost exactly.

60. 26.40.9: *ea fato quodam data nobis sors est, ut magnis omnibus bellis victi vicerimus.*

the relationship of the Second Punic War as a whole to earlier events in Roman history. Moreover, both his position as consul and his unique personal experience of all Rome's disasters give a particular authority to Scipio's narrative and, by extension, to the historian's.[61] Again a claim about the gods that, after the historian's own exposure of Scipio's falsification of supernatural signs at 26.19.4, Livy's audience cannot but regard as suspect occurs at a point where the interdependence between the *imperator* and the historian appears most clearly.

The beginning of Scipio's campaign in Spain provides an especially appropriate occasion for confronting the problem of how the historian should treat the gods, since Polybius made his account of this event a showpiece of uncompromising rationalism. The *novus imperator*'s first address to the troops points out what the full consequences of Livy's adopting such a position would be. For Scipio's use of the gods here cannot be written off as a simple political trick designed to win the crowd's support; his entire account of the war abounds in references to supernatural causes. To discredit them or treat them as mere rhetorical maneuvers would thus deprive Rome's greatest defeats and victories of much of their religious dimension. But in the course of the speech, the Polybian position receives an important qualification, one that Livy chooses to place in the mouth of Scipio himself. After referring to nocturnal visions and other divine messages promising Roman victory, Scipio then shifts to arguments based on strategic considerations: "My mind too, my greatest "prophet" [*vates*] up to now, foretells that Spain is ours. . . . Reason, which does not deceive [*ratio haud fallax*], supports the same conclusion that the mind on its own divines [*mens . . . divinat*]." Although these sentences function primarily as a bridge from one well-worn rhetorical topos to another, they also give Scipio a chance to offer his own response to the historiographic debate set up by Polybius about his religious attitudes. By claiming his *animus* as his greatest *vates,* Scipio is not quite coming down on the side of *ratio;* rather, he obliterates the conflict between reason and superstition. Both ways of looking at the world work together to establish his point and enhance his credibility.

Livy's treatment of the lunar eclipse that occurred just before the battle of Pydna similarly attempts to reconcile *ratio* and religion by attribut-

61. And incidentally to affirm that account through autopsy: "I myself was present at all the disasters, or those at which I was absent I have felt more than anyone" (*maximus unus omnium sensi*).

ing a supernatural quality to what in another context might have been described simply as a clever leadership strategy (44.37.5ff.). The military tribune, C. Sulpicius Galus, renowned for his knowledge,[62] warns the Romans beforehand that the eclipse will occur. He informs them that an eclipse is a natural event, predictable according to certain laws, and thus not a sign from the gods. The Romans therefore are not frightened by the eclipse, but the Macedonians, who have no warning, are terrified and believe that the phenomenon portends the fall of the Macedonian dynasty. But if the eclipse has been stripped of its supernatural character, the knowledge by which Galus averts the portent itself seems "almost divine."[63] Again, it is instructive to contrast Livy's treatment with those of his predecessors. Polybius has the Romans simply inspired by the portent, whereas the Macedonians are discouraged by it; such foolish superstitions prove the moral that "many trivial things are a part of warfare."[64] Cicero uses the episode in the *De re publica* to illustrate the utility of knowledge even of subjects like astronomy to the statesman. Thus he necessarily highlights Galus's intervention and the decisive role played by his *ratio* in averting disaster. But here too *ratio* is placed in opposition to religion; the measure of Galus's accomplishment is that he "thrust away fear and empty religious scruples from troubled men."[65] The synthesis between scientific knowledge and religion suggested by Livy's description of Galus's *sapientia* as "almost divine" is missing from the passage, however much the historian's overall conception may owe to Cicero's own attempts to harmonize scientific and supernatural authority in texts like the *Somnium Scipionis.*[66]

An emphasis on the inseparability of divine and human causation, by which even events explicable in purely human terms take on a divine di-

62. Münzer 1939. Although Galus is not himself the possessor of *imperium* here, Livy remarks (44.37.5) that his address to the soldiers is authorized by the consul himself.

63. 44.37.8: *sapientia prope divina*. Galus's efficacious use of his own knowledge contrasts with the superstition on the part of troops and commander that led to disaster after another lunar eclipse delayed the Athenian evacuation from Syracuse (Thuc. 7.50.4).

64. Pol. 29.16.1: πολλὰ κενὰ τοῦ πολέμου.

65. Cic. *Rep.* 1.24: *hominibus perturbatis inanem religionem timoremque deiecerat.*

66. For the techniques by which Cicero, like Galus confronted with the eclipse, rationalizes the supernatural elements in Plato's Myth of Er, see Zetzel 1995: 223–24. At the same time, Scipio reports his rationalized dream in language that recalls Roman religious practices. Thus the scientifically correct vision of the planets Scipio regards is described as a *templum* (*Rep.* 6.15.2; see Zetzel 1995: 232). Plutarch's treatment of the eclipse (*Aem.* 17.3–6) demonstrates another possible interpretation. There the consul L. Aemilius Paullus, who knows full well the scientific explanation for the eclipse, nevertheless chooses to set his knowledge aside and conducts an elaborate religious ritual. The integration of science and religion characteristic of Livy's version is absent here too.

mension, provides one means by which Livy can adopt a historian's analytical perspective without undercutting the claims to divine favor that the figures in the narrative themselves use to exercise power and interpret their actions. Even if Scipio's statements about the gods result only from his own cleverness, that does not imply that he does not have their backing. The mind can be a prophet too, and wisdom can become divine. But beyond its expediency, this way of representing causation reflects an overlap of powers inherent in *imperium* itself. Livy's treatment of Papirius's actions at the battle of Aquilonia revealed the parallels between his strategic abilities and his handling of divine affairs. Both depend on the consul's ability to control what counts as true for his troops. And in the moments before the battle, the miraculous voice of the crow, which prompts the consul to give the order for battle, signals the continuity between divine and human action. On such occasions, it becomes impossible to separate the contributions of gods and men; both aspects of the *imperator*'s power are equally involved. Even if a battle is won purely through stratagem or trickery, the victory itself is a proof of divine cooperation. No Roman ever won a battle against the will of the gods.

But the fundamental discrepancy between the two modes of representing the past in which Livy's text shares cannot be removed simply by positing a divine aspect to human actions. The first law of historiography, as Cicero proclaimed, was "neither to include anything false nor exclude anything true,"[67] and as we have seen one of the defining characteristics of history as a genre is that the events it describes are true. But truth or falsehood is not a useful criterion for evaluating the representations produced by the *imperator*. Rather, it is the ability of the commander to mobilize all the energies of a society, whether those derive from the gods or from individual *virtus*, that determines his success or failure. On these terms, Papirius's false staging of the arrival of Roman reinforcements is indistinguishable from his statements about the gods. It is the potency of the *imperator*'s representations, revealed in the victories or defeats they engender, that enables them to count as truth. Perhaps the best way to regard Livy's skeptical statements about the gods is to say that rather than attempting to reconcile the tasks of *imperator* and traditional historian, they actually point out the fundamental incompatibility between the two. By showing that the social significance of the magistrate's claims is independent of traditional historical questions of truth and falsehood, Livy moves the statements of a Scipio or a Numa beyond

67. *De or.* 2.62.

the range of skeptical inquiry. At the same time, Livy's treatment of these episodes highlights the role of the *imperator* as representer and the ability of *imperium* to make such representations meaningful, to make them count as history, independent of their truth or falsehood. In doing so, he offers his audience another model for understanding his own work, and links his representations of the past to a different set of *auctores* than written sources.

Livy's own preface lends support to such an interpretation. Again, he uses stories about the gods, essential to Roman legend but incompatible with the genre of history, to introduce what amounts to a programmatic statement instructing the reader how to approach his text:

> Those things recorded about the time before the founding of the city and about its founding that are more suited to poetic legends than to the incorruptible monuments of history, I intend neither to affirm nor refute. This pardon is given to antiquity in order that, by mixing human and divine things, it might make the origins of cities more august [*augustiora*]; and if it ought to be granted to any people to consecrate its origins and to carry them back to divine creators [*auctores*], such martial glory belongs to the Roman people, so that when they claim Mars as their own parent and the father of their founder, the human races will tolerate this with equanimity as they tolerate our *imperium*. But I do not consider it very important how these and similar tales are regarded and evaluated; rather, let each reader pay keen attention to the following things: what the life and customs were, through what men and by what arts, at home and abroad, our *imperium* was both created and increased. [*praef.* 6–9]

This dense and much studied passage has generated a number of readings.[68] I want to start by observing that the issue raised by early histori-

68. Most recently, Miles 1995: 16–19, has similarly interpreted the passage as an opportunity for Livy to introduce the notion of a historiographic tradition based on the transmission of reliable and accurate information about the past and simultaneously to differentiate his own practice from it. This reading forms part of Miles's larger argument that throughout his narrative, Livy continually undercuts the possibility of the kind of accurate and objective knowledge about the past that such *monumenta* seem to provide. This strategy helps to "redirect the reader's attention from the questions about the factual truthfulness of Roman tradition to the issue of its formative influence on Roman identity and character" (Miles 1995: 74). Although Miles expresses his conclusions in different terms and arrives at them by different means, his thesis that Livy uses references to historiographic conventions as a way of highlighting the capacity of his text to influence contemporary Roman society is one that I hope my arguments here will complement. Moles 1993: 148–50, by contrast, regards the differentiation between history and poetry as implying that Livy's own history will be "factually true" but will grant "indulgence" to *fabulae;* this position he presents as a synthesis between Thucydidean and Herodotean approaches to history.

cal traditions, whether tales about the gods are to be affirmed or refuted, is precisely the one introduced by the claims of Numa and Scipio. Again Livy begins by reasserting the generic distinctions that ought to exclude such legends from a history. Yet here too this statement serves as much to differentiate his work from traditional models of writing history as to profess his allegiance to them. Livy is not promising to exclude these stories; on the contrary he is justifying their inclusion. We might expect a Polybius, by contrast, to be very interested in refuting and rejecting "poetic" material.[69]

But Livy makes clear that the tales that ought to be excluded from history for generic reasons possess value and gain acceptance on different grounds. As in his accounts of Numa and Scipio, Livy introduces a system of representation based on *imperium* operating alongside conventional historiography. Here the right to claim divine ancestry depends not on the literal truth of such stories but on military success, just as it is military success that allows Papirius Cursor to establish a monument recording divine favor at the battle of Aquilonia by dedicating the captured *spolia*. The language used to describe the influence of such stories additionally recalls the processes by which *imperium* itself is transmitted. Legends that the gods are the Romans' *auctores* make the origins of the city *augustiora*. Both the noun *auctor*, here used to mean parent,[70] and the adjective *augustus* derive from the verb *augeo*, to increase. Wagenvoort has shown that this verb can be used to signify the "increase" in power conferred upon a king or consul at his inauguration and that he in turn uses to inspire or empower the rest of the state.[71] The tales about divine parentage may be pure fictions, from a historian's point of view, but even fictional gods can be *auctores* in the sense that they contribute to the city's cumulative *auctoritas*.[72] The word *auctor* acquires an additional level of meaning in this context: since *auctor* is also the term Livy uses to describe his historical "source," its use here underlines the connections between the transmissions of authority and of historical data implicit in the rest of the sentence. Paradoxically, even made-up gods can affirm their own existence.

69. Cf. Mazza 1966: 92: "Nei confronti di tale distinzione, Livio non assume però la posizione che aveva, ad esempio, caratterizzato il "polibianista" Sempronio Asellione."

70. This usage is somewhat unusual in classical prose but not extraordinary in light of the "poetic" color it confers. Livy does give the word special emphasis through hyperbaton, *ad deos referre auctores*.

71. Wagenvoort 1947: 12–17; cf. also the comments of Linderski 1986: 2290–91, esp. n. 578.

72. In the same way, Scipio's fictional divine supporters are instrumental in winning him *imperium*.

But if Livy is using this passage to delineate what we might call an alternative system of transmitting information, one grounded in *imperium* rather than the traditional heuristic devices of literary history, then how does Livy position his own historical text in relation to that system? At first he seems to diminish its importance in favor of a more conventional historiographic program of tracing the moral and institutional factors that contributed to the growth and subsequent decline of the state. These legendary stories have their place and are not worth refuting, but the reader should focus his attention on men and customs. Yet even once we return to subject matter less problematic for a historian, the language in which Livy described the legends that gain credence only because of Rome's *imperium* still echoes. *Imperium* is explicitly mentioned as Livy's subject, and although it is an *imperium* that results from human factors rather than the divine parentage of Romulus, nevertheless when Livy speaks of the "birth" (*partum*) and "growth" (*auctum*) of this *imperium,* the historical processes of Rome's development recall the legendary role of Mars becoming *auctor* of the Roman people by fathering Romulus.[73] What is more, when Livy asks his reader to move beyond questions of the truth or falsehood of stories about the gods in order to concentrate on the ethical underpinnings of *imperium,* he is constructing a response to his own text that mirrors the way in which he himself responds to the representations of Numa Pompilius.

The possibility of an analogy between the roles of historian and wielder of *imperium* emerges yet again at the end of the preface when Livy once more highlights the traditional definitions of history as a literary genre. "If we possessed the same custom that the poets do, we would rather begin with good omens [sc. rather than complaints] and prayers to the gods and goddesses, that they might give a favorable outcome to those laying the beginnings of such a great labor."[74] But it was not only poets who began great works with invocations of the gods.[75] The

73. The application of imagery of biological development to the formation and growth of the Roman state forms part of a long tradition. With its use here, cf. specifically Cic. *Rep.* 2.3: *facilius autem quod est propositum consequar, si nostram rem publicam vobis et nascentem et crescentem et adultam et iam firmam atque robustam ostendero,* with Zetzel 1995: 159–60 and 186, and also Pol. 6.57.10. Ruch 1972 argues that such language represents a distinctly Roman conception of the state as a living organism animated by its own vital forces, and that this idea plays a particularly important role in Livy's view of history (Ruch 1968 and 1972: 834–38).

74. *Praef.* 13: *cum bonis potius ominibus votisque et precationibus deorum dearumque, si, ut poetis, nobis quoque mos esset, libentius inciperemus, ut orsis tantum operis successus prosperos darent.*

75. So also Ogilvie 1965: 29.

omens, vows, and prayers with which he would like to begin his history recall the inauguration ritual by which a magistrate received his *imperium*, or the way he secures the support of the gods for a military campaign before he departs from the city through the ritual *profectio* described in chapter 1. In this way, the beginnings of his text, like those of the city itself, are to be magnified through the favor of the gods.[76] Yet does Livy actually invoke the gods here? The location of this passage, at the end of the preface, is certainly an appropriate place for such a gesture.[77] Nevertheless, the sentence remains counterfactual: this is what Livy would do if the conventions of history were like those of poetry, which of course they are not.[78] Thus here too Livy explicitly proclaims his adherence to the conventions of historiography, but he does so in a way that simultaneously introduces the possibility of another set of practices and models for his work and so ultimately raises the question of which category his *opus* belongs in.

III. Camillus the Historian

Livy's location of his text within the tradition of inspiring and renewing the power of the state exemplified by the speeches and representations of Rome's political leaders aims to provide a link to "real" centers of authority that give his work a special status, different from that of other literary accounts of the past. But his connections to that tradition depend entirely upon his own representations of it. Livy held no office; his records of events were not "official" in the sense that tablets posted by the Pontifex Maximus would have been. If Livy's interpretation of the battle of Aquilonia, for example, is confirmed by the consul Papirius's pre-battle speech, if the very act of narrating the battle seems to continue the consul's own efforts to establish permanent reminders of his success, it is because Livy himself has composed his

76. As such this would be one of a number of patterns of imagery suggesting that Livy's work constitutes a "city" in its own right, analogous to the real city whose *res gestae* it traces. See Kraus 1994b: 267–70.

77. Cf. Cizek 1992: 358: "bien qu'il dise qu'il n'invoque pas les dieux, Tite-Live le fait."

78. The point that Livy does not strictly speaking begin with an invocation is well made by Moles 1993: 156. Cf. also his interpretation of the effect: "Indeed it is precisely because the sentence hovers between the hypothetical and the actual that it is so rich in implication."

speeches and recorded his dedication of the *spolia*. And if Livy's text is in competition with other literary accounts of the same events, the verisimilitude with which he can represent Papirius himself endorsing his own version will also contribute to his authority as a historian. But this very circularity only furnishes another point of comparison between Livy and the military leaders he describes. They also had to rely on nothing other than their own representations to construct for their audiences an image of the unseen forces whose "presence" guaranteed victory. The treatment of the defeat of the Gauls at the end of book 5 reveals even more clearly how Livy uses the figures within his narrative as "sources" who lend their own authority to his version of events. It thus provides a concluding illustration of the unique symbiosis between Livy's text and the historical tradition it records.

The defeat at the battle of the Allia had been one of those moments when the connections between the Roman army and the power of the gods was disastrously broken. In contrast to the battle of Aquilonia, where human and divine resources were all portrayed as working in harmony to ensure Roman victory so that the roles of divine aid and simple strategy could not be disentangled, here a breakdown occurs at every level from the gods down to the individual soldier, who deserts his post because he thinks of his own family apart from the interests of the state.[79] The gods, already alienated by a Roman violation of the *ius gentium,* are not invoked; nor are the auspices even taken prior to the battle. And it is the Gallic chieftain rather than the Roman leaders who devises a successful military strategy.[80] Like the Samnites before their own defeat, the Romans in this situation are overwhelmed by "fear" (*pavor*) and "forgetfulness" (*oblivio*). As Livy stresses repeatedly, all the distinctions that set the Romans apart from their enemies have been obliterated. Even before the capture of the city, the Romans have ceased to be Romans.[81]

Camillus's restoration of the Roman state thus begins well before his famous speech with the reestablishment of that nexus of contacts to divine and human authority that makes the Romans what they are. When

79. Luce 1971: 271–72: "Livy makes it clear that the disaster at the Allia was not caused solely, or even chiefly, by military mistakes; it was the result of moral guilt, religious neglect, and political folly on the part of all classes: leaders, senate and people. The military mistakes are therefore explicable in terms only of the general failure."

80. 5.38.4: *adeo non fortuna modo sed ratio etiam cum barbaris stabat.* For Livy's emphasis on this paradox, see Luce 1971: 269 f.

81. 5.38.5: *in altera acie nihil simile Romanis, non apud duces, non apud milites erat.*

he miraculously leads his troops into the Forum at the very instant when the Romans have just weighed out the gold to ransom their city, the combination of *deorum opes humanaque consilia* (5.49.5) that brings about the Roman victory signals the negation of the battle of the Allia. Livy's narrative focuses on how Camillus as dictator uses the resources of the *imperator* to bring about the reversal. By ordering his soldiers to fight "holding before their eyes the shrines of the gods, their families, and the soil of the *patria*" (5.49.3), Camillus creates for each of his soldiers a visual link to the totality of the Roman state.

Camillus's role as the one who restores the lines of contact by which Rome again becomes Roman[82] stands out all the more clearly since the formerly exiled dictator himself had to be personally restored to membership in the Roman state.[83] Livy describes how, after the army at Veii has voted to summon Camillus from exile to take over command, a young soldier volunteers to float down the Tiber, climb the besieged Capitolium, and have Camillus officially recalled and proclaimed dictator by the Senate. Prior to receiving word of his appointment, according to the version Livy prefers to believe,[84] Camillus would not even leave his place of exile. This elaborate procedure is inspired by more than an impractical concern for propriety. The young soldier's journey and the subsequent embassy to Camillus establish a physical link between the dictator and the Capitolium, the "seat of the gods" (*sedes deorum* [5.39.12]), which complements his official establishment as a magistrate.

But at the same time that Camillus reverses the fortunes of the state, he also works an equally dramatic transformation on Livy's own narrative. The sack of Rome by the Gauls was one of the most momentous events in early Roman history, and among the most controversial, with many competing versions.[85] According to some surviving accounts, there was no last-minute rescue by Camillus, and the Gauls withdrew after accepting a ransom payment from the Romans.[86] Polybius has a Gallic chieftain of the mid third century B.C.E. boasting that his tribe had occupied Rome for seven months and returned home "with their

82. Cf. his warning to the Ardeates that if they do not act, Ardea will become Gallia (5.44.7).

83. Miles 1988: 202–3, stresses Camillus's scrupulous adherence to traditional forms and institutions.

84. 5.46.11: *quod magis credere libet.*

85. For a full account of the evidence for these competing traditions and a review of previous scholarship, see Luce 1971: 289–94.

86. Pol. 2.18.2–6, 2.22.5. See Ogilvie 1965: 727. Cf. also Diod. 14.116.7.

spoils."[87] This is the story that Livy is in the process of telling, has indeed already completed,[88] at the end of chapter 48 when the dictator's dramatic arrival and victory negate that version of events. The issue raised by the Gauls after Camillus's arrival is precisely the same as the question raised by the existence of conflicting historical traditions, whether the Romans were ransomed. The Gauls, of course, assert that the treaty has already been fulfilled, but their claim is rendered doubly invalid by Camillus's *imperium*. Not only does the defeat itself demonstrate the true power of the Roman people and its gods and lead to the recapture of the gold that has been paid out, but Camillus also introduces a constitutional argument to prove that the treaty was never actually valid. Once Camillus has been appointed dictator, his *imperium* supersedes that of the lesser magistrates who negotiated the surrender.[89] Thus at the same time that he mobilizes the forces of gods and men to liberate Rome from the Gauls, he is also "rewriting history" by invalidating in his own voice rival versions of the liberation of Rome. The authority of Livy's representation of the past, his emphatic denial that the Romans were ever ransomed, rests on the *imperium* of Camillus himself.

In fact, the historical tradition is all that was ever at stake in Camillus's raid. The resources of "gods and men" are not mobilized to save the city, for Rome is already out of danger. Rather, Camillus acts to ensure that the Romans will not "survive by having been ransomed" (5.49.1). The ransoming of the city, which Livy calls a *res foedissima* (5.48.9), would have left the defeat at Allia stand as a proof of Rome's powerlessness against the Gauls. Their state, a people "soon about to rule over nations" (5.48.8), would have been preserved not by an overwhelming demonstration of invincible military might and divine favor, but by mere wealth. Hence Camillus orders his troops to save the city by "iron not by gold" (5.49.3). Camillus fights to determine how Rome's liberation from the Gauls will be remembered, and Livy by recording the version of events established by his victory, becomes the means by which this end is accomplished, by which the dictator's claims will reach all future readers of his history. His text is as essential to Camillus's *imperium* as that *imperium* is to his text.

87. Pol. 2.22.5.

88. At 5.48.9, he says the "business is finished," and the insulting cry *vae victis,* uttered by one of the Gauls, serves as a fitting conclusion. See also Luce 1971: 296–97, on the unexpectedness of the ending Livy gives to the narrative.

89. 5.49.2: *negat eam pactionem ratam esse quae postquam ipse dictator creatus esset iniussu suo ab inferioris iuris magistratu facta esset.*

CHAPTER 3

Duels and *Devotiones*

In a scene full of political resonances for the first century B.C.E., Livy describes the embassy of the Latin praetor Annius Setinus to Rome to demand for the Latin allies a share in governing the state (8.4–6).[1] Since the Latins provide half of Rome's military forces, Annius argues, one of the consuls and half of the Senate ought to be made up of Latins, although he is willing to concede that Rome should remain the seat of power and that the united peoples should continue to be called Romans. As he had said to an assembly of allies, "where there is a portion of strength, there also is a portion of *imperium*."[2] The call for "one people, one Republic" (8.5.5) may seem to offer a chance for the peaceful incorporation of kindred peoples. The compromise reached at the end of the *Aeneid* proposes a similar fusion,[3] and even the sharing of magistracies has a parallel in the joint kingship of Romulus and the Sabine Titus Tatius. Yet the Roman consul T. Manlius Torquatus regards the Latin claim not only as a cause for war but as sacrilege (8.5.8–10). What Annius's demands fail to take into account is that Roman *imperium* is not simply a matter of strength, that political incorporation is not merely a consequence of kinship, and that the Roman Jupiter is not like the other gods. The Roman political structure, as we saw in chapter 2, de-

1. For an analysis connecting this episode to the issues raised by the Social Wars, see Dipersia 1975; and see also Lipovsky 1981: 130–32.

2. 8.4.4: *ubi pars virium, ibi et imperii pars est*.

3. Cf. *Aen*. 12.820–40. Indeed, Annius's concession at 8.5.6, "let us all be called Romans," closely resembles Juno's insistence on the abandonment of the Trojan name.

pended upon a network of contact, channeled through the persons of Rome's legitimate magistrates, which connected all members of the state to the power emanating from the gods; without this, the Latins, despite all their superficial similarities to the Romans in language, race, and institutions, were inescapably alien.

The Latin commander soon received an all-too-vivid demonstration of the realities of Roman *imperium* and its privileged connection to the divine. Annius's speech was delivered on the Capitoline itself, the sacred center of the state, where the consul's bond to Jupiter was annually established through his *inauguratio,* and the site that Camillus used above all to confirm the loyalty to place that prevented the Romans from emigrating to Veii.[4] In rejecting the Latin demands, the consul directly addresses the statue of Jupiter, summoning him to witness Annius's impiety. After Annius responds by "slighting the power of the Roman Jupiter," he slips and knocks himself out.[5] Torquatus in turn proclaims Annius's fall to be an omen predicting Roman victory. More than that, he claims it as a proof that the divine power (*numen*) of Jupiter, which Annius has explicitly and implicitly rejected, does in fact exist.[6] By these actions, Annius is not only exercising the consul's religious sanction to interpret the omens; his gesture reminds us of the interdependence of political and religious authority at Rome. The consul proclaims the existence of the gods, yet these very gods act to protect the consulate itself from usurpation by the Latins.

Annius's embassy leads to a battle between the Romans and the Latins. Significantly, in light of the Latins' demand for one of the consulships, it requires the combined forces of both Roman consuls to obtain the victory. Two events render the encounter particularly memo-

4. 5.54.7, and see ch. 1, sec. IV. Manlius's reference to Jupiter's *auguratum templum* (8.5.8) not only refers explicitly to the inaugural ritual through which the consuls entered office every year; it also recalls the description of the original inauguration of the temple itself in Camillus's *peroratio.* Again an emphasis on the preservation of rituals and traditions highlights the parallel between maintaining continuity with the past and continually reestablishing the vertical bonds linking Rome's political leaders to the power of the gods.

5. 8.6.1 ff. Levene 1993: 218–20, finds an inconsistency between this act and Annius's affirmation of the gods' power elsewhere (e.g., 8.4.6 and 8.5.4). But the episode as a whole reveals how closely the cult of the gods was connected to place and nationality. Annius slights the *Roman* Jupiter; his piety in the abstract is irrelevant. Indeed, his failure to recognize that the consulship of the Romans is divinely sanctioned and not to be arbitrarily shared with the Latins already amounts to a rejection of the Roman Jupiter. This is Torquatus's point.

6. 8.6.5: *Est caeleste numen; es, magne Iuppiter; haud frustra te patrem deum hominum hac sede sacravimus.* Notice again the insistence on locality.

rable. Torquatus executes his son for fighting a duel against a Latin challenger without his consular permission, and his colleague P. Decius Mus obtains victory for the Romans through the ritual of *devotio,* which requires his own death. Some have argued that the point of the juxtaposition is to contrast the cruelty and extremism of Torquatus with the true piety and patriotism of Decius.[7] But in this context both actions together share the function of illustrating why the political conceptions upon which the Latin claim for citizenship is based are to be rejected. Annius posits a political union based on kinship, but for a Torquatus to sacrifice his son in the interest of the state, not to mention Decius's self-sacrifice, his bond to Rome must transcend the ties of mere kinship.

Both acts also focus attention on the special quality that differentiates the Roman state from the Latins and places it above kinship. Within the text, this is defined as *disciplina,* the obedience to orders that requires the punishment of anyone who fights without his commander's permission.[8] But military discipline is only one aspect of that larger system of transmitting authority through contact on which Roman unity depends. While Torquatus punishes his son for cutting himself off from the state by disobeying orders, Livy's account of Decius's *devotio* highlights the ritual by which the consul places himself in contact with the power of the gods and consecrates himself by the act of touching his own chin. The *devotio* and the combination of duel and execution not only teach the importance of thus maintaining connection with the collective authority of the state; these actions themselves establish such a connection for the spectators who observe them through the medium of visual contact.

This chapter analyzes both duels and *devotiones* as spectacles—that is, as actions whose effectiveness depends on their being witnessed by others. Each "performance" puts on display the hierarchies that give structure to Roman civic life and thus offers an image of the distinctive political system that sets Rome apart from her adversaries. But more than that, these spectacles become the means through which the collective power of the state operates on the spectators, devastating the enemy and drawing the Romans closer to the sources of their own strength. The

7. Levene 1993: 222–23 and Lipovsky 1981: 112–15.

8. For the motif of *disciplina* in this section and its role in establishing a distinction between Romans and Latins, cf. 8.6.15–16: *Agitatum etiam in consilio est ut, si quando unquam severo ullum imperio bellum administratum esset, tunc uti disciplina militaris ad priscos redigeretur mores. Curam acuebat quod adversus Latinos bellandum erat, lingua, moribus, armorum genere, institutis ante omnia militaribus congruentes.*

transforming power of spectacle points to a final similarity between the *devotio* of Decius and the duel of the young Torquatus. Each is directly linked to similar performances of which it is either an imitation or a model. Torquatus's son accepts the Latin's challenge because the consul himself, when young, had earned his *cognomen* by defeating a Gaul in single combat. Decius's son and grandson will also devote themselves in later battles. Thus beyond its own impact, each individual duel or *devotio* reproduces previous successful performances and so defines a pattern of imitation, like a series of beacon fires, by which the uniquely Roman *res publica* perpetuates itself. Such a system of spectacle, which Livy contrasts with the empty and ineffective spectacles of Rome's opponents, itself provides a crucial criterion for differentiating Rome from her enemies.

In the battle against the Latins, one of these actions, Decius's *devotio* is performed properly, while Torquatus's duel, because he fails to imitate previous duels in certain respects, necessitates his punishment. But as we shall see, this negative example is as instructive as successful duels in defining the crucial elements of the performance. What I have said about duels can also be applied to the scene of the consul executing his own son. Here too Livy emphasizes the impact of the sight of the execution on its spectators, and this act too recapitulates an earlier event in Roman history, the first consul Brutus's similar punishment of his sons for disobedience.[9] Indeed, the execution is depicted as a corrective to the failed duel, an alternative spectacle that replaces the act it punishes in the eyes of its audience.

I. *Devotio*

Devotio is a drastic measure in which a magistrate with *imperium,* consul, dictator, or praetor, to prevent imminent defeat consecrates one individual, who thus takes upon himself the impurities of the entire state. This individual then charges into the midst of the enemy, presumably to his death, and by this act ensures their destruction. In fact, we know of only three instances of *devotio* in Roman history, and in each of them, the individual whom the magistrate consecrates is himself.

9. For an analysis of the Brutus episode as spectacle, see ch. 5; and see also Feldherr 1997.

Furthermore, all three consuls were members of the same family: the first is P. Decius Mus, consul at the battle of Veseris (8.9ff.); his son follows his example at the battle of Sentinum in 295 (10.28–9). The case of his son is somewhat problematic: Cicero tells us that he offered his life in the same way against Pyrrhus at the battle of Asculum,[10] and a fragment of Ennius has been taken to describe the same event.[11] However, the summary of the relevant book of Livy makes no mention of it, and the consular Fasti indicate that this Decius was alive some ten years later.[12] Cassius Dio records an extraordinary story in relation to this event that demonstrates the triumph of Greek cunning over Roman religiosity: When Pyrrhus's troops themselves fear that Decius might perform a *devotio,* the king makes inquiries about the ritual and instructs his soldiers that no one dressed in the special garb of the *devotus* is to be harmed.[13] He then sends a message to Decius, letting him know that any attempt to devote himself will be fruitless.

Livy himself provides the fullest account of the procedure for *devotio.* Both Decii request the assistance of the Pontifex Maximus, who prescribes the proper gestures and the exact words of the prayer. At the command of the pontifex, the consul dons the *toga praetexta,* the purple-bordered toga worn by magistrates, and veils his head; sticking his hand up from beneath his toga, he touches his chin, and while standing upon a spear recites the prayer:

Ianus, Jupiter, father Mars, Quirinus, Bellona, Lares, Divi Novensiles, Di Indigetes, divinities who possess power over our troops and the enemy, Gods of the dead, I pray and beseech, I seek and bring prayers that you favor the might and victory of the Roman people and that you afflict the enemies of the Roman people with terror, fear, and death. As I have undertaken with words, so on behalf of the Republic of the Roman people, the army, legion, and auxiliaries of the Roman people, I devote the legions and auxiliaries of the enemy along with me to the Gods of the Dead and the Earth. [8.9.6–8]

Having done this, the consul girds himself in the *cinctus Gabinus,* a way of wearing the toga drawn over the head that was used by magistrates

10. *Fin.* 2.61.

11. Enn. *Ann.* 191–94 (6.xii) Skutsch. See, however, Cornell 1986a, who argues that the book to which the fragment belongs actually includes material from much earlier than the Pyrrhic war and that Ennius is more likely to have described one of the two successful *devotiones* than the abortive attempt of the third Decius.

12. Another difficulty is that the Romans ultimately lost the battle of Asculum, although for their opponent this was to prove a "Pyrrhic" victory indeed. Also, since some sections of the Roman army were more successful than others, the *devotio* of Decius may have affected only the troops under his command.

13. Dio. 10.43 = Zon. 8.5.

with *imperium* in the performance of sacred rites,[14] leaps on his horse and charges into the midst of battle. The enemy are afflicted with terror wherever the consul rides, and when eventually they kill him, their fate is sealed. The consul's body is always buried under the thickest pile of weapons and corpses and so cannot be found until the next day.

How many of these details accurately reflect early Roman religious practice remains uncertain.[15] The idea of charging a man or beast with the impurities of the people and sending it off to exert its destructive influence among the enemy possesses many analogues, from Hittite sacrificial practice to the legend of the Trojan horse.[16] However, Versnel has argued that what has become the archetypal form of *devotio* actually evolved from the more widespread but somewhat less dramatic practice of invoking the gods' power by making over to them the lives and property of the enemy.[17] But whatever the actual authenticity of Livy's description, the act clearly possesses a special significance for his text. The historian explicitly justifies his inclusion of the details of the ritual in terms that remind us of one of the cardinal aims of his history: he has preserved the tradition of an archaic Roman practice into an age when native religion has been supplanted by foreign rites.[18] Indeed, the first step in the ritual itself draws attention to the importance of preserving traditions. The Decii would not have been able to perform their *devotiones* if they too had not had access to an equivalent record of the past through the memory of the pontifex. Thus when the second Decius devotes himself, the ritual prescribed by the pontifex presumably reproduces Livy's account of his father's *devotio.*[19]

Livy's use of accounts of *devotio* to highlight his own role of giving access to the past relates to another important feature of the ritual itself: perhaps no other Roman practice reveals more clearly the importance of

14. Not only of a sacrificing priest (Deubner 1905: 70). See Versnel 1981: 148–49, for evidence and bibliography.

15. Skutsch 1985: 355, regards the prayer formula itself as "a fairly competent antiquarian's product."

16. For parallels, see Versnel 1981, esp. 153 ff. and 164 ff.; and see also Burkert 1979: 52 ff.

17. Versnel 1976. The formula for this type of *devotio* is preserved by Macrobius *Sat.* 3.9.9 ff.

18. 8.11.1: *Haec, etsi omnis divini humanique moris memoria abolevit nova peregrinaque omnia priscis ac patriis praeferendo, haud ab re duxi verbis quoque ipsis, ut tradita nuncupata sunt, referre.* The language of the passage, with its doublets, heavy alliteration, and pleonasm, makes the historian's own description of his task an echo of the consul's prayer.

19. 10.28.14. Ironically, this second pontifex also bears the name Livius, although with a different *praenomen* than the historian.

contact as the mechanism for the transmission of power. The role of contact is first apparent in the physical gestures by which the consul invokes the aid of the gods. The touching of the chin recalls the action with which an object is consecrated or made over to the gods.[20] The spear on which the consul stands either embodies the god Mars,[21] or perhaps, since it is placed on the earth, opens a bridge between the person of the consul and the underworld gods to whom he devotes himself.[22] Between them, the two actions denote the twin sources of power that energize the entire state, the power of the gods and the collective power channeled through the person of the magistrate.

The performance as a whole has a contradictory effect on the consul himself. The *devotus* surrenders more than his life; through being rendered *sacer,* he loses his status as an individual member of the group.[23] Thus the *devotus*'s charge into the midst of the enemy can denote his separation from the Roman host as much as his aggressive intention against the enemy. On the other hand, the gesture of *contactus* binds the individual even more closely to the whole. Not only does he become their substitute, the one whose death ensures the survival of the multitude;[24] he takes upon himself all the religious impurities of the people, so that his death becomes an expiation for them. At the same time, he also assumes their power, becoming the instrument through which the wrath of the gods is brought to bear on the enemy. The *devotus* also makes himself a surrogate for the enemy, whose fate is bound to his own through

20. See Deubner 1905: 71, and esp. Wagenvoort 1947: 34. The chin, which in many European cultures was regarded as a center of life forces (cf. Onians 1951: 233), was surely not chosen just because it is easily accessible when the head is veiled.

21. Deubner 1905: 71–72.

22. If this spear ever comes into the possession of the enemy, a *suovetaurilia* must be performed to Mars as an expiation (8.10.14).

23. Wagenvoort 1947: 32, defines the *devotio* as "a religious *capitis diminutio maxima,*" referring to the legal term used to designate the complete loss of citizen rights. He bases this definition partly on the references to the *caput* of the *devotus* as the object of consecration in other Latin authors (Val. Max. 5.6.5, Curt. 8.6.28, Flor. 1.17.7, and Ps. Quint. *Decl. mai.* 12.11 and 12.18). Livy does not use the term explicitly of either Decius (unless the idea of the loss of *caput* is somehow conveyed through the gesture of veiling the head), but one of the signs by which Decius learns that he will be required to devote himself is that the liver of the victim he has sacrificed, although healthy in every other respect, has had the "*caput* cut from the *pars familiaris*" (8.9.1). On the *devotio* as a rite of separation, see also Versnel 1981: 148–52.

24. For the many levels of ritual substitution involved in the *devotio,* see Versnel 1981: 159. Palinurus, whose life is demanded by Neptune in return for the safe arrival of the Trojan fleet in Italy (*unum pro multis dabitur caput* [*Aen.* 5.815]), provides the clearest example of the logic of this kind of substitution in Roman literature.

the agency of sympathetic magic. Not only does the *devotus* actively terrify the enemy, but the death that he suffers ensures that they too will die.

After the initial ritualized contact charges the consul with both the power and the pollution of the entire state, contact emerges again as the mechanism by which these energies are disseminated among the enemy. Thus the younger Decius says that he will "touch the standards, weapons, and arms of the enemy with deadly curses."[25] The impact of the elder Decius, "like a *piaculum* sent from the heavens for all the anger of the gods,"[26] can be understood in the same terms. He is initially described as bringing a *pestis,* or plague, among the enemy, and throughout the description, it is less the consul's own actions than the superhuman influences he bears with him, *terror* and *pavor* (panic), that overwhelm the enemy. The progress of this fear, which sets in confusion the standards of the Latins and then "penetrates deeply throughout the entire army," resembles the spread of a disease.[27] The enemy "tremble as though stricken by a plague-bearing star."[28]

But in the description of the elder Decius's final charge, the very sight of the consul, in addition to physical contact or proximity, provides a medium through which he exerts his influence on both sides. The appearance of the consul, with his specially arranged toga, mounted on his horse in the midst of foot soldiers, makes him strikingly conspicuous. Livy emphasizes that Decius was "seen by each army" (*conspectus ab utraque acie* [8.9.10]) and immediately draws attention to his *visus* when he is described as "exalted beyond human appearance" (*augustior humano visu* [ibid.]). The simile of the "plague-bearing star" (8.9.12) further contributes to the pictorial vividness of Livy's description of the consul's charge and at the same time links the visual impression Decius produces directly to his destructive power. Even the devastation of the enemy, called *evidentissimum,* "most clear to see," becomes a spectacle for

25. 10.28.17: *contacturum funebribus diris signa tela arma hostium.*

26. 8.9.10: *sicut caelo missus piaculum omnis deorum irae.*

27. 8.9.11: *ita omnis terror pavorque cum illo latus signa primo Latinorum turbavit, deinde in totam penitus acies pervasit.* For the connections between contact and "contagion", see Wagenvoort, 1947, esp. 175–78.

28. 8.10.12: *haud secus quam pestifero sidere icti pavebant.* Another uncanny aspect of the consul's charge, one that makes it inexplicable on purely rational terms, is that while we might expect the enemy to be terrified by the sight of such a terrific figure charging toward them, the actual death of the consul, rather than restoring the enemy's courage, only completes their devastation. Cf., too, the instantaneous demoralization, indeed insanity, that afflicts the Gauls after the death of the younger Decius (10.29.2).

the Roman troops, who immediately take on new vigor, "as if they were beginning a fresh battle with the sign just given."[29]

That comparison of the consul's charge to the signal to begin battle emphasizes the connection between the result of a *devotio* and the powers of *imperium,* a connection already apparent in the requirement that the *devotio* be performed by a magistrate with *imperium.* In fact, the entire ritual can be read as a means for projecting magisterial *imperium* in a particularly intensive and efficacious form. The twin aims of *devotio* signaled in the consul's prayer, to render the Romans powerful and prosperous and to inflict destruction upon the enemy, represent precisely the function of all *imperium.*[30] Papirius at the battle of Aquilonia accomplishes just the same thing. While Decius's cry that "the aid of the gods is required" seems to suggest that the *devotio* procedure marks a movement beyond the standard resources of the commander, it should be remembered that there is a superhuman component in all magisterial authority. What the *devotio* does accomplish, however, is to heighten the immediacy with which the powers residing in the *imperator* are communicated. The person of the *devotus* becomes a particularly transparent manifestation of these powers. The transformations in his appearance all reveal the sources of Roman might.[31] Thus his special way of girding the toga, *cinctu Gabino,* signifies that he possesses *imperium;*[32] the term *augustior* applied to the visual impression made by the consul confirms this connection because of its association with the terms used to describe the "increase" in authority received by the consul at the moment when he enters his magistracy. Yet as we have seen, the *devotus*'s appearance does not simply represent or symbolize his authority; like the visible *insignia*

29. 8.9.12–14. *Evidentissimum* is emphatically placed at the beginning of the sentence.

30. Indeed, even the language with which the consequences of *devotio* are described can be compared to terms applied to the effects of *imperium.* The Romans, after the death of the consul, are said to "charge into battle as if the signal had just been given for the first time" (8.9.13). Giving the signal for battle, a procedure we saw emphasized in Livy's narrative of the battle of Aquilonia, may be regarded as one of the essential acts of the *imperator.* So, too, even the report of the *devotio* of the younger Decius inspires the Roman soldiers who have not actually seen it (*ibi auditur eventus P. Deci, ingens hortamen ad omnia pro re publica audenda* [10.29.5]). The enemy, on the other hand, are said to "grow sluggish" (*torpere* [10.29.2]) as a result of the charge of the younger Decius. This sluggishness often appears among troops exposed to *imperium* that is flawed or ineffectual, or opposed by a conquering enemy, as for example the Romans before the disaster of the Caudine Forks: *sistunt inde gradum sine ullius imperio stuporque omnium animos ac velut torpor quidam insolitus membra tenet* (9.2.10).

31. Wagenvoort 1947: 122, n. 2, suggests a connection between the physical amplification of the *devotus* through contact and the large size of the statue that must be buried as a *piaculum* if the *devotus* survives the battle (8.10.12).

32. Versnel 1981: 149.

displayed in a triumph, it provides the means through which this authority functions.

The role of the *devotus* as someone who manifests or communicates the power of the gods also explains another important feature in Livy's accounts of both Decii. In each case, the *devotio* itself is predicted by an elaborate series of omens. Prior to the battle of Veseris, both consuls in their sleep behold the same vision "of a man larger and more exalted [*augustior*] than of human bearing, saying that by one side the general [*imperator*] and by the other the entire army was owed to the gods of the underworld, and [that] victory would belong to the people whose general devoted himself and the legions of the enemy" (8.6.9–10). This communication operates on two levels. First is the simple sending of a message, which is received by the consuls and finally acted upon when Decius devotes himself. But there is also an important connection between the visual aspect of the omen and the *devotio:* The vision of a figure "more *august* than human," predicts precisely the appearance of the *devotus* himself. Thus the consul is not just obeying the orders of the gods; in his own person, he "broadcasts" the miraculous sight he has seen in the dream, rendering it visible to both armies. Here is another respect in which the *devotus* performs the traditional function of the *imperator* through more emphatic means, for, as we saw in chapter 2, it is always the role of the general to represent the divine realm to his troops.

Before the battle of Sentinum, when the troops have been arranged for combat, a deer pursued by a wolf runs between the two battle lines. "The deer runs toward the Gauls and the wolf toward the Romans. The wolf is received within the ranks; the Gauls kill the deer. Then a Roman soldier proclaims, 'Flight and slaughter have gone to that side where you see the sacred beast of Diana laid low; on this side the wolf of Mars, whole and untouched, reminds us of our martial heritage and of our founder'"(10.27.8–9). The double aspect of the prodigy looks forward to the two components of the *devotus*'s prayer where again the "flight and slaughter" of the enemy complements the inspiration of the Romans. More than that, the prodigy also predicts the mechanism by which the *devotio* operates. The two animals become surrogates for each army, which in turn takes on the characteristics of its representative. When the deer is killed, the Gauls ensure that they will be similarly affected by *caedes;* the Romans recognize the wolf as *victor,* and so they too will be victorious.[33]

33. The soldier's description of the wolf as *integer* and *intactus* is also interesting in this regard. Although the Romans will not be "untouched" in the battle of Sentinum (cf.

The willingness of the Decii to give up their lives in the service of the state has made their deaths virtual paradigms for Roman patriotism, and Livy's account of them has an emphatically didactic function, revealed most clearly in the praise that each receives from his fellow consul.[34] But the *devotio* ritual itself, which Livy describes in such detail, can also offer a new model for how the exemplary figures of the Decii affect the audiences they are designed to instruct. Imitation, after all, plays a crucial role in each narrative, as the enemy and the Romans both take on characteristics possessed by the Decii. The *devotus,* precisely by imitating the past, that is by properly performing the ceremony prescribed by the Pontifex Maximus, becomes an embodiment of the collective power of the state and, by projecting this power through his own person, confers it back to the army as a whole, rendering them victorious where before they were on the verge of defeat. Thus through a kind of sympathetic magic, founded on the possession of *imperium,* the Romans are made more like themselves. The social regeneration, for it is nothing less, accomplished by these *devotiones* is made to depend upon direct contact with the centers of collective power. This explains why Livy uses his account of the first *devotio* ritual to cast his history as the means by which such "transmissions" can be preserved. Admittedly, the *devotio* offers an extreme case, where the powers of the *imperator* clearly operate through superhuman means. In the next section, we shall examine a seemingly less extraordinary genre of regularized performance, the series of duels in books 7 and 8, where the role of *imperium* and its link to the "education" of the individual can be understood in comparable terms.

II. Duels

In spite of the juxtaposition of the stories of Decius and the younger Torquatus in book 8, and the shared willingness of those involved to give up their lives for their country, any intrinsic similarity between duels and *devotiones* seems to be ruled out by their different outcomes. The *devotus* is expected to die in battle, while the youth sent out to fight the enemy champion is expected to win. Nevertheless, Livy's

10.29.18), the same adjectives are used repeatedly to describe the "restoration" of the Roman troops after the *devotio* of the first Decius at the battle of the Veseris (cf. 8.10.4–6).

34. 8.10.4: *memores consulis pro vestra victoria morte occubantis.* Cf. 10.29.19–20.

narratives of the two types of actions share the same general structure. Prior to the duel itself, the young Roman combatant must be given permission to fight by his commanding officer.[35] In each of the two successful duels, this is none other than a magistrate with *imperium*, a dictator in Torquatus's case, a consul in Corvus's. So too a citizen can only be devoted by a consul, dictator, or praetor (8.10.11). After their respective performances, both the living champion and the dead *devotus* are reincorporated into the group by being praised and held up as inspiring examples, again by the commander.[36] The way that the actions of the magistrate frame the exploits of both champion and *devotus* emphasizes the importance of contact in each procedure as the means that allow the individual to act effectively on the state's behalf. Correspondingly, in Livy's account of the duels of Torquatus and Corvus, each champion, like the two Decii, becomes a kind of surrogate for the Roman people as a whole. Their victories not only bring them individual glory but predict, or indeed determine, the outcome of the conflict between Gauls and Romans. Their success acts to validate Rome's intrinsic might and renders the Romans who witness it fiercer and more active; the defeat of each Gaul has an equivalently demoralizing effect on his fellows. When the first Gaul is killed by T. Manlius, fear is said to have rendered the entire army of Gauls motionless (*defixerat*) while the Romans are made *alacres* (7.10.12). The defeat of Corvus's Gaul similarly determines in advance the outcome of the battle in which it occurs.[37] Thus the effect of the duel as spectacle, to invest each side with the attributes displayed by its surrogate, reproduces the combined result of the *devotio*. The difference is that in a *devotio* the *devotus* plays a double role, acting as surrogate for the victorious Romans and at the same time "infecting" the enemy with death through his own destruction. In the case of the duel, this double function is split in half. Each side produces its own champion, so that victory can belong entirely to the Roman and death need befall only the Gallic combatant.

Livy's treatments of the exploits of Torquatus and Corvus give us important clues about the particular concerns of his narrative because we

35. 7.10.2–4 and 7.26.2.

36. For the recovery of the bodies of the *devoti* and their funeral, which is in each case conducted by the *devotus*'s partner in *imperium*, see 8.10.10 and 10.29.19–20; for the praise and celebration with which the victorious champion is received by his fellows, cf. 7.10.12 and 7.26.10.

37. 7.26.8: *adeo duorum militum eventum, inter quos pugnatum erat, utraque acies animis praeceperat.*

can compare them to parallel accounts from other annalists, which survive as excerpts in the text of the second-century antiquarian Aulus Gellius. The fragment recording the duel of Torquatus is especially valuable: it is directly attributed to the first century B.C.E. historian Claudius Quadrigarius, and close verbal resemblances make it likely that Livy modeled his account on it directly.[38] It would thus provide the only point in the first ten books where we can compare Livy's treatment of an event verbatim with that of one of his "sources." The Corvus narrative is more difficult to use.[39] Gellius does not attribute it directly to Quadrigarius, as we would expect, since this author was one of his particular favorites,[40] and probably reaches him only through having been previously excerpted, and in some measure recast, by another compiler.[41] Comparisons between both sets of parallel versions reveal that the crucial elements of Livy's construction of the duels—the role of the commander as the one who both enables the young Roman to fight and later praises his victory, and the corresponding influence the duel acquires over the outcome of the larger conflict between Gauls and Romans—were not indispensable components of a fixed narrative tradition. Claudius Quadrigarius makes no mention of Torquatus's request for the dictator's permission to accept the Gaul's challenge, a moment Livy ac-

38. Aul. Gell. *NA* 9.13.7–19 = Claudius Quadrigarius fr. 10b Peter. For the argument that Quadrigarius is in fact Livy's source for the duel, despite the differences in his treatment, see Luce 1977: 224–27.

39. Aul. Gell. *NA* 9.11 = Claudius Quadrigarius fr. 12 Peter.

40. See Holford-Strevens 1990: 179 ff.

41. In spite of Gellius's assertion (*NA* 9.11.2) that the story is told *in libris annalibus*, the way the quoted fragment begins suggests that its immediate source was not an annalistic text but a collection of *exempla*. The beginning of the true excerpt from Quadrigarius on the duel of Torquatus, *cum interim* (9.13.7), shows that it forms part of a continuous narrative of the battle. It could fit in precisely at the point where 7.9.8 begins in Livy's version. The Corvus excerpt however was not taken from a narrative of the events in the *ager Pomptinus,* which are summarized in the second sentence of the selection (9.11.4). The consular dating is included; this would be unnecessary in an annalistic source, where that information would have been given at the beginning of the account of that year. The link to what preceded the excerpt in its source is provided by the phrase *adulescens tali genere editus.* This would seem to derive either from some parenthetical description of the deeds of famous noble men or more probably from a collection of narratives arranged by subject (e.g., "How Noble Families Won Their Names"; indeed, Wiseman 1986: 98, with n. 58, notes that one later collector of *exempla,* Aurelius Victor, had a special interest in the origins of noble *cognomina*). *Talis* can perform a similar linking function in the work of Valerius Maximus (cf. 3.3.4: *talis patientiae aemulus Anaxarchus*). Therefore for all its archaizing tendencies of language (Holford-Strevens 1990: 179, n. 10), it is possible that this account, far from being a source for Livy's text, may have even been retailored to conform to his version of events.

centuates by including the dictator's exhortation in direct speech. The "annalistic" treatment of Corvus's duel does state that the tribune asked the consul's permission but leaves out the later speech of the consul urging his soldiers to "imitate" their champion. Neither account implies that the duel has any greater consequence than to win glory and a new cognomen for its victor.[42]

The full significance of Livy's reformulation of the duel can best be viewed against the background of the varied cultural associations that the institution of dueling possessed in the Late Republic. Stephen Oakley has demonstrated the frequency and importance of single combat in Roman military practice and made clear that such duels cannot be regarded simply as a response to foreign challenges.[43] Oakley collects over thirty examples of single combats and suggests that during the peak period of the Middle Republic, such combats could have happened as frequently as once a year.[44] The evidence he compiles, together with the wealth of parallels adduced from other cultures, make it possible to trace the variety of connotations the practice acquired within Roman culture.

One of the tendencies that emerges from Oakley's analysis is the link between participation in single combat and the competition for power and prestige within the Roman aristocracy. Both Manlius Torquatus and Valerius Corvus rise to the highest positions at Rome. More than that, their exploits yield the honorific surnames (*cognomina*) that will distinguish their respective families throughout their history. Indeed, it has been suggested that the story of Valerius Corvus arose as a response to the glorification of the hero of the Manlii.[45] At the same time, Oakley points out that the Romans were unique among ancient cultures in their attempt to circumscribe the personal glory won through single combat

42. A point also observed by Fries 1985: 99–100, and Walsh 1961a:71.

43. Oakley 1985: 392, provides a summary of previous scholarly opinions and acknowledges his debt to Harris 1979: 39, n. 1, as the only other scholar to draw attention to the prevalence of single combat at Rome. The opposite notion, decisively refuted by Oakley, that the institution of dueling was associated with a lack of discipline and therefore an essentially alien practice, belonging above all to Rome's Celtic opponents, will be found, e.g., in Bayet and Bloch 1968: 109–11.

44. Oakley 1985: 397.

45. Holford-Strevens 1984: 148, suggests that the story was worked up by Valerius Antias for the purpose of glorifying the Valerii. But he does not think it was actually invented by Antias. According to Suetonius *Tib.* 3.2 (= Oakley ex. 9 [1985: 394]), the Livii Drusi also claimed that their cognomen derived from Drausus, the name of an enemy chief killed in battle. However, nothing in the language of the passage allows us to be certain that the killing took place in the context of a formal duel.

by emphasizing that the champions accepted challenges only with the permission of their commanding officer.[46] For our purposes, though, the stress on *disciplina* is best treated as only one of many possible ways of interpreting single combat rather than as an overarching Roman cultural strategy for regulating individual ambition. It is possible to imagine a version of the Torquatus story designed solely to commemorate the young man's heroism and prowess. In fact, such a version survives in the account of Claudius Quadrigarius.[47]

A brief survey of the accounts of duels fought in the decades surrounding the Social Wars, a period when the traditional models of aristocratic authority were being tested by the rise of Marius, reveals that the practice could be subjected to competing interpretations and had in fact become a significant locus for demonstrating or debunking the importance of noble ancestry. Thus L. Opimius, presumably connected with the consul responsible for the destruction of Gaius Gracchus, is reported to have fought a duel with one of the Cimbri.[48] The anti-Sullan hero Sertorius similarly challenged the soft aristocrat Metellus Pius to a duel. Unlike Opimius, Metellus refused and was derided by his troops.[49] During the same war in which Opimius accepted the chance to distinguish himself through single combat, Marius himself was said to have been challenged to a duel by a Teuton and to have ostentatiously rejected that challenge in a manner that parodied the entire institution. "When a Teuton challenged him and demanded that he advance, Marius responded that if he wanted to die, he could go hang himself. After the Teuton insisted, Marius placed before him a gladiator of

46. Oakley 1985: 404–7 contrasts his approach with the conclusions esp. of Neraudeau 1979: 249–58, that dueling, as a definitively un-Roman practice, was associated particularly with the impulsiveness and energy of the *iuvenes,* who had to be held in check by the *disciplina* of their elders.

47. Oakley's interest in recovering the attitudes of the Early and Middle Republic has perhaps led him to underestimate Livy's own role in making the duelist's request for his commander's permission a canonical element in duel narratives. Oakley 1985: 406, declares that this theme "is regular in the literary sources," but of the seven passages he cites, five come from Livy himself and the other two are of a later date and quite possibly influenced by Livy's practices. So, too, he sees Livy's addition of such a scene to Quadrigarius's narrative as evidence that the emphasis on discipline had become "a *topos* of single combat." One could equally say that it reflects Livy's desire to construct such a *topos.*

48. Ampel. 22.4 (= Oakley ex. 24 [1985: 396]). Münzer 1931 suggests that this L. Opimius was the son of the consul in 121 B.C.E. and also that he fought the duel in order to restore the reputation of his family.

49. Plutarch *Sert.* 13.3–4 (= Oakley ex. 26 [1985: 396]). Plutarch's defense of this refusal, based on Theophrastus's dictum that a general should die like a general and not a foot soldier, represents his own opinion, not Metellus's.

contemptible stature and almost worn out with age and told his challenger that if he beat the gladiator, he himself would fight the winner."[50]

By the time Livy came to write his own versions of the duels of Torquatus and Corvus, the practice of single combat itself seems to have all but died out. With the exception of an encounter during the Jewish War,[51] the last recorded instance of single combat took place during Caesar's Spanish campaign of 45 B.C.E.[52] But the decline of the actual practice of single combat does not mark the end of its cultural significance; in addition to Livy's narratives, the statue of Valerius Corvus, complete with crow, erected in the Forum of Augustus testifies to the importance that these episodes assumed during the early Principate.[53]

How then are we to understand Livy's representations of single combat, particularly his interest in the relationship between the young champion and his commanding officer, in this context? We can rule out any idea that Livy was sending a crude message about the new political reality by subordinating the accomplishment of the individual champion to the superior authority of the magistrate. The explicit moral function of these episodes, both in Livy's text and in the Augustan Forum, was not to check ambition but rather to inspire imitation; Corvus is held up as a model of behavior whom his consul instructs the other Roman soldiers to emulate. The innovation of Livy is not to have wrested dueling itself away from the surviving *nobiles* as a means of personal advancement, but, like Augustus in his Forum, to have taken control of the stories told about these events, converting them from self-glorifying family narratives to paradigms of patriotic action that had broader, national application. We shall see that even within the story of Torquatus, Livy signals the transition from family glory to the interest of Rome as a whole as the

50. Front. *Strat.* 4.7.5 (= Oakley ex. 23, [1985: 396]): *C. Marius Teutono provocanti eum et postulanti ut prodiret, respondit, si cupidus mortis esset, laqueo posse eum vitam finire; cum deinde instaret, gladiatorem contemptae staturae et prope exactae aetatis obiecit ei dixitque, si eum superasset, cum victore congressurum.* However, Marius too was subject to radically different interpretations. Thus when Plutarch in the early part of his biography celebrates Marius's rustic origins and essential valor in a manner reminiscent of the glorification of the early heroes of Rome, he notes that Marius himself defeated an enemy in single combat at the battle of Numantia. This brave action contrasts with the general corruption and laxity of the rest of the army. See Plut. *Mar.* 3.1–2 (= Oakley ex. 22 [1985: 396]).

51. Jos. *Bell. Iud.* 6.168–76, cited by Holford-Strevens 1984: 148; see Oakley 1985: 410.

52. *Bell. Hisp.* 25.3–5 (= Oakley ex. 30 [1985: 396]).

53. Even if it is an accident of transmission, it should be borne in mind that with the exception of the excerpts preserved in Gellius, one of which may well be most immediately derived from an imperial compilation, all of our accounts of duels date from after the end of single combat as a Roman military institution.

motive that impels the youth to accept the Gaul's challenge. The motif of the commander's permission therefore has nothing to do with limiting individual accomplishment; on the contrary, contact with the collective power of the state in the person of the magistrate is what enables the individual to be successful and allows him to act not just on his own but as a true representative of the entire state. It thus gives his victory a historical significance it would not otherwise have possessed.

Another aspect of dueling facilitates Livy's translation of single combat from a manifestation of individual or familial prowess to a sign of the broader superiority of the Roman state over its opponents: the idea that single combat had a quasi-judicial function and served to resolve disputes by legitimating the claims of the victor.[54] We have already seen on a larger scale how the victory of the Romans over their enemies itself validates their motives; the gods would not have aided them unless their cause was just. Nicolaus of Damascus attests the existence among Italian peoples of a form of trial by combat to resolve disputes between individuals: "Whenever the Umbrians have a dispute against one another, having armed themselves, they fight as if in a war, and those who slaughter their opponents are thought to have made the juster claim."[55] A similar principle has been discovered in archaic Roman judicial procedures like the *vindicatio,* an ancient form of judgment to determine ownership of slaves or moveables that required both disputants formally to state their claim in the presence of witnesses while simultaneously touching the slave in question with a rod.[56] After this, the magistrate compels both parties to release the slave and to state the basis of their claim. Even the response to this question is standardized. The claimants offer no other proof than the simple fact of having performed the rite (*ius feci*). As Gernet points out, in this case, not only do actions have a ritualized, linguistic function but the words themselves have a palpable physical effect. The performance of the act of *vindicatio* is the prerequisite for decision. The right of ownership is obtained not by offering a compelling account of the past but by participating in the present encounter.

In addition to their own physical resources, participants in a trial by combat can invoke the aid of the gods themselves by oaths, which Gernet interprets as originally serving simply as a means of engaging the divine powers in support of one's claim.[57] Whoever wins the duel will now

54. See also Fries 1985: 17–18, with bibliography.

55. Nicolaus of Damascus, *FGrH* 90 F 111 = Stobaeus *Ecl.* 3.10. 69.

56. Gernet 1981: 216–39. The source for the *vindicatio* episode is Gaius *Inst.* 4.16.

57. Gernet (ibid.) here refers to Greek law, but the oath was also a common and powerful feature of Roman legal practice. The Roman oath, which is much more specifically

have his right affirmed by the gods who have given him victory. Something similar is accomplished in Livy's account of Torquatus's duel when the consul, in giving the combatant permission to fight, also invokes the aid of the gods on his behalf. This action, almost a consecration of Torquatus, in addition to providing him with greater resources to fight, necessarily raises the stakes of the competition and assures that a victory will be attributed not just to the might he inherits from his ancestors but to the power of the Roman gods.

III. Torque and Crow

If the story of Valerius Corvus's miraculous fight with the Gaul did originate as a doublet of the earlier duel of Torquatus, then it is remarkable that Livy has treated both episodes so fully given their temporal proximity to each other.[58] The number of identical narrative elements (challenge, request for permission, the combat itself, aftermath) further reinforces the similarity between the two scenes, and Corvus himself refers to Torquatus as a precedent, again ensuring that we read the second duel with the first one in mind (7.26.2). Thus, far from treating it as a liability to be disguised, Livy has made this repetitiveness one of the crucial features of his presentation.[59] Each scene emphasizes elements that complete the other narrative, so that the full meaning of both emerges only when they are taken together. While Torquatus's duel highlights the power of men, Corvus's victory results from the aid of the gods. In the Torquatus episode, the commander speaks in his own voice before the duel, emphasizing the moment when the champion requests permission to fight. In Corvus's case, it is the

linked to the power of *contactus*, whether expressed by touching an altar or by raising the hands to heaven, made the bond between god and swearer all the more explicit. See Wagenvoort 1947: 50 ff.

58. If Holford-Strevens 1984: 148 is correct in this suggestion, then it is possible that Livy was in fact the first historian to include accounts of both duels in his narrative. The elements of the story itself, however, may have a much earlier provenance. Bayet and Bloch 1968: 114 ff., have suggested that the legend of the fighting raven in fact betrays the influence of Celtic beliefs in a battle goddess who could appear in this form. For more on the history and development of the narrative, see Köves-Zulauf 1984 and Fries 1985: 146–51.

59. For the contrary interpretation, see Fries 1985: 149: "Der zeitlich geringe Abstand, die Ähnlichkeit der Situation der Torquatus- und Corvus-Episode stellen Livius vor die Aufgabe, den Eindruck einer Doublette zu vermeiden und die Besonderheit der jeweiligen Vorgänge zu betonen."

complementary scene, where the consul praises the victor, in which the magistrate speaks.

At a deeper level, the exemplary function assumed by each champion explains the interdependence of the two scenes. Livy has transformed Quadrigarius's narrative to stress the links between the individual achievement of Torquatus and the entire state. The momentum by which his deed becomes "public" reaches fulfillment when another youth, not a member of his own family, imitates his behavior. By this principle, no historical event is complete in itself, the great deeds of the past always demand to be renewed by being repeated in the future. Each of the two duels emphasizes one of the reciprocal aspects of this process of imitation.[60] The Torquatus duel focuses on the production of a spectacle that both forges a link between the individual and the power of the group and "broadcasts" this power in a manner that has a transformative effect upon its spectators. The Corvus duel by contrast is about the reception of messages, the interpretation and reproduction of signs.

Comparisons between Livy's description of the Torquatus duel and Quadrigarius's frequently emphasize that Livy has paid greater attention to the visual impression created by the duel.[61] The space in which the combat occurs is clearly delineated before the Gaul's challenge almost in the manner of an ecphrasis.[62] Livy presents the fight itself through the eyes of those looking on and correspondingly provides a greater variety of visual stimuli, like the embroidered clothing and gilded armor of the Gaul,[63] for his audience.[64] These changes are generally regarded as purely stylistic choices designed to make his narrative more vivid and

60. Naturally, of course, Torquatus's action was itself inspired by the earlier deed of his father, and Corvus's action is also meant to be an exemplum for others.

61. The stylistic comparison between Livy and Quadrigarius has been undertaken countless times. My reading owes most to von Albrecht 1989: 86–102, esp. pp. 90–92, who provides a full bibliography. See also Fries 1985: 99–105. Livy's portrayal of the Torquatus duel as spectacle is explicitly noted by Borzsák 1973: 59–60. For an analysis of the duel as a self-contained "dramatic" incident see Pauw 1991: 36.

In light of the attention that has been focused on the visual density of Livy's version in contrast to Quadrigarius's, it is interesting to note that it is precisely the quality of visual realism that is responsible for Gellius's concern with Quadrigarius's narrative. "The philosopher Favorinus used to say that when he read this passage, his mind was shaken and affected by emotions no less than he would have experienced if he himself had actually seen their combat [*quam si ipse coram depugnantes eos spectaret*]" (Aul. Gell. *NA* 9.13.5). See Borzsák 1973: 60.

62. 7.9.7: *Pons in medio erat.*

63. Quadrigarius's Gaul is naked except for his torque.

64. 7.10.6; *cf. aestimantibus.*

dramatic. However, Livy's interest in reproducing the visual impressions produced by the duel goes beyond the level of presentation; he explicitly draws attention to the "theatricality" of the scene in a manner that gives the question of spectacle a thematic importance within the episode.[65] Not only does the appearance of each fighter provide crucial clues to the characteristics of the nation to which he belongs, with the boastful and avaricious Gaul ranged against the controlled and resolute Roman, but as in the battle of Aquilonia, the very manner in which each side makes use of visual communication becomes a criterion for distinguishing between them. In the Gaul's case, the discrepancy between the appearance he gives and his actual effectiveness in combat betrays the same inability to produce meaningful visual signs that marked the Samnite "linen legion." The Roman wins after moving past this outward appearance to the vulnerable body it conceals by "twisting himself between the Gaul's arms and body."[66] The Gaul's gold and finery is a pure distraction, and Torquatus's decision to leave the splendid corpse of his opponent undespoiled with the exception of a single neckband, a choice that will surprise anyone familiar with the common result of duels in Greek epic, appears as an implicit rejection of mere appearance.[67] In his description of the Roman, on the other hand, Livy faces the problem of making "visible" the absence of any purely visual characteristics. The Roman is physically unremarkable, average size, and his weapons are chosen for use rather than show. Correspondingly, Livy describes the Roman primarily in terms of his action and accomplishment; it is precisely the movement of the Roman that uproots the statuesque and largely immobile Gaul. At the same time, Livy's description of the Roman provides an "image" of his inner qualities, his "heart full of courage and silent wrath."[68]

For the Roman side, the process of watching itself takes on a particular dynamic property: it becomes a medium for an exchange of energy between the individual and the group that has the power to transform

65. 7.10.6: *et duo in medio armati spectaculi magis more quam lege belli destituuntur.*

66. 7.10.10: *totoque corpori interior periculo volneris factus insinuasset se inter corpus armaque.* The phrase *inter corpus armaque* and the colorful verb *insinuasset* represent Livy's additions to Quadrigarius's description.

67. Heinze 1933: 101 f., sees Torquatus's refusal to cut off his opponent's head, as he does in Quadrigarius's version, as a sign of Livy's attempt to soften the cruelty of the earlier version. But while Livy does not draw attention to this act, the Celtic torque was not a simple necklace but a heavy band of twisted metal, which would perhaps have been most expeditiously removed through decapitation.

68. 7.10.8: *pectus animorum iraeque tacitae plenum.*

both. As we have seen, Livy alters the earlier account of the duel by introducing the idea that the two champions act as representatives for their entire peoples. It is the Gaul who introduces this theme by claiming that the duel with "the man whom Rome considers the bravest" will "show which race is better at war" (7.9.8). Torquatus, by contrast, betrays no awareness that the duel possesses any such national consequences; what he wants to put on display is the honor of his family.[69] His request for the dictator's permission to accept the challenge, beyond illustrating the value of *disciplina* per se, offers the means by which this essentially personal impulse acquires a larger importance. The dictator responds with the words, "Be successful in your virtue and piety toward your father and fatherland. Go forth and with the gods' help render the Roman name unconquered."[70] The dictator's command, by coupling father and fatherland, translates Torquatus's action to one where family motives go hand in hand with patriotism. In proportion to the increase in the stakes of the combat, the dictator's words also lend the youth greater resources with which to fight. The gods will be aiding him, and the expression *macte virtute,* translated above as "be successful," although something of a formulaic phrase, may yet retain some of its original sacral meaning, "be filled, be increased."[71] The fashioning of Torquatus into a surrogate for the group as a whole is completed when his comrades all participate in arming him (7.10.5). Thus from the Roman perspective, the spectacle of the combat itself comes at the culmination of the process that binds the individual to the larger group. In return, by watching his victory, the Roman spectators are brought into contact with their collective might. Rendered *alacres,* they are freed from the immobility that marked the

69. 7.10.3: *volo ego illi beluae ostendere . . . me ex ea familia ortum quae Gallorum agmen ex rupe Tarpeia deiecit.* The verb *ostendere* responds to the Gaul's own use of *ostendat,* "to show which nation is best in war" (7.9.8). The entire career of Torquatus illustrates the process by which family loyalty is harnessed to and eventually superseded by patriotism. We first meet him as a young man whom his father has banished from the city because of his slowness of speech. When a tribune attempts to use this mistreatment against the father, the young man roughly threatens him and forces him to swear an oath at knifepoint to withdraw the accusations—as Livy says, a deed praiseworthy for its piety, even if hardly a model of civic behavior (7.4–5). Yet this is the same man who in the interest of preserving state order will be prepared to sacrifice his own son.

70. 7.10.4: *macte virtute ac pietate in patrem patriamque, T. Manli, esto. perge et nomen Romanum invictum, iuvantibus dis, praesta.*

71. As such the phrase often formed part of a prayer and was addressed to the god who was "enriched" by sacrifice. See Wagenvoort 1947: 46, n. 3, who defines *mactare* as meaning both "to strengthen (the gods) by sacrifice" and "to strengthen a sacrifice for the gods," and Fowler 1911: 182–83.

first stages of their conflict with the Gauls, and they too run forth from their posts, as originally Torquatus had,[72] to retrace his journey toward the dictator. The Gaul by contrast stands resolutely alone; there is no mention at all of his fellows until the fear and astonishment engendered by their own response to the spectacle paralyzes them (7.10.12).

The properties that the process of watching possesses within the narrative in turn explain Livy's own adoption of a visually vivid narrative style. By enabling his own audience to become spectators of the duel, he makes it possible for them to share in the exchange of energy experienced by the participants. Indeed, Livy's narrative can go beyond the purely visual by directing the attention of the reader toward the inner qualities that the Roman does not put on display, his "heart full of courage." The account of the duel differentiates between two possible modes of spectacle; the socially cohesive experience of the Romans stands in contrast to the meaningless and ineffectual display of the Gaul. How does Livy ensure that the "spectacle" he produces will not be taken as the stylistic equivalent of the Gaul's performance, a purely decorative intrusion within the course of the larger narrative? The initial attitude the historian adopts toward the combat suggests that this is indeed how it is to be regarded. When Livy says that the encounter between Torquatus and the Gaul was more of a spectacle than a battle, he himself seems to be detaching it from his narrative; it is a show, not a serious combat. Like the Gaul's gesture of sticking out his tongue at the Roman, which Livy can only describe with the qualifying comment that such behavior is not worthy of forming part of his narrative yet has been recorded by his predecessors (7.10.5), it is an element that Livy must both include and somehow excise from his text. Again Torquatus's adoption of the Gaul's torque provides a model for Livy's approach. This single Gallic artifact can acquire a Roman historical significance as a marker of the defeat of the people who produced it. Like the armor taken from the Samnite linen legion, its splendor must first be dimmed by blood. In the same way, Torquatus's defeat of the Gaul gives his outrageous performance a place in Roman history precisely as a record of the failure of the quintessentially alien behavior of Rome's opponents.

In the Corvus episode, the language of signs and revelation punctuates the narrative, just as the imagery of spectacle did the account of Torquatus. The crow that miraculously perches on the Roman's helmet

72. 7.10.12: *Romani alacres ab statione ... progressi.* Cf. 7.10.2: *T. Manlius ... ex statione ad dictatorem pergit.*

and helps him to defeat the Gaul is an "*augurium* sent from the sky."[73] As a result of this miraculous apparition, the human aspect of the duel is said to be made less *insigne,* marked or conspicuous (7.26.3). The same word had first been used to describe the Gaul, "conspicuous for his height and weapons."[74] But as the balance shifts from human resources to divine power, it is the Roman champion who after his victory becomes "conspicuous" because of the spoils of the defeated Gaul.[75]

But like all signs from the gods, the apparition of the crow must be acknowledged and accepted by the human to whom it is sent. In the version of the duel recorded by Gellius, the apparition of the crow is treated as nothing so formal as an *augurium,* but as the intrusion of "a certain divine power" (*quaedam divina vis* [*NA* 9.11.6]) that operates on its own. Livy by contrast emphasizes the role of the human tribune in receiving the divine message. At first, the crow is presented simply as a crow that alights on the Roman's helmet. It is only once Corvus recognizes the crow as an *augurium* and formally entreats the goodwill of the god who sent it that the behavior of the bird becomes "miraculous" and it begins to fight on the Roman's behalf. But the emphasis on the transmission of signs does not stop there. Once Corvus receives the sign from the gods, he becomes a sign himself. After the tribune has defeated the Gaul, the consul Camillus presents this victory to the soldiers as a token of divine benevolence and urges his soldiers to fight more confidently (7.26.7). The crow therefore becomes only the first miraculous sign, the influence of which is transmitted to ever-larger audiences. In acknowledging the crow as a sign, the tribune is made "joyous" (*laetus* [7.26.4], a word we have met before used to describe the recipient of a message from the gods). When the victory is interpreted for the soldiery, the same word is used of them and emphasized by anaphora.[76]

The pattern of resemblances traced here recalls the treatment of Decius's *devotio,* where the consul becomes an image of a sign sent from the gods, and his "performance" in turn causes the spectators who witness it to take on his own characteristics. Indeed, by assuming the cognomen *Corvus,* the tribune himself becomes the "Crow." The motif of resemblance in the Corvus narrative is explicitly emphasized by the consul

73. 7.26.4. Later it is a *prodigium* (7.26.5).

74. 7.26.1: *magnitudine atque armis insignis.* Cf. the similar transfer of the adjective *insignis* from the conspicuous Samnites to the Roman commander who defeats them in Livy's acount of the battle of Aquilonia discussed in ch. 2, sec. I.

75. 7.26.7: *insignem spoliis tribunum.*

76. 7.26.7: *laetum militem victoria tribuni, laetum tam praesentibus ac secundis dis.*

himself in a manner that assimilates it to the process of imitation that provides the mechanism by which all historical events are meant to transform their audiences: the soldiers are told to "imitate him,"[77] a phrase that looks back to the central purpose of Livy's own history, to provide *exempla* for his readers to "imitate."[78] The parallel between the imitation of a historical example and the transmission of divine signs is confirmed when we recall that the initial impetus that drove Corvus to accept the Gaul's challenge was his emulation of Torquatus. And once again, as in the narratives of the sack of Rome and of Torquatus's duel, the Gaul, whose blindness to divine signs is graphically represented by the crow's pecking at his eyes, serves as a foil to highlight the distinctively Roman ability to recognize and interpret such signs effectively.

IV. The Duel of the Younger Torquatus

These earlier narratives form the background for the younger Torquatus's encounter with his Latin challenger (8.7). Together, they have defined a double tradition that binds each individual champion to the collective authority of the state through contact with magistrates and gods and to a pattern of successful behavior extending through time, of which his own action provides but one manifestation. In conforming to the demands exerted by the political hierarchy and the weight of historical precedent, the individual becomes an instrument for disseminating the influence of each tradition, and this provides both the means and the significance of his victory. As we have seen, the younger Torquatus's duel occurs in a context that puts at risk both the historical supremacy of the Romans over the Latins and the privileged connection to the larger power of the gods upon which that supremacy depends. Yet Torquatus, far from asking the consul, his father, for permission to fight, ignores his specific instructions that no Roman is to engage the enemy without orders. Had Torquatus lost his duel, the outcome could therefore have been easily explained and would have possessed an educative value as an illustration of what happens when soldiers fight without permission. But the outcome of this encounter turns out to be far more dangerous for the authority structure of the state and even calls into

77. Ibid.: *hunc imitare.*
78. *Praef.* 10: *inde . . . quod imitere capias.*

question the value of the historical tradition: Torquatus wins despite the fact that he is fighting without authorization. Thus his very victory, far from affirming the superiority of Roman over Latin, as he had hoped, can be read as a justification of the Latins' position: there is no power beyond force, and the idea that Rome's dominance has any kind of external guarantee from the gods is a sham; therefore it is only right that the Latins, who have shared equally in Rome's victories, should also have a share of *imperium*.

Torquatus's son belongs to a cavalry squadron sent out to reconnoiter. A band of Tusculan cavalry meets and recognizes them, and the leader of this band, Geminus Maecius, taunts the Romans. The young Torquatus responds by an appeal to both axes of authority, the hierarchical and the historical, in his assertion of the superiority of Rome. He claims that Roman victory will be assured by the presence of Jupiter along with the armies of the consuls, and, as his father had before him (8.5.10), invokes the battle of Lake Regillus as a historical precedent for the victory of the Romans over the Latins: "The consular armies will be here in time, and with them will be Jupiter himself, a witness of the treaties you have violated, who has even more power. If you had more than enough of us at the battle of Lake Regillus, this encounter too will curb your taste for doing battle with us."[79] But having correctly recognized the sources of Roman power, Torquatus then makes a mistake. Maecius challenges, "Do you wish then, until the day when you move your armies for the great attempt, to fight with me yourself in order that the outcome of our battle make clear by how much the Latin knight excels the Roman?"[80] And Torquatus, "moved by anger or shame or the ineluctable power of fate" (8.7.8), accepts.

The duel that the young Torquatus fights under these circumstances is very different in character from that of his father:

> Thus forgetful of the command of his father [*imperii patrii*] and the order of the consuls, he is driven headlong into a contest where it did not matter much whether he conquered or was conquered. When the other riders had withdrawn, as if at a spectacle, they drove their horses against one another in

79. 8.7.5–7: *Aderunt* (*sc. exercitus consulares*) *in tempore, . . . et cum illis aderit Iuppiter ipse, foederum a vobis violatorum testis, qui plus potest polletque. Si ad Regillum Lacum ad satietatem vestram pugnavimus, hic quoque efficiemus profecto ne nimis acies vobis et conlata signa nobiscum cordi sint.*

80. 8.7.7. Again we recognize the use of single combat not only to distinguish between two combatants but to establish a permanently valid assessment of the two peoples represented.

the area of empty field that lay between them. As they clashed with their opposed weapons, the spear of Manlius flew over his opponent's helmet; Maecius's glided over the neck of Manlius's horse. On the second charge, when Manlius rose first to deliver his blow, he planted his missile between the ears of the Latin's horse. Feeling his wound, the horse reared up and shook his head with such force that he unseated his rider, whom, while he leaned upon his shield and spear and was raising himself from a bad fall, Manlius stabbed through the throat so hard that the spear came out through his ribs and pinned him to the ground. Gathering up the spoils and returning to his fellows, he headed straight for the camp, accompanied by his rejoicing squadron, and to his father's tent, uncertain of his fate and destiny, whether he deserved punishment or praise. [8.7.8–12]

Here, too, the fight takes the form of a *spectaculum,* yet unlike his father's battle with the Gaul, it is a *spectaculum* entirely without consequences, a mere spectacle. Since Torquatus fights entirely alone, without contact with the *imperium* of the magistrate or the aid of the gods, his victory will prove nothing about the real sources of Roman power, it can only be meaningless. As opposed to the reserve and discipline of his father, which stood as a foil to the extravagant display of his opponent, the son appears from the first as out of control, "driven headlong" to battle rather than choosing it; the errant casts of the combatants and panic of the stricken horse aptly represent the absence of any restraining influence. Correspondingly, the narrative itself is constructed as a flamboyant pastiche of Homeric elements; the repeated throws, wounded horse, and the anatomic specificity in the description of the final blow all suggest the world of epic.[81] What is missing from this narrative, apart from the description of the "rejoicing squadron," is any reference to the effect the duel possesses upon its spectators.

Unlike his father, this Torquatus does not limit himself to a single token of victory but gathers spoils from his fallen opponent. The youth's enthusiasm for *spolia,* of the sort that were frequently displayed on the façades of the houses of the nobility,[82] aptly connects the misplaced interest in insubstantial visual signs illustrated in the account of the duel to a flawed conception of the relationship between family glory and the needs of the *res publica.* Pointing to the *spolia,* the young man tells his fa-

81. For the motif of the repeated throws, cf., e.g., *Il.* 3.346–60, 7.247–50, 22.273–90; *Aen.* 10.776–86; for the death of the horse, cf. *Il.* 8.83–86, 16.467; *Aen.* 10.892 (again the Mezentius-Lausus episode, which offers an interesting foil to Livy's treatment of fathers and sons in this narrative). See also the analysis of the passage's vividness in Pauw 1991: 37 and 47, n. 24, and Fries 1985: 154–65.

82. Rawson 1991: 582–98.

ther that he chose to engage in combat in order to live up to the precedent of his own earlier duel, "so that all would say that I was truly born of your stock" (8.7.13). Torquatus's mistake is not so much to have placed his desire to exalt himself and his *gens* above obedience to the orders of the consul as to have failed to realize that there simply ought to be no difference between the demands of family and *patria*. This was one of the lessons of his father's duel, where the dictator's formal command to fight served to fuse duty to the family with patriotism. Torquatus was to be of "outstanding *pietas* toward father *and* fatherland." By winning his duel, he had earned both praise from the dictator and an honorific cognomen. The unity of the authority of family and state ought to have been especially clear to the young Manlius, since the consul whom he should have obeyed and the father whose example he wished to emulate were one and the same person.

The speech in which the consul sentences his son to death for disobedience elucidates the relationship between the misinterpretation of visual signs and the breakdown in the patterns of order upon which the survival of the state depends:

> Since, Titus Manlius, you have respected neither the *imperium* of the consul nor the supremacy of your father, and have fought against the enemy contrary to orders and outside of your position, and, as much as you could, eroded that military discipline by which the Roman state has stood until this day, and have led me into the necessity of neglecting either my own interest or that of the *res publica*, we shall be afflicted by our fault rather than the nation pay the penalty for our sins. We shall be a severe *exemplum* but a healthy one for the youth [*triste exemplum sed in posterum salubre iuventuti erimus*]. I am indeed moved by the natural love of fathers for their children and by the appearance you give of virtue deceived by a false image of honor, but since the *imperia* of the consuls must either be sanctified by your blood or be henceforward violated with impunity, I would think that not even you, if you have any drop of my blood, would deny that you must restore through your punishment the military discipline that has been compromised by your error—go, lictor, tie him to the stake! [8.7.15–19]

His son was lured into fighting this battle by a "false image" (*vana imago*) of glory (8.7.18), which finds a corollary in the sight of the *spolia* with which the consul has just been confronted. In participating in the duel, however, his son was not just a victim of deception; through the excitement aroused by the combat and his own use of signs to commemorate his victory, he has helped perpetuate the "empty image of glory" responsible for his own mistake. He himself has become in his father's words a "*specimen*"(8.7.18). Thus in contrast to Valerius Corvus, the sight of whose victory served to communicate the power of the gods responsible for his success to all the spectators of the duel, the young Torquatus has set in motion a sequence of visual signs that, if left unchecked, is in danger of deceiving those who witnessed it and drawing them away from the *disciplina* that links them to the *imperium* of the state. Another of the dangerous consequences of the youth's action afflicts the father himself. By assuming that the chance to win glory for his family justified disobedience to orders, his son had created an opposition between the service of family and state. His disobedience compels his father in turn to choose between personal interests and affections and the demands of public duty. By presenting the punishment of his son as something that his family's tradition of obedience requires, and by compelling the young man himself to acquiesce in the principle that necessitates his death on the basis of heredity, the consul attempts to make the execution a sight that will paradoxically restore the alignment between family honor and the interest of the nation.

To correct his son's error, the consul produces another spectacle, the young champion's execution, to be witnessed by precisely the same audience who exulted in his success. This spectacle ought to put on display all the personal and national qualities conspicuously absent in the duel itself. Personal fortitude, family honor, and the authorization of the consul unite in an image which will restore and "sanctify" (*sancienda* [8.7.19]) that bond between each individual and the power of the state that is the secret of Roman difference. Unlike the empty and ultimately insignificant duel, the execution will take its place within the "official" tradition of Roman history, recalling one of the founding acts of the *res publica,* Brutus's execution of his sons: it will be a *salubre exemplum,* designed not just for its immediate audience but to provide a model for the future as well.

We are forced to speak about what the spectacle of the execution ought to reveal rather than what it does reveal because Livy avoids describing the actual moment of Manlius's execution and allows his audience to see it only as it is reflected in the eyes of those who watch it:

All were stunned [*exanimati*] by such a ruthless command and were silenced by fear rather than moderation, just as if each one saw the ax prepared for him. And so they stood in silence rooted to the spot [*defixi*], their senses, as it were, overwhelmed by astonishment. Suddenly after the blood poured forth from the victim's neck, their voices rose in such an unrestrained cry that they held back neither from mourning nor from curses, and the youth, covered with his spoils, was given a funeral with all possible marks of the favor of his fellow soldiers and burnt on a pyre built up outside the camp. And "Manlian *imperia*"were not only terrifying in the present but served as a cruel example for the future [*exempli etiam triste in posteritatem*]. But nevertheless the very ruthlessness of the punishment made the soldiers more obedient to their leader, and since guards and watches and the stationings were conducted with greater care, this severity was beneficial in the final battle. [8.7.20–8.8.1]

The very absence of narrative specificity about the execution itself creates an opposition between this scene and the duel, with its carefully descriptive detail. The technique provides a corollary to the absence of external signs with which Torquatus had confronted the merely visual magnificence of the Gaul. But if the spectacle itself has vanished from Livy's text, the decision to describe the spectators rather than the action shifts the emphasis of the scene to the effect of spectacle. Nowhere in Livy's text is the sympathy that develops between audience and the object of spectacle more clearly evoked. So strongly do the spectator's identify themselves with Manlius that they actually seem to take his place as victim; they see the axes raised against them. As in the other spectacles discussed, the audience take on the characteristics of their surrogate. He is deprived of life; they, too, are *exanimati*. During the very time when the victim is immobilized by being bound to the stake, they are described as "rooted to the spot" (*defixi*). As such, the young men who had before identified only with the victor of the duel come to assume the posture of the defeated, whom Manlius pinned to the ground (*adfixit* [8.7.11]) with his spear.

Livy's emphasis on the horror experienced by Manlius's fellow soldiers has been read as an implicit criticism of the consul's severity. Torquatus, in contrast to his fellow consul Decius, mistakes cruelty and extremism for duty, and the fact that the youth of Rome will never be reconciled to his authority, even going so far as to spurn his triumph,[83] seems to suggest that the execution has failed to be anything other than an exercise in violence.[84] But nothing in the text leads us to look for compromise or reconciliation. The consul predicts that the *exemplum* he produces will be both *triste* and *salubre,* and indeed it is the very cruelty of the penalty that is the key to its effectiveness. As Livy puts it, the *atroc-*

83. 8.12.1: *iuventutem et tunc et omni vita deinde aversatam eum exsecratamque.*

84. Lipovsky 1981: 112–15, supported by Levene 1993: 222–23, a reading that seems to me at odds with the sympathetic focus on the consul's own internal ambivalence and anguish in the speech Livy composes for him.

itas of the punishment makes the soldiers more obedient. The consul's remedy relies upon the same mechanism of sympathetic contact by which the influence of *imperium* communicates itself in duels and *devotiones.* The punishment of the victim here becomes the punishment of the audience who, having identified with his success in the duel, now experience his execution as their own. If we, Livy's audience, have rejoiced in Manlius's success without perceiving its illegality, then the *exemplum* is as much for us as for the soldiers who were actually present. Thus it is by recreating the full impact of the spectacle on those who witness it that Livy most effectively communicates the influence of the *exemplum* through his text.

The execution therefore, rather than harmonizing the social and ethical tensions resulting from Manlius's disobedience, necessarily articulates them with the greatest clarity. For this reason, even in the midst of the consul's *exemplum* a rival spectacle is produced, which enshrines an image of precisely the values that have necessitated the punishment. Manlius's comrades immediately give the victim a funeral where the tokens of victory, the *spolia* that occasioned his death, are again placed on triumphant display in such a way as almost to conceal the corpse itself and allow the youth's glorious accomplishments to obliterate the traces left by his punishment.[85] Like the burial of an epic hero, the scene concludes with the construction of a pyre, a monument in this case both to the son's glory and the father's cruelty. The episode therefore generates a double historical legacy; the image of the young man's victory and the consul's cruelty are infixed in the disciplinary *exemplum* he produces. Yet by ensuring that the *exemplum* continues to be felt as *triste,* they also preserve it as *salubre.*

The execution of Manlius is not the only such doubled spectacle that appears in Livy's text. In the next chapter, we shall see that similar scenes occur precisely in contexts that require Roman society to redefine itself by simultaneously excluding outsiders and cementing new bonds of loyalty between insiders. These spectacles perform the same "initiatory" function as the execution of Manlius, which is designed to restore the soldiery to obedience to the *imperium* of the consul. A clue to the nature of these spectacles is to be found in the remark of a later historian, Valerius Maximus, that the young Manlius perished *in modum hostiae,* "like a sacrificial victim."[86]

85. 8.7.21: *spoliisque contectum iuvenis corpus.*

86. Val. Max. 2.7.6. Sacrificial overtones are also present in Livy's text, particularly in the consul's comment his son's death will "sanctify" the *imperia* of the consuls (8.7.19).

CHAPTER 4

Sacrifice, Initiation, and the Construction of the *Patria*

Livy begins his narrative with the destruction of Troy and the flight of the survivors to Italy. However, Aeneas was not the only Trojan leader to found a new city in the West. There were two men, Aeneas and Antenor, whom the Greeks spared because of ties of hospitality and because both argued for the return of Helen and the restoration of peace:

Now, first of all, it is sufficiently established that, after Troy was captured, the other Trojans were slaughtered, but in the case of two men, Aeneas and Antenor, the Greeks held back from exercising their rights as conquerors [*omne ius belli . . . abstinuisse*] both as a result of ancient ties of guest friendship and because these two had argued for peace and the return of Helen. Then through various accidents, Antenor, together with a population of Eneti, who had been expelled from Paphlagonia by sedition and were seeking a new leader after the death of their king, Pylaemenes, entered the innermost reaches of the Adriatic Sea, and, when the Eugenaeans, who dwelt between the sea and the Alps, had been driven out, the Trojans and Eneti took possession of their lands. And so the place where they disembarked is called Troy, and the region is known as Trojan; the people as a whole are called the Veneti. Aeneas, driven from his home by the same misfortune, but with the fates leading him on to the beginnings of greater things, went first to Macedonia, then was borne to Sicily, seeking a permanent settlement, and from Sicily held his course to the Laurentian fields. This place, too, is called Troy. [1.1.1–4]

Two elements in Livy's account will particularly surprise the reader of the *Aeneid*. First is the emphasis on personal propriety and obedience to *ius* on the part of both Trojans and Greeks. This Aeneas does not fight his way out of the burning city; it is mutual respect for ancient tradition that ensures his survival. But more remarkable is the suggestion of an alternative Trojan inheritance in Italy. Antenor as well as Aeneas founded a new race, and although "the fates led Aeneas on to the beginnings of greater things," there is no qualitative distinction between the two, no plan of Jupiter, nor any reference yet to divine birth. Antenor's descendants are the Veneti and the place where he lands is the historian's own birthplace, Padua. Livy's initial pairing of Aeneas and Antenor therefore reminds us that the Roman national myth is not unique or inevitable, that there are other possible pasts, and particularly that the historian himself, who was a citizen of Rome but a native of Padua, is thus in a position to choose between the heritage of Antenor, which he abandons after two sentences in the narrative, and that of Aeneas, which he will follow for 142 books.[1]

Implicit at the beginning of the *History* is the choice between two *patriae,* Rome and Padua, and the creation of Rome as a nation is synchronized with the historian's adoption of Roman nationality, as represented by the decision to narrate the *res* that follow from Aeneas's foundation.[2] Moreover a change in national identity is necessary not only for the historian but for Aeneas himself, who begins life as a Trojan but must find a new nation. Indeed, the first four sentences of the narrative present an array of conflicting and overlapping national identities, each set in motion by war or sedition and blurred by the process of wandering: the Eneti too are expelled from their land, and the Trojan refugees take on their name; their original settlement is called Troy, but as such becomes one of three places that can be so designated. In these respects, the Trojan emigration predicts a crucial pattern in the development of the Roman state. Throughout its history, and particularly during its beginnings, Rome grows through absorption. New territories necessitate the incorporation of new citizens. Romulus himself, the next founder of Rome, comes from Alba, and his fellow citizens are exiles and fugitives.

1. For the connection between Livy's own origins and the origins of his narrative, see esp. Bonjour 1975b: 96 and 248 ff.

2. For a discussion of how Livy in these sentences draws attention to the difficulties of creating and interpreting a historical narrative through the interplay between direct and indirect statement, see now Miles 1995: 20–31. The parallel between the complexity of the narrative and of the events it describes, revealed most significantly at 1.1.6, where the report or *fama* Livy confronts itself becomes "twofold" (*duplex*), suggests a further similarity between the actual process of founding Rome, which itself necessitates wanderings and doublings of identity (Trojan, Aboriginal, Latin, Enetian), and the construction of a unified history out of the maze of stories these wanderings have produced. For more on the "overlap of text and subject" in Livy's narrative, see Kraus 1994b: 269 f.

In striking contrast to the Athenian national myth, in which the first kings are born from the soil itself, and where birth is stressed as a criterion of citizenship, Romans are made, not born. Thus it is particularly appropriate that the first event in Roman history is the destruction of a previous fatherland, Troy.

The making of citizens was not just a matter of historical interest in Rome of the first century B.C.E. Rather, the historian's treatment of the past highlights a crucial issue in contemporary political life. After the incorporation of the Italian allies, the citizen population had grown from 395,000 in 115 B.C.E. to about 1.5 million in 28 B.C.E., according to a conservative estimate.[3] Not only did this vast population of new Romans, who were already *cives* of their own cities, have to think of themselves as members of the Roman *patria,* but in the face of such expansion, the very term *civis,* which had originally described a participant in a tangible community of peers, required redefinition for all citizens. Nor is it inappropriate to adopt the perspective of the individual citizen here. The Romans themselves recognized that the subjective dimension, the individual's identification of himself as a Roman citizen, was fully as important as issues of law and public procedure in questions of citizenship. Thus Cicero in the *Pro Balbo* claims that "our right of changing citizenship [*ius civitatis mutandae*] . . . depends not only on public laws but also on the will of the private citizen." (*Pro Balb.* 27).[4]

But the civic identity of the newly enfranchised was only the most obvious dimension of a much larger issue. Both the Late Republic and the Early Principate perceived a crisis in public participation, whether real or not.[5] Loyalty to one's native state could hinder full identification with the *res publica,* but so could political factionalism, or philosophical precepts, or the love of leisure. Friends, family, books, or even the body could equally usurp the rightful place of the community as the center of loyalty and attention.[6] A Lucullus ostentatiously opting out of his polit-

3. See Brunt 1971: 13–14, for the statistical evidence. The census figure for 28 B.C.E. is given in *Res gestae* 8.2 as over four million, which Brunt assumes is only conceivable if it includes women and children.

4. On the vast problems of citizenship, see the standard treatment by Sherwin-White 1973 and particularly Nicolet 1980: 21–23. The meaning and derivation of *civis* is discussed by Benveniste 1969: 1.335–37.

5. For three very different introductions to the processes by which Augustus himself fosters the construction of an inclusive national identity, see Syme 1939: 440–58; Eder 1990, esp. 118 ff.; and, regarding the sphere of religious activity, Gordon 1990.

6. For Roman anxieties about the dangers of pleasure for the state as a whole and the antithesis between indulgence in pleasure and the conduct of public duty, see esp. Edwards 1993, esp. 190–200.

ical career and Augustus's upbraiding of an unproductive, alienated aristocracy demonstrate but two aspects of this phenomenon.[7] Thus the importance of citizenship as an issue in Livy's text is not restricted to those in his audience who, like Livy himself, were not native Romans. The reintegration of the *patria* involved the incorporation of those within as well as of outsiders. *Luxuria,* the force that has corroded the Roman state, shuts off the individual from the collective life of the state, and history, as I argued in chapter 1, seeks to reestablish this contact.

This chapter analyzes how the transition between non-citizen and citizen is accomplished in an extended episode from Livy's first book, the defeat and incorporation of Alba Longa, ancestral city of the first Roman king and thus a vital link between Rome and Troy. To a greater extent than Rome's other early enemies, the Albans shared links with the Romans that rendered it difficult to differentiate them as foreign enemies, and their incorporation is ultimately presented as a reunification of what is essentially one nation. In this respect, the conflict between Rome and Alba bears a special relevance to the internal struggles from which Rome had just emerged at the time when the *History* was composed. Indeed, Livy makes the comparison explicit by saying that the struggle between Rome and Alba was "most like a civil war" and even "almost like a war between fathers and sons" (1.23.1). The last description not only conjures up the most terrifying image of the civil strife of the author's own day but also extends the significance of the conflict from the level of national identity to the more intimate sphere of the family, just as the civic conflicts of the first century were shown to disrupt society at every level.[8]

7. For Cicero's criticism of those *nobiles* who retreated into luxury in moments of political necessity, see esp. *Att.* 1.18.6: *ceteros iam nosti; qui ita sunt stulti ut amissa re publica piscinas suas fore salvas sperare videantur.* For Augustus's attitudes and policy toward the elite, see Nicolet 1984. Of course, Augustus also had an important interest in limiting and restricting the terms in which the members of the aristocracy took part in government, and indeed the "degeneracy" of the aristocracy, so compellingly portrayed by Syme 1939: 490–524 and 1986: 64–81, was itself arguably the product of the *princeps*'s own monopolization of the honors and prerogatives that provided the traditional impetus toward political action.

8. The correlation between civic discord and the disintegration of the family emerges particularly in Appian's catalogue of the horrors of the proscriptions in 43 B.C.E. (*BCiv.* 4.17–29). In episodes involving the treachery of son against father (4.18), slave against master (4.26), and wife against husband (4.23–4), the chaos of the state is seen to depend upon and coincide with the breakdown of natural ties. The link between civil war and the destruction of the family manifests itself in a different way in the stories of family members who were destroyed for not abandoning their kin; in these cases, the violence of the civil war literally directs itself against the family group. Thus, for example, the two Egnatii, father and son, are decapitated with a single blow, while their bodies continue to embrace (4.21). Some of the imaginary situations that furnish the topics for rhetorical exercises in

Throughout Livy's account of the fall of Alba, the bond between the individual citizens and their *patria* is forged and tested by making them spectators at acts of violence. First, Albans and Romans watch a duel between two sets of triplets representing each city, whose outcome will determine which side will possess *imperium* over the other. After the duel, the Romans look on as the victorious Horatius kills his sister for mourning one of the dead Albans, and then face the possibility of witnessing the execution of their own champion. Then the rebellious Albans are compelled to be spectators as their dictator, Mettius Fufetius, is ripped apart by chariots. And this event in turn leads to the physical transferal of the Albans from their native city to Rome, their new *patria*, in a scene that stands out in Livy's text for its descriptive power.

The link between spectacle and civic identity, which receives recurrent emphasis and exploration throughout this portion of Livy's narrative, can in turn tell us something about the function of the *History* in addressing the social crises of its own age. If these spectacles contain the mechanism for establishing the bond of citizenship, then the historian by reproducing them for his own audience is doing more than describing the past, or even analyzing it in terms of contemporary anxieties. His text possesses a performative dimension, a power to effect the same transformation among his own readers and listeners. But before turning to the narrative itself, we must explore more fully how the Romans conceptualized the bond between the citizen and the Republic and how these conceptions underlie the model of patriotic participation adopted in Livy's early books.

I. The Boundaries of the *Patria*

At Rome every five years, when the censors drew up their list of Roman citizens, the members of the state assembled on the Campus Martius, and a pig, sheep, and bull were led around them in a circle and then sacrificed. The same ritual performance, called a *lustratio*, was used to prepare an army for battle and to purify the weapons and trum-

Seneca's *Controversiae* also advert to the social consequences of the civil wars. In *Cont.* 10.3, a woman hangs herself outside her father's door after he refuses to forgive her for not having abandoned her husband, who had died fighting for the losing side during the civil wars. Cf. also *Cont.* 7.2.

pets before and after each campaign. In 28 B.C.E., after a lapse of forty-one years, Augustus restored the census, together with the performance of a *lustratio,* as a part of his renewal of Roman civic rituals after the end of the civil wars.[9] Whatever proportion of Roman citizens had actually experienced such a lustration, the frequent depictions of the scene in art,[10] its recurrence throughout the Roman religious calendar, and Augustus's very interest in restoring it show how profoundly the performance was associated with the constitution of the civic body. The ritual's structure both expresses and gives shape to the Roman conceptualization of what it means to become a citizen.

The *lustratio* used to be thought of primarily as a purificatory ritual and many attempts were made to connect it etymologically with the root that means cleanse.[11] But as Versnel emphasizes, lustration rituals generally take place at the beginnings of enterprises rather than at their conclusions. The army is lustrated before, not after, a battle, when there is no blood guilt to be purged. In consequence, Versnel argues that in addition to its purifying or apotropaic elements, the act of *lustratio* also possessed a constitutive function, defining the group preparatory to collective action.[12] Within the ritual, it is most obviously the gesture of encirclement by the procession of priests and victims that differentiates the group from the outside world. The exclusionary as well as inclusive nature of *lustratio* appears from the instructions that survive in an Umbrian inscription from the city of Gubbio, where the ceremony begins with the explicit and elaborate listing of foreign peoples who are commanded to depart.[13] The second element of the *lustratio,* the sacrifice, may be rationalized as a gift to the gods for their protection of the lustrated body,[14] but, as discussed more fully later in this chapter, sacrifice itself can function as a mechanism of social bonding and in this respect complements the constitutive function implied in the gesture of encirclement.

But the use of lustration, as of sacrifice, extends far beyond rituals involving the entire state. The earliest reference to lustration describes its

9. *Res gestae* 2.8. See Liebeschuetz 1979: 96.

10. See Ryberg 1955: 104 ff., and, for a reading of the *census* depicted on the altar of Domitius, Torelli 1982: 9 ff.

11. For a full discussion of the etymologies that have been proposed, see Ogilvie 1961: 33–35, and see also Versnel 1975: 103 and 112, n. 53.

12. See Versnel 1975: 100–103, who gives full bibliography on the subject.

13. *Tab. Ig.* IB. 16f., cited in Ogilvie 1961: 38.

14. Deubner 1913: 130.

application to a farmer's field,[15] and the combination of animals used in the procession suggests an agricultural origin. Moreover, its use was not limited to Rome; as we have seen, the most detailed description of lustration comes from an Umbrian city. Even the individual body was lustrated both nine days after birth (eight days for females) and nine days after death.[16] In the case of the lustration of babies, the obvious protective function of the practice is once again coupled with a constitutive dimension. It is at the ceremony of the *dies lustricus* that the baby is given a name and thus acquires an identity.[17] The multiplicity of possible *lustrationes* creates an image of each individual enclosed, not just within the magic circle of the state, but within any number of different rings, each of which define him as a member of a particular social entity, such as a local community or a particular family. At the smallest level, even the body emerges as microcosm of the whole.

A map of affiliations similar to the one suggested by these overlapping *lustrationes* also underlies discussions of conflicts of loyalties in Cicero's ethical writings. Although his native town of Arpinum had obtained citizenship three generations before his birth, and he himself was even awarded the title of *pater patriae* for his services to Rome, Cicero is still at pains to define the relationship between his native place and the Roman *res publica*. As book 2 of the *De legibus* begins, Atticus is surprised to hear Cicero refer to Arpinum as his *patria,* and Cicero responds by asserting that "everyone from the towns has two *patriae,* one of nature, and one of citizenship."[18] Already the problem of terminology arises; Cicero must create the terms *patria naturae,* "natural fatherland," and *patria civitatis,* "fatherland of citizenship," to articulate the division of what had been a unitary idea. Ultimately, it is not the venerable opposition between *nomos* and *phusis* that justifies greater allegiance to the larger *patria* but the larger extent of the community. "It is necessary that the *patria,* where the name of *res publica* is a marker of our common citizenship, stand first in our affections; for which we ought to die and to which we ought to devote ourselves entirely and upon which as an altar we ought to set and as it were sacrifice all our goods." In the *De officiis,* a much larger set of possible societies, extending all the way to the human species, is again sorted by size. The inner core is defined by the family,

15. Cato *Agr.* 141.

16. See Wissowa 1902: 329, n. 1, for testimonia.

17. Versnel 1975: 103.

18. Cic. *Leg.* 2.5. For a further analysis of this passage and Cicero's treatment of the conflict of loyalties it reveals, see Bonjour 1975b: 78–86.

with the husband and wife at its center. The emotional bond within the family is based both on a natural desire for propagation[19] and, at a further remove, on *benevolentia* and *caritas* arising from the sharing of *monumenta maiorum,* religious rites, and burial places.[20] On the basis of this organization, it seems as though the nearer bond should predominate. Yet after apparently leading to this conclusion, at the climax of the whole discussion, Cicero says that no bond is *carior* or *gravior* than that which links us to the *res publica.*[21] Here the order of rating these associations is suddenly reversed. In contrast to the centripetal tendency of the previous discussion, the Republic is now to be valued most highly precisely because it surrounds all other forms of community. "The one *patria* has embraced [*complexa est*] all the loves [*caritates*] of all."[22]

But Cicero's appeal to *caritas* as a motive for patriotism contains the kernel of a paradox that would recur frequently in Roman discussions of civic participation.[23] It has been argued that the new allegiance to Rome presented no conflicts for the new citizens because it existed "on a different level" from the previous citizenship to the native state.[24] In the sense that Roman citizenship supplemented rather than replaced municipal citizenship, it was not in direct competition with it. However in the *De legibus,* the distinction between "legal" citizenship and "natural" or affective citizenship does not imply a qualitative difference in the kind of bond that obtains between the citizen and his two *patriae;* it is on the same subjective scale of dearness or *caritas* that the more distant state must prevail over the smaller.[25] And the reality of this conflict is revealed

19. Cic. *Off.* 1. 54: *libidinem procreandi.*

20. Ibid. 1. 55.

21. Ibid. 1. 57.

22. Ibid. 1.57.

23. The importance of loyalty to the native place as a theme in Roman literature is studied in detail by Bonjour 1975b. Among the most significant treatments of the role of love of the native place in the formation of Roman patriotism is Livy's overview of the transformation from monarchy to republic (2.1), on which see Phillips 1974, esp. 89, and Feldherr 1997.

24. Cf., e.g., Nicolet 1980: 44, 47.

25. Cf. Bonjour (1975b:64) on the relationship of the two *patriae:* "Il est évident que le *de legibus* (2.5) ne fait qu'une différence quantitative, et non qualitative dans la *caritas* selon qu'elle se rapporte à la grande ou à la petite patrie." On the word *caritas,* see Hellegouarc'h 1972: 148–49. Based largely on Cic. *Part.* 88, scholars have proposed various distinctions between the terms *amor* and *caritas.* Both may be applied to family, but while *amor* is the natural result of *usus* and *familiaritas, caritas* implies some choice and is therefore especially suitable to affection for more distant or abstract persons and organizations. But for our purposes it is enough that *caritas,* too, describes an affective bond that is here applied both to the family and to the *patria.*

when Cicero immediately qualifies his ringing call for patriotism: "However, the *patria* that bore us is dear in almost the same way as that which receives us."[26] Thus Cicero's formulation seems less a schematized resolution of this possible conflict of loyalties than a diagnosis of an abiding tension in the construction of each individual's civic identity. Yet there is a still larger contradiction in this model of patriotism. It is not sufficient simply to serve the *patria* because we understand that it protects and enfolds those nearer groups like wife and family whom we love "naturally." Cicero demands that we feel even greater love for the state than we do for other associations: we must, in other words, think of the Republic in the same terms in which we think of the family and even subordinate to this entity those nearer bonds on which patriotism itself is originally based.

The canonical images of Roman patriotism highlight the rejection of these "inner circles" for the interest of the state. Cincinnatus leaves his farm to become dictator; Brutus presides over the execution of his sons for treason; and Mucius Scaevola, in what is effectively a declaration of Roman citizenship,[27] burns off his hand. Livy constructs the Cincinnatus episode, which is explicitly directed at those who prefer wealth to *virtus* (4.26.7), to emphasize particularly the passage into the public space, from which Cincinnatus's farm is symbolically separated by the Tiber River. His famous gesture of putting on the toga recalls the assumption of the *toga virilis* by every youth as he entered manhood. And the procession that receives the dictator, after he has been carried across the Tiber "on a public ship," recapitulates the transition: "Three sons went to meet him, next intimates and friends, then the majority of the Senate."

Such *exempla* not only teach the subordination of the smaller unit in the interests of the larger state but also reinforce both the interdependency and the parallelism between family, state, and body. As we shall see in chapter 5, at the moment when Brutus puts the interest of the state ahead of his paternal feeling, his relationship to the *patria* is redefined as that between a father and his children. Other explicitly didactic moments of Livy's early books similarly encourage a perception of the state not just as the protector of the family or body but *as* a family or body. For example, after a performance of the "Great Games," the plebeian Titus Latinius receives a prophetic dream warning him that the city is in danger because the games have not been properly conducted (2.36).[28]

26. Cic. *Leg.* 2.5.
27. 2.12.9: *Romanus civis sum.*
28. The same story is also recounted by Cicero (*Div.* 1.55).

Before the spectacle began, a *paterfamilias* had had his slave killed in the circus. Latinius is afraid that he will be laughed at if he tells anyone about his dream and so disregards it. A few days later his son dies. When he hesitates even longer, his own body is stricken with disease. The event implies more than the interconnectedness of family and state; it suggests that the *res publica* is a family or body in macrocosm.[29] The same point lies behind the famous parable of the belly and the limbs, which the patrician Menenius Agrippa tells to a group of plebeians who are trying to sever their bonds to the Rome and form a new city (2.32.8–12). When the limbs, or plebeians, begrudge food to the belly, which represents the patricians, they themselves begin to fail. Thus the inherent comparability of the state to the family or the body provides a constant resource for the generation of collective loyalty; plebeians blind to the functioning of the state as a whole can be made to perceive its indissolubility when projected onto the level of the body.[30]

Nor is this message directed only at controlling the lower classes; patricians as well as plebeians are inclined both to place concerns for their honor above the welfare of the state and to miss the integral connection between family and *res publica*. Thus the patrician rebel Coriolanus, in the scene that concludes the complex of episodes beginning with Latinius's dream, abandons his attack on Rome when his mother makes him realize that by becoming an enemy to the state, he has also changed his relationship to his family.[31] When Coriolanus attempts to embrace her, his mother asks whether she comes as a captive to a conqueror or as a mother to a son (2.40.6). The lurid possibility that Coriolanus's mother might become his slave, and, as such, his concubine, reveals in

29. Conversely, the original religious impropriety of punishing a slave in the circus arose from a failure to understand that this "domestic" issue could have any bearing on the piety of a public festival; cf. Livy's comment, *velut ea res nihil ad religionem pertinuisset* (2.36.1).

30. 2.32.8–12. Lincoln 1989: 145–48, describes Agrippa's parable as a strategic inversion of the normal analogical relationship between body and state. Usually, the patricans are associated with the head, but Agrippa reverses this and links them to the belly, a body part with less positive connotations. However, he then overturns the hierarchies implicit in the image of the body itself by insisting that the belly is in fact an important and valuable organ. As a result, the plebeians are returned to the state and accept patrician hegemony. Although interesting as a reading of the parable, Lincoln's account does not capture the full importance of the episode in the context of Livy's narrative, where the emphasis is less on hierarchy than on unity. It is not so much the relative order of bodily parts as simply the acceptance that there is an inseparable organic relationship binding the components of the *patria* together that provides the key to the preservation of the state. Moreover, this lesson is as important for the patrician Coriolanus to learn as it is for the plebeian secessionists.

31. For a full analysis of this episode, see Bonjour 1975a.

the most powerful way the complete inversion of the structure of the *familia*.

One further demonstration of this pattern of interdependency from Livy's second book suggests a more complex relationship between the entities of body and state (2.23). An old soldier who has been reduced to abject misery by debt slavery hurls himself into the middle of the Forum. Exhausted, he can only point to the scars he has earned in battle. When he finally begins to speak, he chronicles how public misfortunes and unjust economic practices have reduced him to misery. The exigencies of recent wars, raids, and the taxes required to maintain Rome's military endeavors have forced him from his ancestral farm (*ager paternus avitusque,* 2.23.6), which, through the adjectives applied to it, becomes emblematic of the family as a whole. Finally, after having been cast into slavery, his misfortune, "as though a disease [*velut tabem*] reached his body" (2.23.6), in the form of the marks of the lash, which he then reveals to the crowd. The speech illustrates the predictable pattern. Evils afflicting the state work inward to destroy the family and waste the body until the body becomes a "text" where the health of the community can be clearly perceived. Indeed, this "text," with its division between the honorable scars won in foreign wars and the shameful lash marks that testify to domestic misfortunes, mirrors the traditional annalistic alternation between foreign and internal affairs employed in Livy's own history.

A closer look at how Livy has structured his narrative suggests that the relationship between body and state serves as more than an intellectualized schema of similarities employed for solely didactic purposes. The impact of the state on the body can be thought of less as a series of causes and effects projected inward than as a kind of quasi-magical sympathy by which the body receives influences from the whole. Livy's description of the interaction between the individual soldier and the crowd highlights a mutual exchange of energy affecting both the spectators and the object of their gaze. After hurling himself into the Forum, the old soldier seems able to take no further action. Indeed, he appears hardly human; the narrative breaks him down into his constituent parts, filthy clothes, a disgusting bodily condition, a long beard, and disheveled hair. This condition is explicitly stated to have "made his appearance wild."[32] That a capable human form slowly emerges from this image of impo-

32. 2.23.3: *obsita erat squalore vestis, foedior corporis habitus pallore ac macie perempti; ad hoc promissa barba et capilli efferaverant speciem oris.*

tence and subhumanity is largely due to the activity of the spectators themselves. By being recognized, the old man is given an identity and a past. Finally, he himself takes part in the process by pointing out his wounds, witnesses (*testes*) of his past public service.

As the presence of the crowd of onlookers reanimates the old soldier, they themselves begin to take on a coherent shape and purpose. At first, there is no mention of the number or organization of the onlookers. We become aware that there is in fact an audience only when the old man is recognized by someone (2.23.4). Yet as the soldier, now identifiable as such, becomes active and is about to speak, we are informed that a crowd, *turba,* has gathered and has come to approximate the form of a political assembly (*prope modo contionis* [2.23.5]). Moreover, after he finds a voice, the crowd too becomes articulate, responding with *clamor* to his revelations (2.23.7). Finally, the crowd breaks its bounds and aggressively invades the whole city.

In this case, the effect of the spectacle of the old soldier is not to reunite the state but to create essentially an alternative state, which is only reconciled several years later by the parable of Menenius Agrippa. Nevertheless, the scene is important for our purposes because it recapitulates the concentric social groups by which an individual can be defined, and suggests the reciprocal interdependence among them. Moreover, it demonstrates the role of visual contact as the locus of exchange where this interdependence is brought into play and where the various "rings" influence one another. Both of these ideas play a large role in Livy's depiction of the fusion of Alba and Rome.

II. The Horatii and Curiatii

The Roman victory over the Albans was practically bloodless even for the losers. There was no siege, and in place of a formal battle, both sides had agreed to let the contest between them be decided by the outcome of a combat between two sets of triplets. Thus when the Roman troops come to destroy Alba itself, they are confronted with a paradox; technically, the city has already fallen, but its appearance is unchanged:

> There was none of the uproar and terror that usually belongs to captured cities, when after the gates have been broken down, the walls laid low by battering rams, and the citadel taken by force, the cries of the enemy and the

rush of armed men through the city throw all things into confusion with fire and sword, but a sad calm and silent sorrow so cast down the spirits of all that they kept asking one another what they should leave behind and what they should take with them, their own judgment failing out of fear, and now they stood in the doorways, now they wandered aimlessly to look upon their homes for this last time. [1.29.2–3]

Aeneas left Troy when it was already burning, but the Albans are suddenly forced to abandon both their city and their homes intact in order to make the journey to Rome. Although the Albans' plight in one sense is the opposite of that of the Ciceronian persona, for whom the native place of Arpinum will continue to be a lingering alternative, Livy's treatment of the scene emphasizes the moment when local ties are surrendered and the Albans become members of a new state, which, unlike the city they must renounce, is invisible.

But as the outcry of the knights ordering them to leave pressed in upon them and the crash of the buildings that were being destroyed on the edges of the city was heard and the dust rising from distant places had filled everything as if with a cloud, snatching up whatever they could, they went out leaving behind their household gods and the buildings where they were born and raised. [1.29.4]

These Albans had not been present at the loss of the duel that ended the autonomy of their city, nor when their dictator had been torn apart by chariots for violating the treaty. They experience the fall of their state as a ring of destruction, which gradually closes in on each individual spectator, advancing from "the farthest parts of the city," until, like a cloud, it blocks out the sight of their homes.[33]

Alba possesses a special relationship to Rome unlike any other enemy. Not only was it the "native *patria*" of the first Roman king, but many of Rome's great families, including the Julii themselves, came to Rome only after its fall (1.30.1–2). By relating this detail just after the description of the sack of the city, Livy blurs the boundary between Roman and enemy. In becoming Romans, the Albans bind themselves to the *imperium* of the victorious city alone; Albans as a category cease to exist. But by the same token, it becomes impossible to demarcate the pathetic experiences that befall the Albans as something belonging to a distinct, enemy people.[34] The Roman nation is as much a legacy of the destruc-

33. For another analysis and interpretation of this scene, see Walsh 1961a: 171–72.

34. Thus the destruction of Alba resembles nothing in Livy so much as the sack of Rome itself by the Gauls at the end of the first pentad. Again, there is the silence (1.29.3; cf. 5.46.1) and the paradox of a city that is at once captured and untouched.

tion of Alba as of the victory of Rome. In fact, despite the destruction of its secular buildings, Alba continues to survive as a religious center, an eternally "absent" city.[35] In this sense, Livy's narrative of its destruction constitutes a challenge in perspective for his contemporary audience. If allegiance is strictly defined by citizenship, there is no question but that the audience will identify itself with the Romans; even the Albans themselves at the moment when their city is destroyed are technically Romans. But the claims of ancestry and heritage, the very factors that move the defeated Albans, resist a purely nationalist interpretation. The conflict between Rome and Alba, a quasi-legendary event, which on its own could not possibly inspire any strong feelings in the first century B.C.E., becomes a means of articulating and responding to one of the central crises of Livy's day, the fault lines implicit in the construction of a Roman national identity.

However, the problem of distinguishing between Alba and Rome is not confined to Livy's audience; it is explicitly addressed at the beginning of the historian's account of the Alban war.[36] Not only does Livy emphasize the similarities between the institutions and ancestry of the two peoples,[37] but even the motives of the conflict are the same for both sides. "By chance it happened that Roman shepherds were plundering Alban land, and the Albans were plundering Roman land in turn. . . . Embassies were sent on each side at almost the same time" (1.22.3–4). And beyond the immediate causes of war, both sides are motivated by a similar desire for conflict. Tullus Hostilius, the new Roman king is eager for glory and also fears that the Romans have been debilitated by too long a period of peace. The Alban dictator emphasizes this point in his address to the Romans: "If the true cause of the war rather than its pretenses [*speciosa dictu*] must be declared, the desire for glory has driven two related and neighboring peoples to arms" (1.23.7). Such an admission, which the audience knows to be largely valid for the Roman side,

35. Livy concludes his account of the sack by describing the preservation of the temples of the gods (1.29.6, another similarity to the scene in Rome after the Gallic sack), and at 1.31.1–4 recounts the prodigies that led to the foundation of the *feriae Latinae,* an annual festival celebrated on the *mons Albanus,* which is described as the continuation of a traditional Alban observance. For the existence of Roman priesthoods entrusted with the preservation of Alban rituals, see Wissowa 1902: 448.

36. For a complementary treatment of the Alba episode as part of a larger pattern of structural oppositions between the division and unification of peoples that recurs throughout Livy's first book, see Konstan 1986, esp. 205–210.

37. Cf. 1.23.1, and 1.24.9, where the repeated reflexive adjective highlights the correspondence between Roman and Alban institutions.

seriously undercuts the logic of the "just war," by which the Romans interpreted victories over their opponents as proof that their own claims for restitution were legitimate and their conduct of negotiations formally correct. Beyond that, as we saw in chapter 2, military success validates the society as a whole, from the physical prowess of its individual soldiers to the propriety of its political and religious practices, and ultimately to the historical tradition that gave rise to them. But since the Albans share the same institutions and history, the kinds of distinction that the Romans used to define a foreign enemy are rendered meaningless.[38]

The first attempt to establish a distinction between Roman and Alban consists of a trick involving the diplomatic procedures leading up to the declaration of war. Both sides had sent embassies demanding restitution simultaneously, but Tullus Hostilius puts off the Alban ambassadors with excessive hospitality until he is informed that the Roman claims have already been rejected by the Alban king. Therefore the Romans can legitimately (*pie* [1.22.4]) declare war. "Announce to your king," Tullus tells the Albans, "that the Roman king calls upon the gods as witnesses of which people first rejected the embassy, so that they might exact all the losses of war against them" (1.22.7). This trickery may seem dubious or even impious, but the Romans expected their leaders to be clever manipulators in the dealings between men and gods.[39] Not only will the king's claim be confirmed by the eventual Roman victory, but his use of appearances to trick the Albans, particularly his sudden revelation to the ambassadors that they are being watched by the gods, foreshadows the other decisive moments in the conflict.

Mettius Fufetius, who has become leader of the Albans after the death of their king, explicitly poses the question of discrimination between the two peoples just as the two armies are on the verge of battle (1.23.7–9). He dismisses both sides' claims about the responsibility for the conflict as mere pretenses (*speciosa dictu*) and exposes the true causes of the war as a mutual desire for power (*cupido imperii*). Given this shared ambition, the task, he says, is to "find a way to decide which people will rule the other without a great slaughter of either" (1.23.9). For the empire of the Etruscans, their common enemies, surrounds both peoples. In making this appeal to fear of a common enemy, Mettius employs the same argument that will be frequently used in resolving inter-

38. Cf. the issues that arise at the beginning of the Latin War (8.4 ff.), discussed in ch. 3.

39. See Porte 1989: 178 f.

nal disunity at Rome, the exposure of an encircling Other whose presence defines the warring factions as allies.[40] Mettius goes on to describe the relationship among the three peoples through the metaphor of a spectacle: "Be mindful . . . these two armies in battle will be a spectacle [for the Etruscans], so that they will attack conqueror and conquered together, weary and depleted" (*Memor esto, iam cum signum pugnae dabis, has duas acies spectaculo* [*sc. Etruscis*] *fore ut fessos confectosque simul victorem ac victum adgrediantur* [1.23.9]). The Etruscans will be able to watch unconcerned as the two armies weaken themselves to the point of being able to offer no resistance. The spectator, this model implies, detached from the action he observes, occupies a position of superiority and is able to gain from the conflict of those he watches without risk. This view of spectacle is of a piece with Mettius's earlier dismissal of the demands of the ambassadors as "specious." The Roman king, as we have seen, far from dismissing appearances as irrelevant, is eager to win his competition with the Albans even on the level of the *speciosa*. Thus the Romans' belief in the efficacy and validity of appearances already appears as a crucial difference between the two peoples, and in fact the manipulation of appearances will play an ever-larger role in the subsequent contest.

The result of Mettius's speech is that both sides agree to solve their dispute through a duel between two sets of triplets, the Horatii and Curiatii, whose outcome will decide "which people will rule which." Initially, the Albans seem likely to prevail, as they kill the first two Romans and face the last with a three to one advantage. But finally the survivor manages to overcome all three of his opponents. The actions of the Horatii exemplify the conceptions of patriotism just analyzed. Like Mucius Scaevola and other exemplary figures, such as Torquatus and Corvus, the triplets agree to risk their own lives in the interest of their *patria*. Furthermore, the progressive isolation of the surviving Horatius, first from the state as a whole and then from his slaughtered brothers, draws attention precisely to the concentric levels of social affiliation out of which, according to the Ciceronian model, patriotism is built.[41]

40. For the origins and development of the theory that the absence of a powerful external threat hastened the internal decline of the Roman state, see Earl 1961: 7 ff., and Harris 1979: 127 f., 266 f.; for its manifestations in Livy, see Luce 1977: 271 and Miles 1986: 3–4. Note, too, that the first passage in Livy's text to discuss the moral and political implications of such fear occurs just a few chapters before this speech, in the description of Numa's religious program (1.19.4).

41. Cf., again, the situation of the *devoti,* described in ch. 3, who are also simultaneously set apart from the larger group and made its representatives.

But the Roman's victory depends on drawing together the interests of family and state as well as placing them in the correct hierarchy. Thus when he kills the last Curiatius, Horatius cries that he "has given two [Albans] to the shades of his brothers, and now slays the third in order that the Romans shall rule the Albans." In contrast, for the last Alban, the family loss keeps him from fighting effectively; he is "already defeated by the slaughter of his brothers."[42] Moreover, Horatius's very body takes on an important quality of the state as a whole, its indivisibility. Although his two brothers have been killed, Horatius is *integer* and is later described as *intactum*.[43] This "wholeness" contrasts with the Albans' disintegration at every level. The climax of the fight comes after the first two Romans have been killed and the Albans surround the survivor.[44] Here Horatius makes the crucial decision to separate the brothers by fleeing, a device that leaves an indelible visual trace in the three monuments of the dead Albans, "separated by intervals," which Livy describes at the end of the battle (1.25.14). By separating his opponents, Horatius has moved from a contest between groups to one between individuals, where the integrity of his body can prevail over the wounded Albans.[45]

By agreeing to have their conflict settled by a duel while the rest of the armies simply look on, the Romans and Albans have effectively set up a spectacle very similar to that imagined by Mettius Fufetius. Both armies avoid mutual destruction by choosing surrogates to fight for them and participate only as spectators, free from danger. But unlike the hypothetical Etruscan spectators, the two armies are not disconnected from the fate of those they watch. As Livy describes the duel, he emphasizes

42. 1.25.11: *victusque fratrum ante se stragi.*

43. 1.25.7: *integer*; 1.25.11: *intactum.*

44. As Ogilvie 1965: 106, and Burck 1964b: 149 ff., point out, Livy's economical treatment of the deaths of the first two Romans contrasts markedly with the far more prolix narrative of Dionysius of Halicarnassus (*Ant. Rom.* 3.13–20). Dionysius alternates the deaths of the Romans and Albans and heavily emphasizes each reversal, peppering his account with no fewer than eight speeches. Not only does Livy's treatment heighten the excitement, but it additionally draws attention to the motif of separation, and to the superiority of the Romans over the Albans as individuals. For an analysis of Dionysius's presentation of the scene, see Walker 1993: 363–70. Walker argues that Dionysius's explicit use of theatrical terms to describe the combat operates programmatically to focus attention on his own text's capacity to produce spectacle and to draw together the experiences of the spectator in the text and the reader. Solodow 1979: 258, contrasts the abstractness and academic frigidity of Dionysius's treatment of the spectators' responses with Livy's success in "making us feel that we too are present at [the] scene."

45. 1.25.7: *Ergo ut segregaret pugnam eorum capessit fugam, ita ratus secuturos ut quemque volnere adfectum corpus sineret.*

the same set of reciprocal links between spectators and spectacle, crowd and individual, that we saw in the episode of the old soldier. Thus rather than distancing the watcher from the event, spectacle forms a bridge between the spectators and their champions by which the larger and smaller groups are brought into contact with one another. The crowds encourage and inspire their champions and in turn respond to their defeats and victories with an excitement or despair that makes them collectively mirror the attributes of the individual.

Livy's account of the spectators' anxiety as they watch the duel goes back to a very famous literary model, Thucydides' description of the battle in the harbor of Syracuse, where the land armies can only look on as the naval combat decides their fate.[46] But one crucial difference between the two narratives reveals Livy's particular emphasis. Thucydides' account focuses on the inability of each spectator to gain a clear understanding of the course of the battle as a whole because of the limited perspective from which he views it. Those who happen to see the Athenians winning are encouraged; those who see them being defeated are despondent. As a result, the experiences of the spectators, described in highly physical language, depend entirely on the emotions generated by their limited perceptions of events, rather than the influence of the complete events themselves. Even though Livy's narrative of the duel has the combatants chase each other for great distances over uneven terrain, there is never a moment when they are out of sight of either army or where either side is in any doubt about who is who.[47] Thus Livy has sacrificed strict verisimilitude in order to keep the link between spectators and spectacle unbroken.

The exchange between the spectator armies and the individual combatants, like that between the crowd and the soldier, impacts equally upon watcher and watched. At the simplest level, the armies inspire their champions by shouting encouragement, and conversely the successes or failures of the individuals inspire or distress the larger groups. But Livy's vivid description lends these effects an air of physicality that suggests a more radical sympathy between crowd and individual: the responses of the spectator armies mimic the very combat that the duel was designed to prevent. The watching armies are "raised up, held suspended, in their

46. Thuc. 7.71.3–4.

47. Contrast Dionysius's statement in his account of the episode (*Ant. Rom.* 3.19.2) that the spectators' ability to perceive events clearly was hampered by the distance from which they viewed them. See also the discussion of the thematic function of this lack of clarity in Dionysius's narrative in Walker 1993: 368 f.

mind they are stretched out[48] toward the unpleasant spectacle." When the battle begins, "mighty terror binds the spectators, and while hope is inclined on neither side, their voice and *spiritus* grow dull" (1.25.4). This sentence gives the effect of their anxiety not only an air of uniformity but also an almost anatomical specificity. The experiences of the group are thus described in terms applicable to a single individual.[49] Moreover, the dulling of the spectators' *spiritus* mirrors precisely the experience of the dying Horatii, who are described with the cognate word *exspirantes* (1.25.5).[50] Correspondingly, Livy describes the combatants as like a battle line (*acies*) bearing the courage (*animi*) of great armies (1.25.3). The few actors lose their individual identities and an awareness of their individual fates in assuming responsibility for the destiny of their cities. Conversely, each of the spectators must individually experience the physical effects suffered by the bodies that represent them.[51]

Livy also correlates the process of watching with the fulfillment of the purpose for which the duel was designed, to allow for a distinction to be made between the two peoples, "to decide which will rule [*imperent*] which" (1.23.9). The first five sentences of his description contain no proper nouns or adjectives, referring only to "each side" or simply "they."[52] At the beginning of the combat, not only do Albans and Romans share the same experiences, but the narrative makes it literally impossible for the audience to distinguish one side from the other. Correspondingly, Livy has already remarked that although he follows those who say that it was the Horatii who fought for Rome, there are other versions that call the Curiatii the Roman champions, an admission that further blurs the distinction between the two sides almost at the expense of the authority of his own narrative.[53] The

48. I follow Gebhard's reading *intenduntur* ("are stretched out") at 1.25.2 rather than the manuscripts' *incenduntur* ("are enflamed") to preserve the consistency of the imagery. See Ogilvie 1965: 112–13, for parallels and discussion.

49. Cf. the similar observation of Fries 1985: 71–72.

50. This event in turn renders the Romans *exanimes,* as if dead themselves (1.25.6).

51. Wilhelm 1936, esp. 77–78, also describes the correlation between the experiences of the groups and their individual champions and analyzes it as a survival of "magical thinking," or a belief in sympathetic magic, which Livy's account of the duel has "probably unconsciously" (1936: 82) preserved.

52. 1.25.1–5.

53. Livy, like the spectators themselves is dragged in each direction by the rival versions, *auctores utroque trahunt* (1.24.1). On the effect of Livy's declaration, cf. Konstan 1986: 210: "I would like to suggest that the union of two populations is here figured as the collapse of distinction between individuals: the lone surviving Horatius is an image of the new unity of Rome and Alba."

indifferentiability of the two sides persists until the instant when an action on the battlefield inclines the advantage toward one side. Two of the Horatii are quickly killed by the Albans. Thus an inequality is established, which is immediately registered both among the spectators, who necessarily respond differently, and in the narrative itself, where the terms *Albani* and *Romani* allow the reader to tell the two sides apart for the first time (1.25.5).

But the spectators' responses do not just provide an index of difference recording the progress of the combat. After the Roman champion has won the victory by dispatching all three Albans himself, the two armies are described as burying their dead "with not at all the same spirits [*nequaquam paribus animis*], since one side has been enriched with authority [*aucti imperio*] and the other has lost its independence" (1.25.13). This description reflects the final exultation and despair that the two sides have respectively experienced as spectators and simultaneously shows that the larger purpose of the duel, the apportionment of *imperium*, has been accomplished. In other words, the duel has not just resolved the dispute in favor of the Romans; it has imposed a difference distinguishing them from the Albans.[54] Just as the champions were inspired by them, the spectators have been empowered by visual contact with their champions. This is revealed by the phrase *aucti imperio* used of the Romans. As we have seen, Wagenvoort interprets *imperium* as the strengthening force communicated by a leader to his troops,[55] and *augeo* is the proper verb for its transference.[56] As in the case of Torquatus and Corvus, so too the champions here become the means for a reciprocal exchange of *imperium*. The Horatii and Curiatii are summoned to fight by their commanders (1.24.2) and receive the encouragement of their respective armies (1.25.1); in return the sight of Horatius's victory in combat has increased the *imperium* of his entire people.

54. Cf. Wilhelm 1936: 78: "Soll die ganze Abmachung [sc., the decision to settle the dispute through the battle of champions] einen Sinn haben, so erhält sie ihn nur von einer Anschauung aus, für die mit dem Falle der albanischen Kämpfer die Entscheidung zwischen den beiden kämpfenden Mächten wirklich und wesentlich *schon gefällt ist*" (emphasis Wilhelm's).

55. Wagenvoort 1947: 59–72, esp. 66.

56. On *augeo,* see above, ch. 2, sec. II and n. 70. That the *animus* in particular should be the site where this new charge of *imperium* manifests itself is appropriate in light of Livy's earlier reference to the *animus* as the psychic organ most affected by the act of watching (*animo intenduntur* [1.25.2]). On the *animus* and its special receptivity to sensory impressions, see Onians 1951: 171.

III. The Death of Horatia

Livy's description of the duel presents two diametrically opposed vantage points on the unfolding action, that of the victorious Romans who identify with the eventual killer of Curiatius and that of the Albans who identify with the victim. It is nationality alone that determines which of these irreconcilable perspectives each spectator adopts. There is obviously no question of a pro-Curiatius faction among the Roman troops. Thus the act of watching becomes a communal exercise that makes the experiences of all the spectators uniform, so that the entire nation responds as one individual, a unity that corresponds to the "wholeness" of the one man who represents them on the field. Not only does civic identity alone determine loyalty but it incorporates and harmonizes with the individual's other motivations. When the last Horatius kills the Curiatii, he is both benefiting his *patria* and avenging his brothers; there is no distinction between what he owes the state and what he owes his family. The sequel to Horatius's victory reverses all of these tendencies. Again, an alternative perspective on an act of violence is introduced, but no longer can the opposite viewpoint be relegated to those outside the *patria*. Moreover, this discrepancy in response results precisely from the spectator's inability to adopt a national, as opposed to personal, perspective.

As Horatius enters the city bearing the triple spoils of the defeated Albans, his sister, who, we are now told, was betrothed to one of the Curiatii, begins to mourn and tear her hair. Her brother immediately kills her, with the cry, "Away to your betrothed with your untimely love, forgetful of your brothers living and dead, forgetful of your *patria*"(1.26.4). Livy's narrative focuses the discrepancy between Horatia's response and that of the "nation" on the interpretation of a visual sign. Horatius carries before him the weapons of the defeated triplets as *spolia* to commemorate his victory on behalf of the nation and thus to anchor his personal accomplishment in the history of the Roman people. Among the trophies is Curiatius's *paludamentum,* a soldier's cloak, which as a military garment was an appropriate spoil of victory. Horatia however recognizes the cloak as one that she, like a good Roman wife, has woven with her own hands.[57] As the public celebrates the vic-

57. Another example of how woven garments can become public *monumenta,* recording the history of the state, is offered by the famous linen corslet of Cossus, which Augustus supposedly saw in the temple of Jupiter Feretrius and used to correct Livy's assertion

tory of her brother, Horatia alone pronounces the name of Curiatius.[58]

Initially, the conflict between Horatius and Horatia seems based exclusively on an opposition between family and state, which in turn depends on gender difference: the woman views the event only in terms of family connections and personal affection, while the all-male army champions the national perspective. But the actions and attitudes of neither character allow themselves to be so neatly characterized. Horatius's own act of killing his sister violates both the laws of the state and the structure of authority within the family: it is only the father who possesses the legal right of life and death over Horatia. Conversely, the exclamation with which Horatius accompanies his deadly blow refuses to cede the realm of the family to his sister. In killing the Curiatii, he was avenging his brothers, whereas Horatia is equally disloyal to family and state. Moreover, as Georges Dumézil points out, by casting Horatia's behavior as shamelessness,[59] Horatius makes it the moral responsibility of the male members of the family to punish her, even if such behavior is technically illegal.[60]

Horatia's rejection of her brothers out of loyalty to her future husband expresses a potential conflict for any Roman bride at the moment when she moves from the family of her brothers into the *patria potestas* of her father-in-law; in this respect too, her actions can be understood as

---

that Cossus had been a mere military tribune when he won the *spolia opima* (4.20.5–11). This passage has been among the most discussed in Livy's text both as evidence for the historian's relationship to Augustus and as an indication of the date of the first pentad. See esp. the recent interpretation by Miles 1995: 40–47, who also provides bibliography.

58. 1.26.2: *nomine sponsum mortuum appellat.*

59. Dumézil 1942: 106–7. Solodow 1979: 266, attempts to refute Dumézil's point by denying that there is any suggestion that Horatia is behaving shamelessly here (in contrast to Horatius's explicit charge of immodesty prior to killing his sister at Dion. Hal. *Ant. Rom.* 3.21.6). Yet in the context of general Mediterranean conceptions of female modesty, as surveyed by Cohen 1991: 112–15, the public conspicuousness with which Horatia expresses her love for a man to whom she was not married itself could render her behavior suspect. Indeed, one Roman's definition of female virtue couples an insistence on sexual continence with a larger ability to control emotions and not to give way to outbursts of grief (Musonius 3, cited in Treggiari 1991: 103). So, too, Horatius's reference to his sister's *immaturus amor,* explicitly presents his sister's affection as "untimely," a word that not only connotes the inappropriateness of Horatia's outburst in the context of his *ovatio,* but also suggests that her love for Curiatius is itself premature. This is not to say that such view of female propriety went unchallenged at Rome (cf. the debates on the public demeanour of women in Livy [34.2–6] and Tacitus [*Ann.* 3.33–34]), much less that Livy himself endorsed it, simply that Horatia's behavior and Horatius's language bring the issue into play.

60. For the notion that a woman's reputation also affected the reputations of the male members of her family, and that consequently it was the duty of fathers, husbands, and brothers both to avenge any attacks upon their female relatives' honor by outsiders and also to control the conduct of the women themselves, see Cohen 1991: 117–20.

illustrating tensions that lie exclusively within the family sphere.[61] Indeed, the very site of the murder bears an association with this critical moment in a girl's life. The *tigillum sororium,* which according to Livy's narrative will be established to commemorate Horatius's purification after the murder of his sister, is actually named for the temple of Juno Sororia, whose cult title derives from the verb *sororiare,* used to describe the swelling of a girl's breast at puberty.[62] And puberty for most Roman women coincided with marriage.

But just as both Horatia and her brother are impelled by their differing familial allegiances, so too at the national level the schism between them reflects not an opposition between "family" and "state" but an internal contradiction within the logic of patriotism itself. Although devotion to the *patria* must eventually take precedence over family loyalty, patriotism arises out of the very love of wives and children that it eventually supplants. So in the preface to Livy's second book, he describes how the national unity of the Romans took time to develop, because it was only very gradually that a wandering people was sufficiently united by their affection for wives and children and love for the "place itself" (2.1.5).[63] A practical example of how such unity can be forged from family bonds emerges in Livy's account of the famous rape of the Sabine women. In the midst of the Sabines' retaliation, their daughters intercede on behalf of their new husbands, the Romans, and the two peoples merge rather than becoming enemies.[64] Horatia occupies exactly the same mediating position between the Romans and Albans. She thus represents those more intimate ties that engender patriotism and serves as a reminder of an alternative means of bringing about the unity of the two peoples, which in this case is implicitly rejected. Paradoxically her brother can only demonstrate his fully developed patriotism by killing her.[65]

61. On the "tensions between lineal and conjugal loyalties" in the Horatia episode and elsewhere in the first book, see also Konstan 1986: 211–12.

62. Festus 380 L. See Ogilvie 1965: 117, for further bibliography, and see also Coarelli 1986: 110–17.

63. See Phillips 1974: 89, and Feldherr 1997.

64. And in the world of Late Republican politics, marriage alliances often prevented hostility between political rivals.

65. In doing so, Horatius's behavior is the exact opposite of that of those Romans and Sabines to whom the Sabine women made their appeal. At 1.13.3, the women invite their husbands and fathers to kill them, as the cause of the conflict, rather than do battle amongst themselves. This appeal so moves (*movet,* 1.13.4; cf. *movet,* 1.26.3, of Horatius's anger at his sister's behavior) the combatants that they immediately cease fighting.

By presenting the Curiatii as potentially linked to their rivals by ties of kinship, Horatia's presence in the narrative challenges the radical differentiation between the Alban and Roman champions that was won by the duel. The Curiatii are no longer defined exclusively as "other," foreign enemies, against whom violence is legitimate. Livy articulates this challenge by presenting it as an alternative spectacle, which "interferes" with the reception of Horatius's victory both by contemporaries within the narrative and by his own audience. As Solodow has shown, the description of Horatius's slaughter of his sister contains several echoes of his killing of the last Curiatius.[66] In neither case does the victim offer any resistance, and Horatius accompanies each killing with a pithy exclamation imposing a meaning on the death.[67] The verb used for the killing of Horatia, *transfigit* (1.26.3), is a cognate of *defigit* (1.25.12), which describes the death of Curiatius. References to Horatius's *ferocitas* also draw together the two scenes.[68] The response of the Romans to the killing of Horatia explicitly juxtaposes the two actions. "The deed seemed appalling [*atrox*] to patricians and plebeians, but his honor, still fresh, blocked out the act" (*sed recens meritum facto obstabat* [1.26.5]). The word *obstabat* suggests that Horatius's honor, on visual display in the form of the *spolia* he bears, literally obstructs the viewer's contact with the scene of the murder. Horatius's father will use precisely the same device to persuade the people to spare his son. He points to the visual signs of Horatius's public victory the *Pila Horatia*,[69] and at the same time conjures up the image of his ovation, almost returning to the very instant before Horatia herself blocks (*obvia* [1.26.2]) her brother's progress.[70] The same doubling of visual signs is preserved for posterity, not only by Livy's narrative, but in the more tangible form of the *sepulcra* with which Livy ends each half of his account. The three *sepulcra* of the Curiatii remain on the battlefield on the Roman side "separated in space just as the

66. Solodow 1979: 253–54.

67. Cf. in this context also the cry with which Romulus kills his sibling, Remus, again at the boundary of the city: *sic deinde, quicumque ulius transiliet moenia mea* (1.7.2).

68. 1.25.1, 1.25.7, 1.25.11, and 1.26.3. Indeed, Dumézil 1942 interprets the whole narrative complex as the Roman form of an Indo-European myth concerning the regulation of the warrior's battle rage.

69. 1.26.10: *spolia Curiatiorum ostentans.*

70. Ibid.: "He whom you saw [*vidistis*] just now adorned, celebrating his *ovatio,* in his victory procession." Correspondingly, the effect of the speech on the crowd is less to persuade through rational argument than to create a moving visual impression. They spare his son "more out of admiration [*admiratione*] for his virtue than because of the justice of the case" (1.26.12).

battle was fought," but there is also a tomb for Horatia, similarly placed at the spot where she fell, the Porta Capena, at the entrance to the city (1.26.14).

But what can such a careful articulation of opposite viewpoints tell us about the functioning of Livy's text? Dumézil, who also argues that the killing of Horatia forms a necessary complement to the duel, finds analogues for such structural ambivalence about the warrior's role in an array of myths from other Indo-European cultures. The god Indra, for example, in Indian myth establishes cosmic order by slaying the demon Vṛtra and a three-headed monster. However, Vṛtra and the monster are also Brahmans; thus their persons are inviolate, and Indra must be punished for Brahmanicide. In a similar way, Horatius becomes at once the savior of the state and a murderer.[71] Dumézil was interested in the myth itself and necessarily treats Livy's narrative only as a means to its recovery. Solodow, who argues that the ambiguous treatment of the episode is unique to Livy and represents his individual development of the historical tradition, dismisses Dumézil's analysis precisely for failing to take into account Livy's originality. Here I want to suggest that the antitheses in Livy's account of Horatius, whatever they may tell us about the historian's personal views, correspond to a larger structure of oppositions in Roman religious institutions, one that can elucidate not the distant origins of the Horatius legend but the contemporary significance of Livy's text.

Livy's narrative itself offers a model for understanding its complexities. Between the speech of Mettius Fufetius and the beginning of the duel, there is a detailed description of the sacrifice that confirms the treaty between Romans and Albans (1.24.3–9). Far from being a mere antiquarian diversion, the account of the Fetial sacrifice sketches a set of relationships among its various participants that anticipates the tensions that will arise later in the episode.[72] Like the mythical narratives studied

71. Dumézil 1942: 122–24. Dumézil also points out that in Indra's case, the same action, the killing of Vṛtra made him both hero and criminal, while for Horatius this ambiguous status is the result of two separate but related actions. He attributes this difference to a Roman desire to demythologize the motif. Yet at the same time that Horatia's death makes Horatius a criminal, her mourning offers a new and much more ambiguous perspective on the duel itself, one that also blurs the dividing line between members of the community and outsiders.

72. For other views on the function of this digression, see Ogilvie 1965: 110: "It is a quite extraneous addition to the story of the Horatii"; Stübler 1941: 174 ff., for whom the elaborate description of the ritual emphasizes that the Roman's coming victory is a divinely sanctioned indication of Rome's superiority; and Fries 1985: 69, who sees the inclusion of the ritual as a device to build suspense for the duel itself. The closest parallel to the interpretation offered here is that of Wilhelm 1936: 79 f., who argues that the use of ritual substitution in the Fetial rite, the pig's role as substitute for the people, results from precisely

by Dumézil, sacrifice possesses an inherently contradictory structure, in the sense that it suspends its audience between an identification with the one who performs the sacrifice and with his victim. The establishment of a sacrificial paradigm behind the narrative also anchors Livy's text to a central socio-religious institution that became a particular focus of interest in the Augustan period precisely because of its intrinsic, practical connections to the issues of unification and alienation.

Livy's description of the treaty ritual by which the Albans and Romans bind themselves to honor the outcome of the duel is the fullest that survives for this procedure.[73] The ceremony begins with an elaborate dialogue in which the Fetial priest first asks the king for authority to strike the treaty. When the king grants it, the Fetial then demands the *sagmina,* a sacred piece of sod kept on the Capitoline. After another affirmative response, the priest asks to be made a messenger of the Roman people. The king approves, and the priest touches the head and hair of a certain Sp. Fusius with the sacred sod, making him *pater patratus,* the man who will actually perform the sacrifice and proclaim the treaty. The *pater patratus* recites the terms and then "strikes" the treaty by sacrificing a pig with a prayer to Jupiter to strike the Roman people, should they ever violate their promise, just as he strikes the pig.[74]

The first parts of the ceremony emphasize the hierarchical transference of authority from the king to his individual executor. The language of request and command (repeated archaic imperatives, *posco, iubeo*) punctuates the king's empowerment of the *pater patratus.* Correspondingly, the gesture of touching the *pater patratus* with the *sagmina* literally places him in contact with a piece of living earth that has been ritually transferred from the highest, most sacred, and militarily most powerful point in the city.[75] At the same time that these rituals set the bearers of power apart from the other members of the community, they also enable them to act as representatives of the entire Roman people. The king

---

the same kind of magical logic that allows the champions to act as surrogates for their respective armies.

73. For a fuller description of the *fetiales,* with testimonia, see Wissowa 1902: 475 ff., and Latte 1960: 121 ff.; and see also Wiedemann 1986, who argues that the original function of the priesthood was to maintain and enforce treaties, and that the more flamboyant ceremony in which they declared war by hurling a spear into foreign territory (see Livy 1.32.5–14) was very much an Augustan construct.

74. Livy chooses not to describe the recitation of the oath itself, on the grounds of its length (1.24.6). This is somewhat surprising if his motive for including the ritual is purely antiquarian. Rather, the omission suggests that the significance of the ritual for Livy lies in the processes of authorization and sacrifice that he does describe.

75. See Wagenvoort 1947: 19–21, on the *sagmina.*

himself first demonstrates his ability to speak on behalf of the *populus Romanus* in his prayer that his action be accomplished "without fraud on my part or on that of the Roman people" (*quod sine fraude mea populique Romani Quiritium fiat* [1.24.5]). This is spoken in response to the Fetial's own request that he himself be made a "royal messenger of the Roman people" (*regius nuntius populi Romani*) and his companions "vessels" (*vasa* [1.24.5]). The *pater patratus* in turn speaks on behalf of the entire people in agreeing to the treaty. The sacrifice of the pig represents the culmination of the unification of the power of the Roman people in the *pater patratus;* not only is he able to speak for the entire people, he enables them to strike with one hand.

But the violence effected by its representative is simultaneously reflected back on the community. If the Romans should ever violate the treaty, the striking of the pig, accomplished through their own surrogate, will become the fate of the people as a whole. Hence for the treaty to be effective, it is necessary for the Roman audience to identify not only with their representative, the *pater patratus,* but also with the victim; they must be able to visualize his death as their own. Both priest and victim are therefore marked out as surrogates for the community of spectators.

This doubling of the surrogates, made explicit in a treaty sacrifice where the spectators are compelled to see the victim's death as their own, is by no means anomalous. Other sacrificial practices also establish a ritual link between sacrificer and victim that sets them apart from the other participants. Both were differentiated by their costume and decorations, the priest with his veiled head, and religious insignia, the victim adorned with fillets and garlands. In particular, the red color frequently worn by priests provided a visual link with the blood of the victim.[76] Moreover, both priest and victim were required to possess certain attributes of the god to whom the sacrifice was offered.[77] A final point of resemblance, which has particular relevance for Livy's text, is the purity required of both priest and victims.[78] The victim was not only to be free from all

76. Thus Fowler 1911: 176–77, notes that religious officials who took no part in sacrifice, such as the Vestal Virgins, did not wear red.

77. Dumézil 1970: 580–82, and Scheid 1985: 39–43, characterize certain Roman priests, in particular, the Flamen Dialis, as living statues, stand-ins for the gods themselves. This explains the various ritual taboos that fenced off the priest of Jupiter from quintessentially human activities. The victim, too, was chosen for his similarity to the god. Thus generally male animals were sacrificed to male deities, and females to female deities. Black victims were sacrificed to the gods of the underworld, and white to the celestial powers. See Wissowa 1902: 348, and Latte 1960: 380.

78. Wissowa 1902: 351, and Latte 1960: 381.

blemishes but never to have drawn the plow; priests had to wash their hands ritually and could not participate in sacrifices if there had been a death in the family.

A glance back from the account of the treaty ritual to the larger narrative of the duel in which it is embedded reveals similarities in both function and procedure that suggest that the Fetial sacrifice can be taken as the complement or even the template for the workings of the duel. Not only is the treaty ritual instrumental in fulfilling Mettius Fufetius's goal of containing violence by compelling the Romans to abide by the outcome of the battle of surrogates, but the sacrifice itself operates by channeling violence, which is conceptually projected against the whole people, on to just one victim. "Strike the Roman people," the *pater patratus* asks Jupiter, "just as I strike this pig." Correspondingly, as the duel itself approaches its decisive moment, images of sacrifice supplant those of combat. If Livy's goal had been simply to provide a gripping military narrative, we might have predicted that the battle with the last Alban would be the most closely fought of all. But Livy defuses any such expectations by making the outcome a fait accompli; indeed, he removes all possibility of viewing the final encounter as a military event with the explicit statement that it was "not a battle."[79] Rather than submerging Curiatius's death in the suspense of a duel, with the audience wondering which of the two will prevail, Livy isolates and focuses attention on the act of killing itself. Moreover, the gesture of preceding the final blow with a speech recalls the action of the *pater patratus,* who makes his prayer at the precise moment before he slays the victim.[80] And when Horatius speaks of "giving" (*dedi, dabo*) the Albans either to the souls of his brothers or for the victory of the Romans, he is using the language of a sacrificial offering.

The Horatii, appointed to use force against the enemy on behalf of the state or conversely to be killed as substitutes for the entire army, bring together in their own persons the roles of *pater patratus* and sacrificial victim. Like that of the *pater patratus,* their designation as champions takes place through the intervention of the king.[81] But the triplets also possess the most crucial characteristic of the sacrificial victim; they consent to meet death of their own free will.[82] Finally, this pattern of re-

79. 1.25.11: *nec illud proelium fuit.*

80. It was also at this moment, just before the victim was slain, that the priest would recite the prayer at a sacrifice (Latte 1960: 388).

81. 1.24.2: *cum trigeminis reges agunt ut pro sua quisque patria ferro dimicent.*

82. Ibid.: *nihil recusatur.*

semblances also offers a new significance for Livy's emphasis on the whole (*integer* [1.25.7]) and untouched (*intactus* [1.25.11]) condition of the last Horatius.[83] This freedom from blemish approximates both the ritual purity of the presiding priest at a sacrifice and the perfection of the sacrificial victim himself, whose health and suitability are tested before the ceremony begins.[84]

The progress of the narrative from Fetial ritual, to duel, to murder, and finally to punishment, builds upon the essential incompleteness and instability of any sacrificial act. Each act of violence both unites and divides the communities, both controls and perpetuates violence. Thus we see the duel from the perspective of Romans and Albans, and even the unity of the Roman "point of view" breaks down when Horatia refuses to acknowledge the legitimacy of Curiatius as a victim. The ambiguity is only reduplicated when the conqueror of the Albans now slays a victim who is indisputably a member of the community, thereby superimposing an improper "sacrifice" upon the image of his victory. This imbalance can only be corrected by yet another use of controlled violence, which inevitably reproduces the same tensions. The king, to whom Horatius is brought for trial (1.26.5), correspondingly acts in a way that both emphasizes scrupulous adherence to established procedures and defers responsibility for the death of Horatius. In accordance with an ancient law, which Livy quotes, *duumviri* are appointed to pass judgment on Horatius.[85] Thus, just as in the treaty sacrifice that preceded the duel,

83. Not an uncommon pairing in battle descriptions (cf. 5.38.7, 10.14.20, 10.27.9, and 10.36.3) but given a special significance both by the sacrificial precedent and by the emphasis on dismemberment in the following story of Mettius Fufetius (see below).

84. Cf. the attention to the purity of the *sagmina* in the account of the Fetial ritual (1.24.4–5). Of course, by the time he is ultimately dispatched, the last Curiatius is not *intactus,* but nor would the victim be at the final moment of the ceremony.

85. Solodow 1979: 255–56, n. 11, draws attention to an ambiguity at this point in Livy's narrative. The quoted law describes the function of the *duumviri* as *iudicare* (1.26.6), a word that can mean either "judge" or "convict." The *duumviri* interpret it in the latter sense and so suppose that they have no choice but to condemn Horatius (1.26.7). Solodow, who considers it "odd" that *duumviri* would be appointed only to condemn, not to judge, argues that the *duumviri* themselves are mistaken, and that their own refusal to act as judges forms part of a larger narrative strategy by which Livy deliberately avoids having any character within the narrative explicitly pass judgment on Horatius's act. But analogies to sacrificial procedure suggest that there is nothing unusual in having the king appoint surrogates solely for the purposes of condemnation, and I would suggest that the *duumviri*'s insistence that they have no choice but to find Horatius guilty serves as yet another means of avoiding responsibility for his death. For the importance of avoiding blame for the victim's death in sacrificial logic see, most conveniently, Burkert 1966: 106 ff., with bibliography.

the king's role in the proceedings is only to empower agents, not to act himself. The reason Livy gives for the appointment of duumvirs is itself instructive; Tullus wishes to avoid being the source (*auctor*) of a judgment that will be displeasing to the crowd—in other words, to avoid being perceived as the killer of someone with whom the crowd identifies.

After having appeared as the champion who strikes down the Curiatii on behalf of the Roman people, and then as an "impure sacrificer," Horatius by the sentence of the duumvirs is made a victim.[86] An appeal to the people (*provocatio*) and a moving entreaty by his father avert his actual death. However, this entreaty gains its effect by essentially enacting the spectacle of Horatius's execution. After legitimizing the death of Horatia, and pointing to the spoils won by his son as victorious surrogate for the *patria,* the elder Horatius then constructs a scene of execution, in which his son can only be an object of sympathy. "Go lictor bind the hands that, once armed, bore *imperium* for the Roman people. Go veil the head of the liberator of this city" (1.26.11). This attention to the various parts of Horatius's body, following the formula of the sentence of execution, constitutes a kind of dismemberment of the individual whose "integrity" was the key to the nation's triumph. Correspondingly, Horatius also defines the audience who watch the dismemberment of the victim by calling it "a spectacle too hideous for even Alban eyes to bear." Thus again the spectacle of the execution is imagined as an inversion of the triumphant duel. Romans watching the execution of Horatius would be adopting the perspective of Albans.

In his defense, Horatius's father also restores the balance between state and family by reconstructing the patriotic argument that the state holds the family and individual in a protective embrace. He complements the display of his son's victory spoils by putting his arms around

86. The term *princeps,* used of Horatius as he processes into the city after his victory (1.26.2), also forms part of the same pattern of imagery, for it too possesses sacrificial connotations. Scheid 1984: 951–53, demonstrates that the Latin word *particeps,* "one who receives a share," the original meaning of which had previously been connected with the division of booty after victory, also recalls the division of meats after a sacrifice. In fact, Scheid suggests that the division of booty is itself "a particular application of a more general principle" (1984: 952) delineated in sacrificial practices. The *particeps* is defined as a member of the community by receiving a share at the sacrificial banquet, and the share he receives in turn signifies his status within the community. So, too, *princeps,* an equivalent term signifying the "one who takes the first share or occupies the first rank," also describes rank within the group in terms of the "portion" received. The explicit reference to the *spolia* Horatius bears as *princeps* suggests that these connotations of the title may be operative here.

him, and by making the famous appeal to sympathy for a father's love so well known in later judicial practice.[87] The people's acceptance of the elder Horatius's plea for the larger entity to protect the smaller therefore reverses the political implications of the killing of Horatia. Here the state acts to preserve the individual on behalf of the family; there the individual had been killed on behalf of the state precisely for upholding the perspective of family. At the same time that the elder Horatius's speech thus reconciles family and national perspectives, he simultaneously reestablishes the autonomy of the family within the state and the father's authority within the family, which had also been overturned by his son's unjustified killing of his sister, by granting that act a retroactive legitimacy. Horatius begins by claiming that he judges (*iudicare*) that his daughter was killed justly (*iure*); if this were not so, he would have exercised his prerogative as father (*patrio iure*) by punishing his son (1.26.9).

But even the sparing of Horatius offers no resolution; a further human death is avoided but the *caedes manifesta* of Horatia still requires expiation. Father and son are ordered to perform sacrifices to expiate the crime, and these sacrifices have been undertaken from then on by the Horatian *gens*. Each "sacrificial" act described in the text has been subject to infinite revision as the perspective oscillates constantly between slayer and victim, and has consequently provoked another act of violence as a response. The institution of an expiatory ritual undertaken by the Horatii both perpetuates and regulates this sacrificial chain by providing for an infinite series of repetitions that bridges the gap between the past and the present, as well as between the historical text and the world of actual ritual practice. Moreover, these ritual enactments are explicitly and recognizably sacrifices in a way that, other than the Fetial treaty, the historical events are not. In the latter case, actual human deaths were related in a manner that recapitulated and emphasized the dynamics of sacrifice; in the former, the level of violence is reduced by the substitution of animal victims for humans. Thus the narrative moves from the ritual of the Fetial sacrifice, which provides the interpretative model for the scenes that follow, to real and unmediated violence, and finally back again to the ritual in which these historical events can be continually reenacted.

The simultaneous conversion of ritual into history and of history into ritual invites us to reevaluate the moral and social function of Livy's nar-

87. Cf., most notoriously, Cic. *Cael.* 79–80; for the principles behind this kind of display, see, e.g., Quint. *Inst.* 6.1.23 ff.

rative. Any attempt to distinguish between "good" and "bad" violence or to distill the moral of moderation from the episode's complexity misses the point that Horatius's killing of his sister is less a counterweight to his victory than a revision or repetition of it, which emerges as an inseparable aspect of the same act.[88] The alternate perspectives articulated in the episode are not just difficult to resolve but intrinsically unresolvable. Nor does the audience in the text really attempt to resolve them; rather their gaze shifts between the two equally compelling but irreconcilable images of Horatius's victory and his crime. But the text's allusions to sacrificial ritual, by moving us beyond the purely literary plane, offer a framework for interpreting these oppositions that does not allow them to congeal into mere ambiguity. As discussed further in the next section, such tensions are an intrinsic part of the structure and syntax of sacrificial ritual. And far from preventing sacrifice from fulfilling its social function, the juxtaposition of irreconcilable perspectives lies at the heart of its unifying power. Livy's technique of articulating these oppositions through the perspectives of actual spectators thus approximates for his audience the effect of being present at the sacrificial procedures prescribed by the people, which at once absolve Horatius from guilt and perpetuate the memory of his crime.[89]

These sacrifices still took place into the Augustan era. Dionysius of Halicarnassus, in concluding his narrative of Horatius, tells us that the Romans regarded the place where the expiation took place as sacred, and that sacrifices were still performed there (*Ant. Rom.* 3.22.8). What is more, the ritual complex surrounding the *tigillum sororium* addresses the same range of social issues as Livy's narrative of the Horatii: the distinctions between insider and outsider, gender divisions, and the tensions involved in the integration of the individual into the citizen body. For, although the Horatian *aition* of the ritual necessarily portrays its function as primarily expiatory, the monument of the *tigillum sororium* also

88. Solodow, who thoroughly analyzes the text's "unresolvedness" (1979: 260), argues that Livy writes in this way in order to reveal the full moral complexities of the episode and to force the reader to make up his own mind about Horatius's conduct; the emphasis on spectator response in the narrative, by making the events more real to the audience, makes them engage the issues with greater urgency.

89. The visual monuments that commemorate these actions also partake of the same structural ambiguities. As we have seen, the tombs of the Curiatii, which record the duel, contrast with the tomb of Horatia (1.26.14). So, too, the tomb that preserves the memory of Horatia's death balances the *tigillum sororium*, the "beam" that, according to the *aetion* given here, absolves Horatius from guilt when he walks under it, "as if sent under the yoke" (1.26.13.). Finally, this image of subjugation stands in opposition to the *pila Horatia* (1.26.10), the spoils of Horatius's victory.

possessed associations with rites of passage.[90] The beam was surrounded on one side by the altar of Juno Sororia, whose cult title suggests a link with a girl's entry into adulthood, and on the other by the altar of Janus Curiatius. Janus's double aspect made him particularly a god of endings and beginnings, and the cult of Janus Curiatius has been connected with a boy's admission into a *curia,* one of the political subdivisions of the citizen body.[91] Not only does passing under the beam literally constitute an entry into the city, but it also symbolizes the moment when an individual ceases to exist solely as a member of the family and becomes a member of the state. Thus, like the *lustratio* with which we began, this ritual too unites the consolidation of membership in a community with the establishment of a spatial boundary.[92]

IV. Sacrifice and Perspective

The initiatory aspect of Horatius's purification ritual takes us back to the larger issues of the entire Alban episode, the movement of the individual toward full participation in a community of citizens. The decision to represent this process through the recreation of sacrificial ritual was not an isolated or arbitrary choice on Livy's part. The very mechanisms of sacrifice, as Livy outlines them in his description of the Fetial ritual, inherently rely on the interaction between a larger group and an individual actor, whom we have seen paired with the sacrificial victim.

90. See Ogilvie 1965: 117, and, for a fuller treatment Coarelli 1986: 110–17, who concludes as follows: "One can see then that this gate [the *tigillum sororium*] was used as much for the rite of passage of initiation—both feminine and masculine—as for the rite of purification that re-admitted into the civic body the warrior returning from battle. But the essential nature of the rites involved is ultimately the same" (1986: 116–17).

91. See Coarelli 1986: 115, with bibliography. *Curiatius* belongs to the same family of words as *Quirites* and *civis* itself, all deriving from the conception of being *co-viri* (Benveniste 1969: 1.335–7).

92. Ogilvie 1965: 117, suggests that by Livy's day, the ritual of the *tigillum sororium* had lost its initiatory associations, and he thus tries to distance Livy's narrative of the Horatii from the "primitive" rites performed there. But as my analysis has tried to show, these initiatory functions are very relevant to the account of Horatius as it appears in Livy's text. What is more, we have no explicit evidence about how these festivals were perceived by an Augustan audience, except for the focus on their expiatory role in Livy and Dionysius, which is almost inevitable given the context in which the rites are described and perfectly consistent with initiation rituals. Nor if we did possess any such testimony would it necessarily provide a complete or accurate description of the ritual's functions (on the methodological issues involved, see Beard 1980: 26).

Moreover, the complexities in attitude and perspective that this double focus raises for the participants essentially reproduce the "patriotic paradox" discussed at the beginning of the chapter. On the one hand, the onlooker can respect the priest's claim to represent the community as a whole and identify with the exactor of violence. The adoption of this perspective not only implies that the spectator defines himself as a member of the group that authorizes and benefits from the killing, but also introduces a seamless model of alignment between the individual priest and the larger community, in the sense that he is recognized as a symbolic agent of the whole. But this unification is bought at the expense of the death of the single victim, with whom the spectator is also asked to identify. Thus the alternative possibility exists of seeing the individual not as the one who manifests the collective power of the community but as its victim.

The inherently paradoxical nature of sacrifice is a fundamental tenet of the theories of René Girard.[93] In Girard's view, sacrifice is primarily a social, rather than a religious, phenomenon. It arises out of a need to control violence rather than to communicate with supernatural forces.[94] The processes of imitative desire constantly force the members of any society into competitions that tend toward violence. Since every act of violence generates an urge for retribution, without some check the accelerating cycle of violence would quickly destroy a society. Sacrifice

93. A few initial qualifications must preface my introduction of Girard's model. Although I believe Girard's theory explains some features of Livy's use of sacrifice extraordinarily well, my aim is not to give an exclusively Girardian reading. Thus my emphases differ from Girard's in a number of respects: Girard does not explicitly discuss the role of visual contact in sacrifice (my use of "perspective" in discussing the spectator's potential for identification with either the victim or the sacrificer is almost the opposite of Girard's more abstract application of the word to differentiate the external perspective of one not involved in the pattern of conflict culminating in sacrificial violence from the internal perspective of the participants [1977: 158 ff.]), and the potential identification between the participant and the sacrificial victim is an important component of other sacrificial theories as well (cf. Burkert 1983: 20 f., 38). Finally, it should be acknowledged that Girard does not directly treat Roman sacrificial practice. Nevertheless, he perceives sacrifice as a universal cultural institution and shows that a similar logic lies behind the practices of diverse peoples. Despite procedural differences, the widespread use of sacrifice is a characteristic that Roman culture shares with a variety of ancient and modern societies, but that separates it from our own, where sacrificial rituals are less immediately apprehensible. Hence the value of Girard's general model of the institution of sacrifice itself is worth the risk entailed by his lack of particular references to Roman practice. For the methodological difficulties involved in the study of Roman sacrificial practices, see esp. Scheid 1984: 949 f., and Habinek 1990. For another use of Girard's theory of sacrifice to explicate the literature of Augustan Rome, see Hardie 1993: 21 f. and n. 5.

94. Girard 1977, esp. 6 ff.

short-circuits this cycle by directing all the violent impulses of the community against a single individual, whom Girard calls the surrogate victim.[95] The actual sacrificial victim in turn substitutes for the surrogate victim,[96] whose killing could result in the spread of violence through attempts at revenge. This sacrificial victim must be sufficiently similar to members of the community for the violence perpetrated upon him to be satisfying;[97] at the same time, he must be from outside the community so that his death will not provoke retribution. The nightmare vision for any society, called the sacrificial crisis, is indiscriminate killing, which comes into being when there are no internal distinctions to direct the flow of violence.[98] This crisis is resolved through the reunification of the community by finding one victim against whom it can inflict violence unanimously. Thus sacrifice constitutes a kind of "good violence," which must be radically distinguished from the uncontrollable violence that it so closely resembles.

Girard's discussion of the social function of sacrifice touches upon Livy's account of the fall of Alba at several points. The initial relationship between the Albans and Romans could well be described as Girard's "mimetic rivalry." As we have seen, Livy emphasizes that for both sides, the desire for *imperium* precedes any cause of war.[99] And it is precisely to prevent this mutual desire from resolving itself through indiscriminate slaughter, in a war that, as Livy points out, would be most like a civil war, that Mettius Fufetius proposes the duel, which is in turn ratified by the treaty sacrifice. With Horatius's murder of his sister, the violence previously exercised against a "legitimate" victim bursts its bounds. The very similarity between the two actions threatens to undermine any possibility of distinguishing legitimate from illegitimate killing. Again, sacrifice ritual is explicitly employed to restore this distinction (by not tolerating a *caedes manifesta*) while avoiding a further divisive death. Although the crisis Livy initially describes is an international as opposed to an internal one, the "otherness" of the Albans is highly problematic, and the ultimate result of the events described is the incorporation of the Al-

95. Girard 1977, esp. 5 and 79 ff.

96. Girard 1977: 101 f.

97. See Girard 1977: 5: "Sacrificial substitution implies a degree of misunderstanding. Its vitality as an institution depends on its ability to conceal the displacement on which the rite is based. It must never lose sight entirely, however, of the original object, or cease to be aware of the act of transference from that object to the surrogate victim: without that awareness no substitution can take place and the sacrifice loses all efficacy."

98. Girard 1977: 39–67.

99. 1.23.7: *cupido imperii.*

bans into one Roman society. The ambiguous status of the Albans as both insiders and outsiders exactly recalls the position of any sacrificial participant, caught between his ties to the society that enacts the violence and his sympathy for the outsider who is its victim. And we shall see that it is as spectators at an act of violence that the Albans experience their final absorption into the *imperium* of the Romans.

In spite of the inherent doubleness of every aspect of the account of Horatius and the Albans, the sacrificial process in this case may be termed successful in the sense that the final union of the two peoples eventually takes place, and the tensions arising from each act of violence are ultimately controlled through displacement into ritual. But another episode in Livy shows an attempt to use violence for similar ends that fails on both counts. This rite is performed by Rome's enemies the Samnites and appears in the context of Livy's account of the battle of Aquilonia, where, as we have already discussed, the Samnites' failure to create a unified military force serves as a foil to the efficacy of the Romans' prebattle spectacles. In the Samnite procedure, the ritual performance does not prevent the death of a human victim but actually precipitates it, and the result of the spectacle is only to fragment the unity of the participants. What is particularly interesting about Livy's account of this episode is that the failure to maintain ritual propriety in this case manifests itself as a transformation of the perspective from which the spectator views the sacrifice.

Before the battle of Aquilonia, the Samnites prepare a special force that will not yield to the enemies' attack but will fight, if necessary, to the last man (10.38.5ff.). An open space in the middle of the camp is enclosed by a linen barrier. After the Samnite leader and priests perform an ancient sacrifice, the best warriors are individually led into the enclosure. Here they are forced to swear an oath cursing themselves and their families if they should either flee from battle or refrain from killing anyone whom they see fleeing. Those who refuse to swear are killed immediately, providing a further incentive for the next subject to take the oath. After this process, a legion made conspicuous by special insignia is constituted from the survivors.

The central passage is the description of the oath taking:

When the sacrifice was completed, the *imperator* ordered that all those most renowned for their deeds and ancestry be summoned by a herald; they were led in one by one. Beyond the other trappings of sacrifice, which might throw the spirit into confusion with superstition, there were also altars in an area covered all around and victims slaughtered thereabout and centurions

> surrounding with drawn swords. Each is brought to the altar more as a victim than a participant in the sacrifice and is compelled by oath not to reveal what he has seen and heard there. They force him to swear with a grim incantation calling down destruction on his head and family and clan if he does not go into battle where the commanders lead, and if he either flees from the battle line himself or fails to kill forthwith anyone he sees fleeing. Some of the first who had refused to swear were butchered around the altars, and, lying amid the carnage of the victims, they served as warning to the others not to refuse.[100]

Even more explicitly than in the earlier episode, Livy portrays this ritual as an initiatory act designed to generate communal bonds; the process of viewing the sacrifice leads directly to the formation of a new group. But here all of the principles and procedures that give sacrifice its efficacy are reversed and overturned. The Fetial sacrifice required that the participant be able to imagine the victim's death as the punishment of a prospective treaty breaker. But that possibility was juxtaposed with an identification with the sacrificer himself who spoke and acted for all the participants. Here that balance is thrown off as the individual's ability to imagine himself as victim outweighs his sense of being a participant. He is threatened with his own death at the altar if he fails to swear the oath. The mitigating substitution of an animal victim for a human is also eliminated, and the mingling of animal and human corpses around the altar forms the final shocking element of Livy's description.[101] For Girard, the failure to maintain sacrificial distinctions between victim and participant led to the disintegration of the community into mutual violence. And indeed the legion constituted by the survivors of the initiation breaks

100. 10.38.7–11: *Sacrificio perfecto per viatorem imperator acciri iubebat nobilissimum quemque genere factisque; singuli introducebantur. Erat cum alius apparatus sacri qui perfundere religione animum posset, tum in loco circa omni contecto arae in medio victimaeque circa caesae et circumstantes centuriones strictis gladiis. Admovebatur altaribus magis ut victima quam ut sacri particeps adigebaturque iure iurando quae visa auditaque in eo loco essent non enuntiaturum. Iurare cogebant diro quodam carmine, in execrationem capitis familiaeque et stirpis composito, nisi isset in proelium quo imperatores duxissent et si aut ipse ex acie fugisset aut quem fugientem vidisset non extemplo occidisset. Id primo quidam abnuentes iuraturos se obtruncati circa altaria sunt; iacentes deinde inter stragem victimarum documento ceteris fuere ne abnuerent.*

101. The juxtaposition of animal and human blood also has a prominent place in other Roman descriptions of perverted sacrificial ritual (cf. esp. Vergil's description of the death of Priam and his son at an altar [*Aen.* 2.512 f.]). Sallust charges the Catilinarian conspirators with the same transgression in the confirmation of their oath by depicting them drinking wine mixed with human blood (*Cat.* 22.1–2). In Dio's account (37.30.3), a boy is actually brought in, sacrificed, and subsequently eaten by the conspirators.

apart out of mutual suspicion as each member "has before his eyes . . . the mixed slaughter of men and beasts and the altars splattered with blood pure and impure."[102]

But the most powerful expression of the reversal of proper sacrificial practice comes through Livy's emphasis on perspective and visual contact. From the beginning, the sight of the scene does not augment the *animus* of the viewer, as did the victory of Horatius, but throws it into confusion (*perfundere* [10.38.8]). The spectator, as he is led to the altar, is literally put in the place of the victim. And Livy's own description, which follows the initiate's gaze, recreates this perspective, focusing on the moment when the transition from participant to victim takes place. Thus the single sentence that describes the scene within the tent ends with the centurions "standing on both sides with drawn swords." The position of the centurions and the part they play in the proceedings is initially ambiguous. They could be sacrificers whose swords are drawn against the victim; they could also be other oath takers, since, as we shall see, the gesture of holding out a drawn sword sometimes accompanies the swearing of an oath.[103] But the participle *circumstantes,* "standing on both sides" or "surrounding," has no expressed object; thus the final possibility, which will in fact be born out, is that the centurions surround not just the altar but the initiate himself, and their swords are drawn against him.

The shift from participant to victim is also correlated with the initiate's progress toward the center of the linen enclosure that encompasses the altar. In the other accounts of spectacles that have been discussed, all of the spectators looked on together, and indeed this common gaze, particularly for the armies watching the duel of the Horatii, formed the basis of the new community. But here the individual, far from sharing the experience with his fellows, is shut off from them both by the linen barrier and by the pledge of secrecy. This physical separateness embodies the increasing social isolation that comes with the initiate's sense of being the object of collective violence. In a *lustratio,* the victims are led around the boundaries of the community, inscribing its members within a magic circle. But in this case, it is the victims who are at the center, and the initiate's motion inward traces the contraction of the group to which he belongs. The oath he swears, which is itself an instrument of further

102. 10.41.3: *quippe in oculis erat . . . promiscua hominum pecudumque strages et respersae fando nefandoque sanguine arae.*

103. Torelli 1982: 10.

isolation, calls down destruction upon his head, his family, and his clan if he breaks it, thus demarcating the smaller groups from the state on whose behalf the oath is taken, just as it makes the swearer both the agent and the victim of internally directed violence.

A set of coins minted by the Italian rebels during the Social War depicts a scene almost identical to the sight that confronts the initiate in Livy's account of the Samnite oath.[104] Four men with drawn swords stand on either side of a sacrificial victim. Since the center of the rebellion lay among the Oscan speakers of the Apennines, it is quite plausible that the procedure shown on the coin is in fact analogous to that in book 10. But the significance of the image is radically different in the two representations. The Italian coins are undoubtedly emblems of unity, designed to reinforce solidarity among the peoples allied against Rome. The gesture of the drawn swords marks the soldiers as oath takers in a manner that relates their bond explicitly to sacrificial practice. The swords all point at the victim, making the soldiers all participate symbolically in the act of killing. This shared killing recapitulates the overall function of the oath itself, to forge the participants into a unified force capable of acting effectively against an outsider. The same intent also lay behind the Samnite ritual, but there the result was precisely the opposite, fragmentation and defeat.

The similarity of the two scenes also allows us to pinpoint the role of visual perspective in determining which of these radically different outcomes the experience of sacrifice will yield. In Livy, as we have seen, the tableau of the armed centurions around the victim is initially ambiguous, combining the possibilities of danger and comradeship. The crucial moment comes when the individual initiate is brought to the altar, for in this case the oath is taken not collectively but individually, and the oath taker affirms his pledge from the position of the sacrificial victim—literally, at the point of the swords. The viewer of the coin can experience no such transformation in perspective; anchored on the perimeter, he watches events from the position of the members of the groups who are bound by the oath.

Such collective oaths were not unknown in Rome itself. Livy tells us that prior to 216 B.C.E., troops from Rome's allies bound themselves by

104. Sydenham 1952, nos. 619–21a, 626, 629, 634, 637, 640, 640a. The interpretation of these scenes as depictions of *coniurationes* confirmed through sacrifice was put forward by Bleicken 1963. The links between the scene depicted on the coins and Livy's narrative of the Samnite oath are stressed by Instinsky 1964: 86–87.

a "voluntary treaty" (22.38.1–5). (The term for treaty is *foedus,* which was also used for the international treaty confirmed by sacrifice between the Romans and Albans.)[105] Not only does the voluntary nature of this *foedus* contrast with the compulsion used by the Samnites, but the actual words of the oath, which Livy also records, differ from the content of the Samnite oath in a manner that corresponds to the inversion of the oath taker's perspective. The Samnite oath both invokes destruction on the family and person of anyone who reveals it and obliges each soldier to kill his fellows if he sees them deserting. The result, as we have seen, is that each soldier imagines his comrades as his prospective killers, and at the crucial moment this internal fear proves stronger than fear of the enemy.[106] It is the last clause that the *coniuratio* oath reverses by compelling the soldiers "not to depart for the sake of flight or fear nor to retreat from the ranks except to take or seek a weapon or to strike an enemy or to save a citizen."[107] Here not only is each soldier made his fellow's savior, but the preservation of the life of the individual is given a higher priority even than the unity of the group.

These contrasting treatments of the oath-taking ceremony demonstrate how a single, simple image can contain a vast potential for either building a society or destroying it. In sacrifice, the violence that unites the group always threatens to break free of the restraints of ritual. The closer the rite approximates disaster, the more powerful is its effect. Moreover, the essential ambiguity of sacrificial ritual relates to two interdependent issues of the utmost importance in Augustan Rome; violence and the integration of the community. The fifty years of civil war that produced the Augustan state could be looked upon as a terrible but finite process whose end was *Tota Italia,* a new unity whose collective might would manifest itself in the conquest of foreign peoples, or else as

105. Crawford 1974: 715, n. 5, states, against Bleicken 1963: 66–67, that "neither evidence nor probability supports the view that the *voluntarium foedus* of Livy xxii, 38, 1–5 involved the sacrifice of a pig." But ancient etymologies that connect the noun *foedus* with the adjective meaning disgusting or hideous, on the grounds that the sacrificial pig died "hideously," show the extent to which the act of sacrifice was bound up with the ratification of *foedera.* (Cf., e.g., Paulus-Festus 84L: *foedus appellatum ab eo quod in paciscendo foede hostia necaretur.* See also Augustine *Dialect.* 6.10 ff. For other etymologies of *foedus,* see below, n. 131.) Moreover, other contemporary literary descriptions of treaty ceremonies, e.g., *Aen.* 8.641, also mention the sacrifice of a pig, especially the fullest account of the ritual, Livy 1.24.4–9, analyzed in the previous section. Thus I find nothing at all improbable about assuming that the word *foedus* at 22.38.5 implies that a sacrifice took place.

106. 10.41.3: *civem magis quam hostem timentes.*

107. 22.38.4: *iurabant sese fugae atque formidinis ergo non abituros neque ex ordine recessuros nisi teli sumendi aut petendi et aut hostis feriendi aut civis servandi causa.*

the ultimate disintegration of that society at every level, an unending sequence of violence that divided families and cities and demanded the renunciation of home, friends, and even children in the service of an ever-shifting *patria*.[108]

The power of sacrifice to embody both of these visions of violence has to do with the multiplicity and pervasiveness of sacrificial imagery in Augustan literature, ritual, and art. In its positive aspect, sacrifice seems to promise the possibility of controlled violence directed outward and the clear definition of friend and enemy. Thus, for example, on the day Augustus entered Rome after the defeat of Antony and Cleopatra, the entire populace offered sacrifice.[109] Extravagant sacrifices followed other foreign victories as well, reaching a climax in the consecration of the Ara Pacis in 13 B.C.E., at which the establishment of peace would be celebrated annually.[110] The suppression of internal threats, such as those of Cornelius Gallus,[111] Murena, and Caepio also prompted sacrifices.[112] Augustus himself became the center of the sacrificial spectacle in the Secular Games of 17 B.C.E. This three-day ceremony began with the *princeps* sacrificing nine ewes to the Fates on behalf of the Roman people. Thereafter every day's program commenced with Augustus and Agrippa presiding over sacrifices to Jupiter, Juno, and the children of Leto respectively.[113]

Nor did this interest in sacrifice manifest itself only in actual ritual practices. Artistic representations of Augustus in a variety of media from statues to coins increasingly depicted the emperor at the center of religious ceremonies, particularly as sacrificant.[114] As Elsner has recently demonstrated in his interpretation of the Ara Pacis, perhaps the culmi-

108. For a complementary analysis of the challenges the Romans of the 20's faced in interpreting the events of their recent past, see Zetzel 1989, esp. 283–14. Zetzel connects the tension between a backward-looking emphasis on justice and punishment and the promise of social rebirth in bk. 6 of the *Aeneid* with alternative attitudes toward the violence and disruption of the civil wars, especially as these alternatives were articulated in the Secular Games of 17 B.C.E.

109. Dio 51.20.

110. *Res gest.* 12.2.

111. Dio 53.23.7. See Raaflaub and Samons, 1990: 424.

112. Dio 54.3.6. Raaflaub and Samons 1990: 426.

113. For an account of the ritual itself and the available sources, see Fraenkel 1957: 365 ff., and the interpretation by Zetzel 1989: 276–82.

114. Cf. the comments of Zanker 1988: 127: "Certainly from the time of the Secular Games in 17 B.C. , and probably much earlier, in the 20's, the *princeps* must have made it known that henceforth he preferred that statues put up in his honor show him togate at sacrifice or prayer."

nation of this pattern of imagery, such representations, far from simply denoting the abstract *pietas* of the emperor, served to recreate and reproduce the sacrificial experience, placing the viewer in the place of participant and making the emperor the focal point of the event.[115] What is more, the diffusion of these images in Italy and the provinces provided a prototype for religious activity throughout the empire and helped create a network of cult practices grounded in the authority of Rome and of the *princeps* himself.[116]

But just as beneficial sacrifice confirmed the restoration of peace and harmony, the image of the corrupted sacrifice, where the boundaries that prevented excessive identification with the victim were violated, had an equal importance in the delineation of public enemies who threatened the social order. Catiline, for example, was accused of using human blood in the confirmation of an oath. There is a story that in 46 B.C.E., Caesar checked the excesses of his troops by having several soldiers sacrificed on the Campus Martius in the presence of the *pontifices* and the priest of Mars.[117] Presumably, as Pontifex Maximus, he presided over the sacrifice. Similarly, Sextus Pompey's close identification with Neptune was turned against him in a report that, dressed in a ceremonial blue robe, he had had men cast alive into the sea.[118]

The story of Octavian's bloodthirsty revenge on the rebels led by L. Antonius at Perusia offers the most interesting demonstration of the political potency of sacrificial imagery during the civil wars. The so-called *Arae Perusinae* are among the most shocking crimes attributed to the young triumvir: "Lucius himself and some others were pardoned, but most of the senators and knights were killed. There is a story that they did not simply suffer death but that after having been tormented, three hundred knights and many senators . . . were sacrificed on an altar

115. Elsner 1991: 52: "In looking at the altar Roman viewers did not simply see images of a sacrifice that once happened. They saw a cultural process in which they themselves became involved."

116. This is the thesis of Gordon 1990.

117. Dio 43.24.4. Clearly, the story as Dio presents it is designed to blacken the figure of Caesar, but was it based on an actual event? Weinstock 1971: 78–79, assumes that it was but argues that the killings themselves were "probably an archaic form of execution rather than a sacrifice." But whether or not Caesar emphasized the sacrificial overtones himself—and it is possible to imagine how they may have formed part of a more positive construction of these events, with Caesar as the restorer of discipline and harmony—the narrative Dio presents certainly requires its audience to imagine the scene as a sacrifice (cf. his term ἱερουργία and the unambiguous ἐτύθησαν).

118. Dio 48.48.5.

consecrated to Julius Caesar."[119] Clearly, the sacrificial setting of these executions springs from anti-Octavian propaganda,[120] and the emphasis on the rank of the victims, which also appears in Suetonius's version of the episode, reveals the audience toward which this fearsome picture was directed: senators and knights would here see themselves specifically selected as victims in an alien, and distinctly dynastic, sacrificial ritual presided over by the triumvir. However, the pro-Augustan version of the resolution of the Perusine conflict, which possibly derives from the emperor's own memoirs,[121] counters this image with another scene of sacrifice, again presided over by Octavian. While Octavian is offering sacrifice, the repentant Antonius approaches with his men:

> [The rebel troops] saluted Caesar as *imperator* and stood separately where Caesar had placed them. . . . When he had finished the sacrifice, crowned in laurel, the symbol of victory, he sat before the tribunal and ordered them to lay down their arms where they stood. He then ordered the veterans [among the rebels] to draw near, apparently to reproach them for their ingratitude and to frighten them. It was already known that he was going to do this, and Caesar's troops, either on purpose . . . or moved by their suffering, as if on behalf of their own relatives, breaking from their assigned position, ran towards Lucius's men and embraced them as fellow soldiers. And they wept and entreated Caesar on behalf [of the rebels], and they did not stop weeping and embracing, with even the new recruits sharing in the sentiment. No longer was it possible to tell the troops apart nor to distinguish them.[122]

Here sacrifice serves not to demonstrate Octavian's barbarousness and implacability but as the locus for political reunification. The terror of Octavian generated in tales of the *Arae Perusinae* by depicting him as sacrificer and the rebels as victims, appears only to be assuaged by a greater sense of community, as the rebels, first kept at a distance, find themselves integrated into the body of participants. The sight of the *imperator* sacrificing melts away all difference, as we shall see that it is meant to do between Albans and Romans.

119. Dio 48.14.4. Cf. Suet. *Aug.* 15.

120. Cf. Syme 1939: 212: "Clearly these judicial murders were magnified by defamation and credulity into a hecatomb of three hundred Roman senators and knights slaughtered in solemn and religious ceremony on the Ides of March before an altar dedicated to *Divus Julius*.

121. The question of whether the ὑπομνήματα referred to at *BCiv.* 5.45 are those of Augustus is debated (see Gabba 1970: xvii–xxiii). Appian refers explicitly to the *princeps*'s memoirs at *Ill.* 14 and *BCiv.* 4.110.

122. Appian *BCiv.* 5.46.

V. Sacrifice and *Imperium*

The emphasis on the social and political aspects of religious ritual that emerged in the preceding section will be recognizable to the student of Roman religion. Not only has the manipulation of religious practice for narrowly political ends been long studied, but on a much broader level the communal nature of so much of ancient religious practice has all but eroded the distinction between our categories of the civic and the religious.[123] Nor were the Romans themselves oblivious to the "social" importance of religion as a means of building ties within a community. For Cicero, shared *sacra* constituted one of the ties that bind an individual to his natural *patria*.[124]

Within Livy's own text, the most explicit description of the use of religious ritual to maintain the social order of the Roman state occurs just a few pages before the events that we have been describing, in the account of Numa Pompilius's religious reforms discussed in chapter 2: after peace has been obtained with all the neighboring peoples, "lest the spirits [of the Romans], which the fear of the enemy and military discipline had held in check, grow soft in peace, first of all—a thing most effective for an inexperienced and, in those ages, unsophisticated people—he thought that fear of the gods must be cast upon them."[125] The terms used here provide a link between the rituals staged under Numa's successor and the social ills that Livy himself treats. The *metus deorum* appears as an equivalent to military discipline; both the Fetial sacrifice and the subsequent execution of the Alban dictator Mettius Fufetius, like the failed Samnite ritual of book 10, take place on the battlefield and enforce a sense of collective identity, which can be measured in adherence to military discipline.[126] At the same time, the specific problems that Numa addresses, *luxuria* and the debilitating effects of *otium,* are emphatically not those of the "rude and inexperienced" Romans of regal

123. For a good introduction to the overlap between the political and religious dimensions of Roman civic life, see Beard and Crawford 1985: 25–39.

124. Cic. *Leg.* 2.3.

125. 1.19.4: *ne luxuriarent otio animi quos metus hostium disciplinaque militaris continuerat, omnium primum, rem ad multitudinem imperitam et illis saeculis rudem efficacissimam, deorum metum iniciendum ratus est.*

126. Cf. also the explicitly disciplinary function of the execution of the death of the younger Torquatus, described in ch. 3.

times but the preoccupations of the first century B.C.E. The discussion of the social utility of religious ritual thus occurs in a context where not only is the distinction between past and present deliberately blurred, but, as we saw in chapter 2, the activities of the king and the historian come to resemble one another. Indeed, the king employs religious ritual to perform precisely the same social function that he shares with the historian, to combat the effects of *luxuria*. This suggests that the reconstruction of sacrificial spectacle can be taken as one of the most important means by which the historian's text directly assumes a political, state-building function.

Beyond its reminiscences of Numa's procedure, Livy's adoption of the sacrificial paradigm for staging the unification of the Albans and the Romans also means that he is communicating in the same medium of religious ritual that Augustus himself, who also appears in the earlier passage as an imitator of Numa, used to accomplish the restoration of the state. But how far is it justifiable to think that a literary text could operate on its readers in a manner resembling the way an actual sacrifice affected its participants? Obviously Livy cannot distribute the sacrificial meats among his audience. Nor will he, like Augustus on the *Ara Pacis*, make himself the center of his audience's attention as the focal point of the sacrificial experience. But visual contact, which has emerged as both a powerful medium for linking the participant to the event and a means of negotiating the antithetical potentials of sacrifice, can be reproduced for the audience of a literary text. If this reproduction achieves less vividness than in the visual arts, not to speak of the unmediated experience of sacrifice itself, perhaps it possesses greater precision since the attentions of the writer's audience can be more strictly controlled.[127]

The overlap between the roles of king and historian suggested in Livy's account of Numa reappears at one of the crucial moments in the process of incorporating the Albans, the execution of Mettius Fufetius. In spite of his pledge to abide by the outcome of the duel and place the Albans under the *imperium* of Rome, Mettius treacherously withdraws the Alban forces in the first battle in which he is asked for assistance and only rejoins the Romans when they are clearly victorious (1.27). Tullus

127. Cf. the comments of Vasaly 1993: 130, on the differences between Cicero's rhetorical use of those scenes and monuments actually before the eyes of his audience and those he must summon up entirely through *enargeia:* "Thus what the visual milieu lost in rhetorical control it gained in direct sensual impact; and what the vividly described environment lost in immediacy it gained in the opportunity it gave the orator to introduce only those visual elements he wished."

punishes this betrayal by having the Alban leader tied to two chariots and torn apart (1.28). The scene in which this punishment takes place recapitulates many of the themes and tensions of the entire episode, from the initial deception of the Alban ambassadors to the deferred execution of Horatius, and offers an explicit, if complex, commentary on the educational functions of the historian and the civic leader.

The Albans' denial of the reality of Rome's *imperium* is bound up with their attitude to the role of the spectator; it was after all through the process of spectacle that this *imperium* was first established over them, and it will be through yet another spectacle that it is confirmed. As we have seen, throughout their dealings with the Romans, the Albans have been constantly at a disadvantage because of their assumption that the spectator is passive and detached from the event he watches and a corollary belief that spectacle itself consists simply of empty display. These conceptions determined both the negligence with which they conducted their initial embassy to the Romans (1.23.5ff.) and the proposal that the dispute with the Romans be decided by a duel. The strategy the Albans employ in betraying the Romans again highlights this attitude to spectacle. By withdrawing to watch the battle rather than actually fighting, the Alban army becomes "a spectator of the competition" (*spectator certaminis* [1.28.1])—a position analogous to the one adopted at the battle of the Horatii and Curiatii—again out of the belief that, as spectators, they will be free from danger.

As in his treatment of the original embassy that came to demand the restoration of stolen property, so too in preparing for the final spectacle of Mettius's execution, the Roman king tricks the treacherous Albans with an outward show of friendship. He addresses them in a kindly way and summons them the next morning to a "lustral sacrifice" (1.28.1). When invited to the assembly by Tullus Hostilius, the Albans are eager to attend and take up the nearest positions because they are struck by the "novelty of hearing a Roman king address an assembly" (1.28.2). But their enthusiasm for "sight-seeing" enables the Roman legion to surround them physically, a gesture that reinforces the point that the Albans are not disconnected from the events they are watching but are as much subject to Tullus's authority as the Roman troops.[128] The physical incorporation of the Albans into the body of citizens is complemented by the sudden reversal of perspective, experienced most completely by Mettius Fufetius himself, who thinks that he has come as a spectator but

128. The Roman troops by contrast are fulfilling the *imperia* of the king by the very act of surrounding the Albans, *imperia exsequerentur* (1.28.3).

finds that his punishment is in fact the spectacle that the audience has assembled to watch.

The symbolic inclusion of the Albans within the Roman state serves as a visual sign of the real purpose of the ceremony the king has orchestrated, the final unification of Rome and Alba. "May it be good and blessed and fortunate for the Roman people and me and you, Albans; I intend to lead the whole Alban people to Rome, to give citizenship to the plebeians, to induct the nobles into the Senate, to make one city, one *res publica;* as once the Alban state was divided into two now let it recombine into one."[129] The sacral resonance of the first phrase, which recalls the language used in the Fetial ritual, reminds us of the performative quality of the king's utterance and of the ceremony as a whole. Tullus's language does not just describe his intention but accomplishes it even as the Romans and Albans are literally being brought together; just as in the Fetial ritual, his statement is a manifestation of his *imperium.*

The statement that simultaneously unmasks the king's purpose and expresses his power occurs at just the moment when the true nature of the spectacle itself has been revealed by the actions of the armed centurions who have surrounded Mettius Fufetius. And the sight of his execution will be the central means by which the king effects the unification of his audience. Tullus had described the event that the Albans were to attend as a *sacrificium lustrale.*[130] Not only does this expression establish the formal parallel between the execution and sacrifice; as Versnel has shown, the lustral sacrifice was, like all *lustrationes,* used precisely to establish a new unity among the group of participants.

The lustral sacrifice is but one of the ritual acts the execution recalls. The reason Tullus gives for killing Mettius is that he violated the *foedus* made with the Romans. The treaty ritual, as we recall, had invoked destruction on whoever failed to abide by it and thus predicts and determines the fate of the Alban. The language of the king duplicates the sacred expressions he used to empower the *pater patratus,* and other terms both in the king's speech and the historian's narrative allude to the earlier ceremony. When Tullus speaks of "trustworthiness and treaties" (*fides ac foedera* [1.28.9]), beyond the alliteration there is also a reference

129. 1.28.7: *quod bonum faustum felixque sit populo Romano ac mihi vobisque, Albani, populum omnem Albanum Romam traducere in animo est, civitatem dare plebi, primores in patres legere, unam urbem, unam rem publicam facere; ut ex uno quondam in duos populos divisa Albana res est, sic nunc in unum redeat.*

130. 1.28.1; for the significance of the phrase and the ironies of its usage here, see Versnel 1975: 98 ff.

to one of the common etymologies of the word *foedus,* as a cognate to *fides.* Others thought that a *foedus* was so named because of the disgusting (*foedus*) ritual by which treaties were confirmed, and Livy makes that connection as well when he refers to the *foeditas* of Mettius's end (1.28.11).[131] In addition to the verbal echoes, the visual tableau Livy constructs by having the centurions encompass their victim recalls precisely the depictions of *foedera* on coins.

In the Fetial ritual, the violence of the sacrifice was an expression of the collective power of the state channeled through the king and his representatives. The unifying aspect of the spectacle derives from the alignment of the group of participants against the outsider or victim at whom this collective power is directed. Thus although the word *imperium* was not explicitly used in the Fetial ritual, the ceremony enacts the transmission of *imperium,* and it is precisely the *imperium* of the Roman king over the Albans that the ceremony of the execution is designed to establish. The link between *imperium* and sacrifice emerges again in Appian's account of the reconciliation of Octavian and the mutineers at Perusia. The situation is strikingly similar to the one Livy describes; again, the two armies are brought together by watching a sacrifice. Octavian has kept his veterans apart, and after the sacrifice they draw near the rebels as though to punish them; suddenly, however, they embrace one another and the end result is that "it became impossible to distinguish between them."[132] Here the participation of the mutineers in the sacrifice over which Octavian presides is explicitly linked to their acceptance of his *imperium.* As they arrive, the troops proclaim Octavian *imperator,* and after the sacrifice he addresses them crowned with the laurel of victory.[133]

The execution of Mettius Fufetius also draws attention to the connection between the ritual performance of sacrifice and the presentation of a historical *exemplum.* In addition to pointing out the connections with the Fetial ritual and the general characterization of the execution as a *sacrificium lustrale,* Tullus emphasizes the educational function of his actions and expresses his consciousness of their historical significance by expanding the audience for his instruction from those immediately present to the entire "human race," implicitly including any possible future violators. His punishment of Mettius is a "noteworthy demonstration"

131. The derivation from *fides* is attested at Serv. Auct. *Ad Aen.* 8.641, Paul. Fest. 84, et al. For the connection with the adjective *foedus,* see Paul. Fest. 84 and esp. Serv. Auct. *Ad Aen.* 1.62: *quod hostia foede necaretur.*

132. App. *BCiv.* 5.46: οὐδὲ ἦν τι διακεκριμένον ἔτι οὐδ' εὔκριτον.

133. Ibid.

(*insigne documentum* [1.28.6]). Indeed, in its crudest form, the very manner in which the Alban is killed "illustrates" his crime: the division of his body manifests the earlier division of his spirit between the Romans and their enemies. In a larger sense his dismemberment emblematizes the division of loyalties experienced by all the Albans, who, as their king is dragged *in diversum iter,* are made "one" with the Romans. Later, Tullus says that he would apply his teaching to Mettius himself if his nature (*ingenium*) were not "incurable" (*insanabile* [1.28.9]). Both the references to *documenta* and the use of the metaphor of health replicate exactly the language in which Livy speaks of his own history in the preface. There, his text is made a source of *documenta* and as such is described as "healthful" (*salubre*). Not only do these echoes draw together the activities of king and historian, they also make clear the interdependence between sacrificial performance and historical instruction. The two aspects of Mettius's death are made inseparable; his punishment (*supplicium*) is the means by which Mettius "teaches."[134]

In all of the sacrificial spectacles we have examined, the socially beneficial aspects of the experience—here epitomized by the king's interpretation of the execution as a moment of unification whose historical significance will be as a constant warning against betrayal—have been balanced by an opposing potential for social disintegration. As incipient Romans, the Albans must view Mettius as a foreign enemy and take part in his killing. So, too, in quelling a later mutiny, Scipio Africanus will require the mutineers to find the sight of their former commanders' deaths a "joyous sight" (*laetum spectaculum* [28.29.8]).[135] But like the victims at

134. 1.28.9: *tu tuo supplicio doce.*

135. This episode shares a number of elements with the description of Mettius's execution, as well as with the scene of the Samnite initiation. Again the spectators, like the Albans in bk. 1, are secretly surrounded by loyal troops, into which group they must be reincorporated, during their commander's speech (28.29.10). The imagery of health and healing, which provides the link between Tullus's description of Mettius as *insanabilis* and the historian's references to the *salubre* effect of his text, there appears even more prominently. Scipio has just recovered from an illness—both the cause and opportunity for the mutiny—and makes the contrast between his own health and the "sickness" of the mutineers the organizing *topos* of his address to them. It is the rebels who have been ill (*insanistis* [28.29.3]), but their approval of the execution of their leaders will be the sign that their health has returned (28.29.8). Finally, the execution that the mutineers witness is explicitly compared to a sacrifice: Scipio describes the mutiny itself as a portent, "which can be expiated by no victims and no supplications without the blood of those who have dared so great a crime" (28.27.16) and will later compare the execution of the rebels to "cutting his own viscera" (28.32.4), an image that at once redevelops the earlier emphasis on healing and places Scipio himself in the position of a sacrificial victim, whose viscera would be torn out and examined after the sacrifice. None of these images, it should be noted, appear in

the Fetial sacrifice, Mettius's death serves as a warning of what might happen to any other potential traitor. In particular, it is as a representative of the Alban people that Mettius is punished; he is made to bear the responsibility for their crime. Thus the construction of the spectacle equally demands the audience's identification with the victim. The emotion that enforces the Albans' obedience is nothing other than the "fear" (*metus*) that results from such an identification. It was "fear of the gods" (*metus deorum*) that Numa had foreseen as the constraining power of *religio,* yet here, as in the response of the Samnites at Aquilonia, fear is directed against more immediate representatives of the state. Moreover, this emotion has a truly unifying effect in the sense that it is "common" to all and obliterates any individual variations in perspective or response.[136]

The double vision required of the Albans is made particularly acute because an execution dispenses with the prescriptions that an actual sacrifice employs to control violence and to diffuse its most threatening aspects. In the Fetial sacrifice, the audience was asked to identify only with the death of a pig, which, however dramatic, has far less immediacy than the death of another human being, much less one's former *imperator.* The relation between sacrifice and execution here precisely reverses the resolution achieved in the trial of Horatius.[137] There, the establishment of a sacrificial ritual arose as an alternative to the death of a Horatius and as a means of controlling tensions that had led to murder. Here, the sacrifice of the pig is reenacted with a human victim. And just as the violence is no longer directed against an animal substitute, so too the role of surrogates in performing the killing is equally diminished. In the Fetial sacrifice, the victim was killed by a *pater patratus* appointed by the king, and the trial of Horatius was similarly conducted by surrogates, appointed precisely to protect the king from direct responsibility for the death of a man with whom the crowd sympathized. In the case of

---

the speech Polybius composes for Scipio on this occasion (11.28–9). For the Augustan resonances of this episode, see Syme 1945: 107–8.

136. 1.28.8: *Albana pubes . . . in variis voluntatibus communi tamen metu cogente, silentium tenet.* The silence that the Albans preserve as a result of their fear may be compared with the ritual silence required during sacrifice.

137. Verbal echoes emphasize the connection between the two scenes and encourage comparison. When the elder Horatius says of the prospective death of his son that "the eyes of the Albans could scarcely endure such a hideous spectacle" (1.26.10), the statement foreshadows the *spectaculum* that the Albans will have to endure. Cf. also the phrase *a tanta foeditate supplicii vindicent* (1.26.11) with *avertere omnes ab tanta foeditate spectaculi oculos* (1.28.11).

Mettius Fufetius, although Tullus does not drive the chariots himself, his role as the one who precipitates the execution is more immediately apparent.[138]

In Livy's account of the execution, these irreconcilable tensions ultimately produce a divergence between the king and the historian as presenters of spectacle. Just at the moment when the chariots have been set into motion,[139] Livy ceases simply narrating the execution and intervenes in his own voice. "All turned their eyes away from such a terrible spectacle. That was the first and last punishment among the Romans of a model [*exemplum*] too little mindful of human laws; in other cases, the Romans can glory in the fact that no other race has decreed milder penalties" (1.28.11). The very statement that the onlookers turn their eyes away, as it breaks the contact between the spectator and the punishment, also releases Livy's own audience from the necessity of "seeing" the culmination of the execution. At this point, Livy himself reverts to the language of the preface, and by doing so emerges as a rival to the king in offering educational spectacles. Not only does he use the term *exemplum*,

138. Indeed, Tullus's own death, which Livy describes just four chapters after the death of Mettius Fufetius, will result from an error in the performance of a religious ritual (*prava religione* [1.31.8]). Moreover, this error derives from Tullus's misinterpretation of a historical text, the *commentarii* of Numa. For another example of kings connected with ritual impurity, see the discussion of the fall of the monarchy in ch. 5, sec. IV.

139. The previous sentence ends with the present participle *portantes* (1.28.10) emphasizing that the action of rending Mettius's body is in progress. It is precisely the image that Livy refuses to have the Albans see that Vergil places on the shield of Aeneas:

haud procul inde citae Mettium in diversa quadrigae
distulerant (at tu dictis, Albane, maneres!)
raptabatque viri mendacis viscera Tullus
per silvam, et sparsi rorabant sanguine vepres.

[*Aen.* 8.642–45]

The words *citae,* recalling Livy's *concitati; in diversa,* for Livy's *in diversum iter;* and *quadrigae,* all in the first line of the description, establish the allusion to the Livy passage. (Moreover, the line before the description of the execution of Mettius begins speaks of "treaties [between Romulus and Titus Tatius] ratified by a slaughtered pig" (8.641), another possible reference to Livy, who, as we have seen, describes the Fetial ritual in detail, but in the context of the Alban treaty.) The pluperfect verb *distulerant* in line 643, while its tense is perfectly appropriate to the ecphrastic context in which it occurs, here also emphasizes that Vergil's narrative begins where Livy's leaves off: the Livian description alluded to in the previous line provides only the preliminary narrative for the scene presented on the shield. For the larger relationship between the shield and Livy's narrative of early Rome, see Woodman 1989, with further bibliography. Ennius (fr. 124 Skutsch), whose account also influenced Vergil's treatment, seems to have had Mettius Fufetius simply dragged by a chariot, rather than torn apart by chariots heading in opposite directions (see Skutsch 1985: 276 f.).

but he shows an awareness of the entire scope of Roman history as well, by setting the execution within the much wider context of all other punishments. Like every other "sacrificial" event that forms a part of this episode, the execution generates two antithetical responses. In the case of Horatius's trial, these responses were articulated as two alternative visual perspectives, one of which focused on Horatius's *decora,* the other on that which was *foedum* or *atrox.*[140] Livy's interruption of the spectacle of the execution introduces a comparable antithesis here. The historian takes control of the perspective of his audience, redirecting its gaze from the *foeditas* of Mettius's death to a "glorious"[141] vision of Rome's past, one where the conflict between the demands of national identity and of "human laws" disappears.

• • •

Throughout the many scenes constituting the complex narrative of the union of Rome and Alba, Livy stresses the parallelism between the rituals and spectacles that accomplish the transition in the civic identity of the Albans and his own literary representation of events. The ambiguous position of the Albans themselves as members of the Roman state and as outsiders both mirrors the divergent possibilities of alienation and solidarity faced by any participant in the rituals by which citizenship and group membership were confirmed and speaks to the crises in civic identity brought about by the transformations of Livy's own era. When Tullus Hostilius claims that, by bringing together Alba and Rome, he is in fact reunifying what had been in the past one city, the Albans find not only their state absorbed by Rome but their history as well. Rome's past now encompasses Alba's, just as Rome's centurions surround her soldiers. This suggests a final point of resemblance between the experience of the Albans and Livy's audience. The Albans attempt to watch the events staged for them by Tullus Hostilius with detachment and separation, but they constantly discover that they are profoundly affected by them, and it is this that prompts their becoming members of the Roman state. In the same way, Livy holds out the promise of detachment to his own audience as they read these episodes. Speaking against those who

140. These pairs are manipulated in various ways by the different characters. It is the elder Horatius's request that his son's *decora* free him from the *foeditas* of punishment (1.26.11).

141. 1.28.11: *gloriari.*

may feel little appetite for the events of the distant past, he claims that he personally "shall seek this reward for my labor, that I may avert my [eyes] from the sight of those evils that our age has seen through so many years" (*praef.* 5). The past seems to offer an alternative object of vision, which enables the historian to turn his eyes away from the present just as the Albans turn their eyes away from the execution of Mettius Fufetius. But, as we have seen, Livy uses the account even of the earliest times as a means not just of describing but of remedying the *mala* of the present. And Livy's audience will find that they are no more detached from the historical *monumenta* that Livy presents than the Albans are from the spectacles of Tullus Hostilius. In adopting Rome's past as their own, they will experience the same transition implied by the historian's own choice of Aeneas over Antenor at the inception of his narrative.

CHAPTER 5

The Alternative of Drama

The preceding three chapters have attempted to show that Livy's interest in visual contact and the vivid reproduction of the visual impressions experienced by spectators within his narrative provides a means by which his text can transfer the state-building and socializing effects of Roman public spectacles to its own audience. In chapter 2, in particular, I argued that Livy deploys traditional definitions of history as a literary genre to signal how his own text goes beyond them to participate simultaneously in the system of communication through which Rome's political leaders manifested their authority to the citizen body. Now I want to reverse the perspective and examine not how Livy uses the political capacity of his history to define his place among other historians but rather how Livy's status as a historian differentiates the "spectacles" his own text offers from other, less beneficial, forms of visual display. This issue relates to larger questions about the efficacy of visual communication within the cultural environment of Augustan Rome, where, according to the analysis of Paul Zanker, a superabundance of contradictory signs necessitated the reconstruction of a coherent and legible visual landscape, and where it was especially the historical associations of monuments, the link they offered to the Roman past, that gave them significance and meaning. This chapter focuses on the relationship between Livy's history and drama, another literary genre whose aim is to produce spectacle, not through vivid description but through direct mimesis of actions, and that has often been regarded as the source of many of the historian's narrative tendencies. I argue that far from claiming the drama as a model for the way he presents Roman history, Livy consistently depicts the theater as antithetical to his narrative in its aims and effects. While based on a traditional opposition between history and drama as literary genres, this attitude to drama takes on a particular significance in light of the ambiguous place that theatrical performances occupied in the political and religious life of the Roman state. Livy exploits Roman cultural constructions of the drama as a socially pernicious and fundamentally alien form of spectacle to highlight by contrast the salutary potential of his own history and its direct link to the centers of Roman power.

Many features of Livy's presentation have been described as dramatic and seen as legacies of those Hellenistic historians who, it is argued, attempted to appropriate the effects of tragedy for their historical narratives.[1] Two qualities of Livy's narrative in particular have been connected with the historian's desire to approximate the effects of drama. The first, as we have seen, is the emphasis on *enargeia* itself, the clarity of description that enables the historian's audience to "see" the narrated action. Second, Livy tends to build his material into discrete episodes that not only possess the "beginnings," "middles," and "ends" Aristotle demanded of a dramatic plot,[2] but also unfold in a series of "scenes," each taking place in a specific and readily imaginable setting.[3] Indeed, scholars have attempted to recover the existence of otherwise lost Roman historical dramas based solely on the arrangement of Livy's narrative.[4]

While such devices may well ultimately derive from tragic practice, Livy's adoption of them by no means implies that he wished his own work to be perceived as an attempt to present Roman history as a dramatic spectacle.[5] Every analysis of the influence of such historians as Duris and Phylarchus on Livy has rightly been accompanied by impor-

1. See the discussion in ch. 1, sec. I, with bibliography (esp. Burck 1964b: 176–233). A recent analysis of the means by which Livy "dramatizes" episodes of the second pentad is offered by Pauw, who also surveys earlier treatments of dramatic elements in Livy's narrative (Pauw 1991: 33–34).

2. For Aristotle's definition of these principles, see *Poet.* 7.1–7 and 8.1–4. For Livy's application of them, see esp. Burck 1964b: 174–95; Walsh 1961a: 178–79; and Ogilvie 1965: 18–19, on Livian episodes as "historical dramas."

3. For examples of this kind of analysis, see the treatment of the rape of Lucretia in Pauw 1991 and Ogilvie 1965: 219.

4. See Corsaro 1983: 112, nn. 21–22, for examples of such reconstructions; and see also Zehnacker 1981: 34.

5. For the opposite view, see Cizek 1992: 357: "Tout particulièrement, Tite-Live rapproche l'historiographie de la tragédie et donc lui assigne des vertus purificatrices et cathartiques."

tant qualifications. Erich Burck's account of Livian *enargeia* makes clear how comparatively restrained Livy's descriptions are. Yes, Livy always makes his audience aware of an action's setting, but these settings are rarely painted with the kind of particularizing detail found in other historians.[6] The death of Lucretia, for example, takes place within a private house, and indeed in her *cubiculum* (1.58.6), but that is all Livy tells us.[7] The result is that the scenes Livy describes mostly take place in a narrow range of highly regularized settings, private house (*domus*), battlefield, senate house (*curia*), forum, assembly space (*comitium*). Together, these typical settings come to define a simplified symbolic geography within which the entire course of Roman history can be mapped. Every senatorial debate or political assembly thus recalls all its predecessors and facilitates the comparisons through time that make each individual event but one facet of a larger tradition. Also, since the settings Livy chooses were still very much a part of the civic life of contemporary Romans, they constantly reiterate the continuities between the past described in his *History* and the lived experience of its readers.

More fundamentally, any borrowing of "dramatic" techniques on Livy's part must be balanced against the historian's direct insistence on the difference between history and drama. We saw in chapter 2 the complex use Livy makes of the conventional distinction between poet and historian at once to signal his awareness of the strictures imposed by the historiographic tradition and to exempt himself from them. A similar ambiguity, with reference specifically to the drama, emerges in a disclaimer Livy makes to justify his inclusion of an improbable episode said to have occurred during the fall of Veii: "In matters of such antiquity, I am content that some events like the truth are accepted as true; it is not worthwhile to affirm or refute these things, which are more fit for the ostentation of the stage, which delights in marvels, than for credibility."[8]

6. Burck 1964b: 197.

7. Contrast the much fuller treatment by Dionysius of Halicarnassus (4.66.1 ff.), who lengthens the episode by having Lucretia travel by carriage to her father's house, where he situates her suicide, and elaborating on both her grief and the astonishment of the bystanders. From Dionysius one can even learn what color garments Lucretia was wearing when she stabbed herself (black, of course).

8. 5.21.9: *Sed in rebus tam antiquis si quae similia veri sint pro veris accipiantur, satis habeam: haec ad ostentationem scenae gaudentis miraculis aptiora quam ad fidem neque adfirmare neque refellere est operae pretium.* The language takes us back to the contrast between history and *fabulae* in the preface itself (*praef.* 6 f.; see ch. 2, sec. II). For the argument that this allusion constitutes a ring, bounding Livy's account of the city's foundation and so preparing for its second foundation at the end of the pentad, see Kraus 1994b: 283–84.

Thus even when Livy incorporates material that he himself defines as appropriate to the stage, he still insists on the generic distinction between history and drama.

The tension detectable in Livy's remark itself possesses a long heritage in Greek theories of historiography. As F. W. Walbank has suggested, Aristotle's famous distinction between history and poetry, especially dramatic poetry, was necessary precisely because the genres were intrinsically so comparable.[9] The boundary between the mythical material that generally provided the subject of tragedy and historical events was never a precise one,[10] and the prominence of "tragic" reversals in Herodotus and Thucydides has prompted comparisons between the techniques of the two historians and the practices of the contemporary stage.[11] So, too, in the Hellenistic period, attempts to differentiate tragedy and history coexist with and result from many historians' systematic use of the compositional methods of tragedy to increase the impact of their own histories.[12] Thus the most extensive contrast between the two genres was articulated in the highly polemical context of Polybius's attack on Phylarchus: tragedy aims at the immediate distraction and pleasure of spectators; therefore verisimilitude, the ability to seem real, is its most important quality. History by contrast aims to instruct "lovers of knowledge" and profit them for all time. This can only be accomplished by presenting the truth.[13] Again, the necessity for Polybius to assert a fundamental difference between two genres testifies to the effectiveness of Phylarchus's "tragic" presentation of events.

Yet in Livy's case, the opposition between history and drama must also be read as part of a larger antithesis operative throughout the work between effective and ineffective visual signs. The stage "rejoicing in ostentation" bears a relationship to historical representation similar to that between the imported statues castigated by the elder Cato and the terra-

9. Arist. *Poet.* 9.2–3. See Walbank 1960, esp. 217 ff. and 233 f., and id. 1972: 34–38.

10. Walbank 1960: 221 ff.

11. For Herodotus, see, e.g., Fornara 1983: 171–72; for Thucydides, the classic treatment is Cornford 1907.

12. For an attempt to reconstruct a theory behind the origins of "tragic history," see Fornara 1983: 124 ff., who argues that Duris of Samos developed a new conception of the aims of history, one that strove to define the distinctive pleasure produced by the historical text based on the terms employed in Aristotle's analysis of tragedy. However, Walbank's critique of earlier efforts to recover precise theoretical bases for "tragic history" applies also to Fornara's argument (Walbank 1960: 233).

13. Pol. 2.56.10–13. Walbank 1972: 34–38, discusses the influence of both Aristotle and Thucydides on this passage.

cotta images of the Roman gods, where again the superficial attractiveness of a foreign tradition stands in contrast to a system of signs whose power derives not from their appearance per se but from their place within the larger authority structures of the Roman state. The dramatic elements I have described may, as is commonly suggested, have made Livy's *History* more enjoyable,[14] but they also raise the danger that his text will become simply an attractive imitation of the Roman past, rather than providing the reader with direct access to it. In scenes like the account of the battle of Aquilonia or the duel between Torquatus and the Gaul, the military victory of the Romans results from and demonstrates their ability to use spectacle as a unifying and empowering force, in contrast to the distracting spectacles produced by their foreign challengers. Here, too, the visual displays of Rome's defeated opponents are described in terms that, as we shall see, recall Livy's attitude to drama. The resulting role of drama, as a foil to the tradition of representation in which Livy's history partakes, in turn recalls the place of the theater within the structure of actual Roman political and religious institutions, which we shall now consider.

I. The Stage and the State

The idea that Roman drama should be perceived as anything other than a public, officially sanctioned spectacle may seem surprising. Of all modes of literary production, drama is intrinsically among the most closely connected to the public life of the state as a whole. Not only did dramatic productions take place within the context of official civic festivals, but in the Late Republic the theater offered the people a crucial opportunity for voicing their political sentiments, and politicians in turn used the production of plays to win popular support. Thus M. Junius Brutus attempted to have the *Brutus* of Accius, a historical drama celebrating the deeds of the regicide, produced at the Apollonian Games in 44 B.C.E., four months after his assassination of Caesar.[15]

14. Cf., e.g., Pauw 1991: 45.

15. On the Apollonian Games in 44 B.C.E., see Cic. *Att.*, 15.12.1, 16.5.1; Cic. *Phil.* 1.36; Appian *BCiv.* 3.23 f.; and Nicolet 1980: 371–72. For more examples and a full account of the political manipulation of dramatic performances, see Nicolet 1980: 361–73, and Frézouls 1981: 193–214.

However, despite the secure location of dramatic performances among the public events of the Roman state, the theater could also be defined as an institution deliberately isolated from the normal conduct of civic life.[16] Although the games were part of an official calendar, they were nevertheless days on which normal public business was suspended. They may thus be considered as publicly controlled lapses in public participation, rather like the conception of *otium*, "time off," which also has a recognized place in the rhythm of public life. So, too, the actors who performed in dramas were rigorously and emphatically excluded from membership in the *res publica*.[17] Yet at the same time that they provide an opportunity for the suspension and inversion of traditional norms, such phenomena create a heightened awareness of the overarching structure of public authority that regulates the transgression of its own rules.[18]

The clearest example of how the theater increasingly became a locus for the manipulation of public opinion during the Late Republic was the frequent translation of the action and dialogue of the stage into a commentary on political affairs. Cicero records many occasions where a particularly pregnant line sparked a demonstration, and himself reaped the benefit of such a display when an actor, "who always took the best parts both in the Republic and on the stage," converted his performance into a plea for Cicero's recall.[19] Such a phenomenon indeed suggests that the segregation between the stage and the *res publica*, if it ever existed, was breaking down, and that the stage was becoming, as Cicero elsewhere suggests, a vital arena for the expression of political views. But this development is by no means incompatible with a theoretical segregation of the stage from the state as a political entity. On the contrary, the politicization of theatrical performances, and the volatility and license of their audiences, through which the stage mounted an increasingly potent challenge to official institutions, made it all the more important to insist on such a separation.[20]

16. The most suggestive treatment of the Roman theater as an alternative institution where the patterns of civic authority are inverted is that of Dupont 1985: 43–68; see also Dupont 1988: 9–25.

17. For a catalogue and analysis of Roman anxieties about the theater, and the resulting exclusion of actors from the citizen body, see esp. Edwards 1993: 98–136.

18. For a similar view of the place of Athenian theater in the structure of civic ritual, see Goldhill 1990.

19. Cic. *Pro Sest.* 120; see Frézouls 1981: 202–3.

20. Indeed, the potential for such politicization may have resulted from the very status of the theater as a space apart; cf. the comment of Nicolet 1980: 364, who describes the political role of theatrical spectacles in a chapter devoted to "alternative institutions": "The theatre was a kind of testing-ground, alongside the *comitia*, where citizens could say what

Thus at virtually the same time that he was praising the artiste who had delivered him from exile, Cicero was also composing, in book 4 of the *De re publica,* a diagnosis of the dangers of just this kind of interpenetration between politics and the theater.[21] Scipio, his interlocutor, praises an ancient Roman law that imposes the most extreme disjunction between the two realms: "Because the entire craft of the theater and the whole stage was held in such disrepute, they decreed that that whole type of men [i.e., actors] not only lack the honor of the rest of the citizens but should even be removed from their tribe [i.e., made non-citizens] by the censor's mark."[22] The complete isolation of all those connected with theatrical performances from the state is accomplished by the political authority of the censors. Scipio also beats back the attempts of drama to intervene directly in political life through openly criticizing public figures again by presenting it as a rival to the legitimate political authority of Rome's magistrates. Even though Greek comedy often attacked men who were truly wicked (*populares homines improbos*), nevertheless it is the place of the censor to condemn them, not the poets.[23] Similarly, it was inappropriate for Pericles, whose political status is described in terms with a very Roman ring,[24] to be attacked on the stage. The Romans met the two-pronged threat of the theater—its propensity both to link itself directly to political institutions, and, in criticizing public figures, to usurp the authority of the magistrates—by forbidding any living man to be praised or blamed on the stage. "For we ought to consider our life liable to the judgments of magistrates, and to legal challenge, and we should not hear abuse except when it is sanctioned that it be possible to respond and to defend one's self in a court of law."[25]

---

they thought without too much risk, and public men could assess their own popularity rating." See also Edwards 1993: 115–16.

21. It must be recognized that these fragments are preserved in the virulently antitheatrical context of Augustine's *City of God,* and that the discussion in Cicero was probably much more balanced. *Rep.* 4.13, for example, describes Greek actors who went on to play an important part in public life as orators and may have been part of a rebuttal of Scipio's sentiments. But, however the issue was resolved, the case against the theater made by Scipio still testifies both to the existence of an anxiety about the role of the theater and the terms in which that anxiety was articulated.

22. Cic. *Rep.* 4.10.

23. Ibid. 4.11. Even though Greek comedy is being discussed, the Roman direction of the speech shows itself in the reference to censors. Notice, too, that the magistrates whose particular authority the stage threatens to usurp are precisely the ones responsible for removing theatrical performers from the citizen body.

24. Ibid.: *cum iam suae civitati maxima auctoritate plurimos annos domi et belli praefuisset.*

25. Ibid. 4.12.

It may be argued against this picture of a theoretical segregation between the stage and the political life of the state that there existed a whole genre of Roman drama, the *fabula praetexta,* devoted specifically to representing episodes from Roman history and even current public events.[26] Nor was the *praetexta* an entirely obsolete form in the Late Republic. We have seen that the tyrannicide Brutus attempted to revive Accius's *Brutus* in 44 B.C.E. And we know of a new *praetexta,* performed only in Spain but available in Rome as a text, by L. Cornelius Balbus to celebrate his own exploits.[27] However, even during the golden age of Roman tragedy in the Middle Republic, *praetextae* were significantly less numerous than tragedies composed on Greek subjects. According to Hubert Zehnacker's count, in the case of the four great tragedians Naevius, Ennius, Pacuvius, and Accius, the titles of only seven *praetextae* survive, compared to eighty-three from other tragedies.[28] What is more, these performances seem usually to have had the clear purpose of glorifying the deeds of the poet's noble patron and his ancestors.[29] Thus the *fabula praetexta* may best be regarded as a not entirely successful experiment in the iconography of power whose use in the service of private ambitions symptomatizes precisely the overt politicization of the drama that was at the root of Cicero's concerns about the theater.[30] Indeed, the two Late Republican performances of *praetextae* that I have mentioned had obvious propaganda value. Accius's *Brutus* would have cast the most favorable possible light on the assassination of Caesar, and Balbus's production is portrayed in extremely negative terms by Asinius Pollio, as a form of self-glorification that surpassed the efforts of Caesar himself.[31]

As Scipio in the *De re publica* stresses the dichotomy between the theater and Rome's political institutions, so Varro in his *Antiquitates rerum divinarum* differentiates the theater from the state in terms of its por-

26. The most complete recent treatments of the *fabula praetexta* are those of Zehnacker 1981 and Flower 1995. Wiseman 1994 argues that *praetextae* were in fact at one time a flourishing genre providing an important and seminal context for historical representation and are thus intimately connected to the development of written history at Rome; see, however, the comments of Flower 1995: 173–75.

27. Cic. *Ad fam.* 10.32.3–5.

28. Zehnacker 1981: 32.

29. So Zehnacker 1981: 41 ff., and Flower 1995, esp. 170 and 190, whose arguments apply primarily to plays on contemporary subjects. As Zehnacker points out, there are only three *praetextae* of which we have any knowledge, Naevius's *Romulus,* Ennius's *Sabinae,* and Accius's *Decius,* where a plausible connection between the play's subject matter and the political context in which it was produced cannot be traced.

30. Cf. the similar conclusions of Flower 1995: 189–90.

31. Cic. *Ad fam.* 10.32.3.

trayal of the gods. Varro distinguishes three forms of theology, which he calls the *mythikon,* the *physikon,* and the *civile,*[32] associated with the poets, the philosophers, and the leaders of cities, respectively. These categories are by no means Varro's own innovation; they reflect a well-established Greek division of the subject.[33] What is most significant for us is that each of the three theologies was given a specific spatial sphere of operation. "The first theology [sc. the "mythical"] is most suited to the theater, the second [the "natural"] to the natural world, and the third [the "civil" or "political"] to the city."[34] Thus here too the theater appears as a realm separate and distinct from the civic space of the city as a whole.

Varro brings up the threefold division of theology in the first book of his treatise as a way of defining his own subject, which will be the civil religion,[35] but his discussion of the *genus mythikon* possesses a moral charge of a piece with negative portrayals of the theater. In particular, his treatise suggests a link between the fears about the dangerous potential of images expressed by Livy's Cato and the ideal of the political segregation of the theater that emerges in the *De re publica.* While Varro recognizes that the theology of the state necessarily borrows elements from both of the other categories, he asserts that it should borrow more from the philosophers than the poets.[36] One crucial distinction that Varro draws between the poet's treatment of the gods and the state religion involves the use of representation. Roman religion was originally aniconic and Varro expresses the wish that it had remained so.[37] The introduction of

32. Varro *Ant. rer. div.*, frs. 6–11, in Cardauns 1976.

33. For a complete discussion of Varro's antecedents, see Cardauns 1960: 33–40, 53–8; 1976: 139–45; and 1978: 80–103. Rawson 1985: 312–16, provides an overview of the *Antiquitates rerum divinarum.* In one of Varro's dialogues, the *Curio de cultu deorum,* the threefold division of theology is placed in the mouth of the Pontifex Scaevola; see Cardauns 1960: 33 ff., for the argument that Scaevola is simply Varro's interlocutor here.

34. Varro, *Ant. rer. div.*, fr. 10 Cardauns: *Prima . . . theologia* [*sc., mythike*] *maxime accomodata est ad theatrum, secunda* [*sc., physike*] *ad mundum, tertia* [*sc., civilis*] *ad urbem.*

35. For this category, he significantly uses a Roman name, although there was a traditional Greek equivalent, *politike.* See Cardauns, 1976: 140–41.

36. Varro fr. 11 Cardauns: *maior societas debet esse nobis cum philosophis quam cum poetis.* Varro's tone here is more prescriptive than descriptive. In general, the contribution of the poetic theology according to Varro's ruthlessly symmetrical formulation has been to make the state religion more comprehensible and acceptable to the people but less true, whereas the theology of the philosopher contains "more than it is useful for the people to examine." Thus it is *utile* for the people to believe that heroes are born from the gods (fr. 20 Cardauns).

37. Varro fr. 18 Cardauns: *antiquos Romanos plus annos centum et septuaginta deos sine simulacro coluisse. quod si adhuc mansisset, castius dii observarentur.* The first image of any god would therefore have been that of Jupiter in the temple of Jupiter Optimus Maximus erected by Tarquinius Priscus. See Cardauns 1976: 147.

images (*simulacra*), whose fictive character suggests a connection with "poetic" theology, necessarily involved a misrepresentation of the gods, since it moved them away from the abstractions of the philosophers at the same time as it reversed earlier Roman traditions. While the poets' anthropomorphization rendered the gods more easily apprehensible, it could also be connected with other *ficta*, such as descriptions of divine thievery, adultery, and periods of slavery to mortals, which Varro describes as "opposed to the dignity and nature of the immortal gods."[38] Though the substance of this remark goes back at least to Xenophanes,[39] it is significant that Varro describes the errors of the poets partly in political terms. As the theater in the *De re publica* illegitimately attacks the political leaders of the state, so the "theology" Varro associates with the theater, as opposed to the city, violates the hierarchy imposed by the Roman structure of political authority where the gods, as superior in status, are possessors of a *dignitas* that deserves respect.[40]

But its connection with the mythical theology of the poets is not the only context in which the theater appears in Varro's treatise. Since theatrical performances themselves constituted part of the cult practices of the state religion, they received their own book (book 10) in Varro's study. We cannot say much about the content of this book based on the one fragment that survives, a reference to certain magistrates' right to use canopies in the theater,[41] but it is natural to assume that, as opposed to the many works in which he treated Roman drama from the perspective of the *litteratus,* here Varro was interested primarily in the rituals of the performance itself. If this is the case, then the treatment of theater in the work as a whole reinforces the contrast between the potentially subversive, or anomalous, content of the plays themselves and the officially sanctioned context of their performance.

The spatial arrangement of the theater reflects a similar tension between the drama on stage and the religious framework in which it was embedded. When in 55 B.C.E. Pompey erected Rome's first permanent theater surmounted by a shrine to Venus Victrix, he attempted to avert criticism by claiming that his edifice was not actually a theater but a temple "at the base of which we have added rows of seats for spectacles."[42]

38. Varro fr. 7 Cardauns: *contra dignitatem et naturam immortalium.*

39. Xenophanes fr. 11 Diels-Kranz.

40. Cf. Varro, *Curio,* fr. 5: *quia sic . . . deos deformant ut nec bonis hominibus comparentur,* where again the improprieties attributed to the gods are placed in a Roman social context. See Cardauns 1976: 142.

41. Varro *Ant. rer. div.* fr. 82 Cardauns.

42. Tert. *De spect.* 10; cf. also Aul. Gell. *NA* 10.1.

However disingenuously this remark was made, it highlights how the orientation of the spaces in which dramatic performances took place reinforced the institutionalized "otherness" of the stage.[43] As J. A. Hanson has shown, the religious context of *ludi scaenici* was, in every case we are able to judge, emphasized by the proximity of the temple of the god in whose honor the festival was held.[44] But within the theater-temple complex, the stage at the bottom of the steps is set against the temple itself, exalted by its podium. The direction of the spectators' gaze within this architectural space thus creates an opposition between watching plays and participating in other forms of religious ritual, especially sacrifice, at least as it was enacted in Pompey's theater.[45] This opposition also appears in the *pompa* or procession preceding the actual dramas, which Tertullian describes as leading "to the stage away from the temples and altars" (*ad scaenam a templis et aris*).[46] During dramatic performances, the spectators turn their backs on the temple itself, literally to look down on the actors whose social rank was correspondingly low. The act of watching becomes a bond that unites all levels of Roman society, from the people to the gods, who are also present as spectators.[47] By contrast, sacrifices were performed on the altar in front of the temple, so that the gaze of the spectators was directed up the steps toward the shrine of the god itself. The importance of this kind of visual contact during sacrifice can be discerned from Vitruvius's discussion of the orientation of the cult statues within temples. The statue should always face

43. Edwards 1993: 122 ff., observes another important aspect of the physical segregation of the theater from the civic spaces of the city: all the permanent theaters in Rome, unlike those of Athens, were built outside the *pomerium*.

44. Hanson 1959, esp. 13–26.

45. And it must be remembered that sacrifices punctuated the *ludi* during which dramatic performances were staged; see Hanson 1959: 86 ff. For Pompey's theater, we have a description of Claudius conducting sacrifice in a way that seems specifically to have emphasized the vertical opposition between the temple at the top of the theater and the stage itself: *ludos . . . e tribunali posito in orchestra commisit, cum prius apud superiores aedes supplicasset perque mediam caveam sedentibus ac silentibus cunctis descendisset* (Suet. *Claud.* 21.1). If earlier Roman theatrical performances did take place on a stage erected below the steps of a temple, this arrangement is unlikely to have been unique to Pompey's theater (see Frézouls 1981: 197, n. 22), although, as Hanson 1959: 87 ff., discusses, it is uncertain where the altars were located in other theater complexes, and in several provincial theaters there is evidence for an altar in the orchestra itself.

46. Tert. *De spect.* 10.2.

47. For evidence that the gods were regarded as spectators at these festivals, see Hanson 1959: 13–15. The importance of the idea is revealed most clearly by the ritual of the *sellisternium,* in which a chair was decorated to accommodate an image or symbol of the god during the performance (Hanson 1959: 82–85), and by Cicero's description of the site of the *ludi Megalenses* as *in ipso Magnae Matris conspectu* (Cic. *Har. res.* 24).

west "so that those coming to the altar to sacrifice might look to the east and the statue in the temple . . . and these images might seem to rise up and gaze in turn upon those making supplication and sacrificing."[48]

The decorations of the Roman stage itself reinforced the sense that it constituted an anomaly within the public spaces of the city. As the plays depicted actions that, in the vast majority of cases, took place outside Rome, usually in a markedly Greek milieu, and focused often on the domestic rather than the political lives of their protagonists, so each of the three genres of stage decoration described by Vitruvius defines a landscape antithetical to the civic context within which the festival itself took place. The comic stage depicted private buildings;[49] the tragic, a distinctively royal palace;[50] and satyric decoration created a non-urban landscape of trees, caves, and mountains. The stage buildings for the temporary theaters of the Republic were built anew every year and offered the magistrates in charge of their construction a chance to win prestige through the fabulous ostentation of the edifices they provided. As a result, the buildings themselves were connected with what was defined as an un-Roman emphasis on luxury and individual self-aggrandizement.[51] Pliny's outraged description of the stage buildings of Scaurus in 58 B.C.E. and Curio in 52 B.C.E. makes them emblems of all the vices that led to the fall of the Republic, especially the canonical two, *luxuria* and *ambitio*, and contrasts the decadent Romans willing to risk their lives for the thrill of riding around in Curio's rotating theater with their ancestors who fell at Cannae.[52] The case of Scaurus suggests another link between the displays on the stage and the private space of the domus. His *scaena* not only represented the luxury of tragic kings but emulated it with its gold, bronze, and, most remarkably, glass, and these splendid furnishings later became part of the decorations of Scaurus's own house.

The foreignness of the stage was made all the more apparent by the careful arrangement of the spectators in the stands to create a contrasting

48. Vitr. 4.5.1. Cf. his prescriptions for the heights of the altars themselves (4.9), which are also designed to facilitate visual contact between the sacrificer and the god. Altars to sky gods like Jupiter should be as high as possible, so that the participants are forced to gaze at the element where the deity himself resides. Similarly, altars to the gods of the earth and sea should be low (*humiles*).

49. *aedificiorum privatorum*, Vitr. 5.6.9.

50. Ibid. Gros 1985: 338, points out that Vitruvius uses the adjective *regalis* only twice in his work, once in reference to the vestibules of noble mansions (6.5.2) and once for the theater (5.6.8).

51. For more on the theater's association with luxury and extravagance, see Edwards 1993: 113–14.

52. Pliny *HN* 36.113–20.

display of the social hierarchy within the Roman state.[53] Well before Augustus's sweeping legislation, the place one occupied in the theater reflected one's position in the state as a whole.[54] (The use of the same Latin word *ordo* to designate both a row of seats and a social class makes the connection almost inevitable.)[55] In even more fundamental ways, the conditions under which dramatic spectacles were watched served to highlight what made the Roman state unique. The very absence of a permanent theater, at a time when many less prosperous Italian cities already possessed one, not only signaled the Roman rejection of luxury, but also served as a reminder of the annual change in magistrates that crucially differentiated the Roman constitution from a *regnum* like those presented on the stage itself.[56] When in 154 B.C.E. a permanent theater was begun by the censors, the consul P. Cornelius Scipio Nasica ordered construction stopped and had the building materials auctioned off.[57] Valerius Maximus explains the resulting *senatus consultum* prohibiting "anyone from building theater seats in the city or within a mile of it or watching the *ludi* while seated, as a way of ensuring that the capacity for standing on their feet that distinguished the Roman *gens* might thus become more widely known." [58]

Augustus's theater legislation, whatever its actual details,[59] was certainly the most comprehensive and elaborate attempt yet to make seat-

53. A point that is the premise of virtually all discussions of the patterns of seating at Roman spectacles. See esp. Rawson 1991: 509–10; Edwards 1993: 111; and Gruen 1992: 202 ff., with further bibliography.

54. The earliest attempt to legislate these distinctions that we know of dates to 194 B.C.E. and is described by Livy himself (34.44.4–5; 34.54). Exactly how the state was to be represented in the arrangement of the audience was naturally the source of much controversy. Thus, according to Livy, the initial attempt to segregate senators was seen by the plebeians as itself a threat to the concord and equality of the state. In this way, even the definition of political hierarchy in the stands becomes an encroachment of *superbam libidinem* (34.54.7), a phrase that, as we shall see, summons up the theatrical excesses of the *regnum* of the last Tarquin, upon the Republican state. For another example of popular resentment against seating regulations in the theater, this time from the Late Republic, see Plutarch *Cic.* 13.

55. Rawson 1991: 508–9.

56. *Annuos magistratus* feature in the first sentence of Livy's description of the Republic after the exile of Tarquin (2.1.1). For a similar analysis of the issues raised by the building of a stone theater at Rome, according to which the annual reconstruction of the theater itself continually reinforced the aristocracy's control over dramatic productions, see Gruen 1992: 205–10.

57. Liv. *Per.* 48.

58. Val. Max. 2.4.2: *ne quis in urbe propiusve passus mille subsellia posuisse sedensve ludos spectare vellet, ut scilicet remissioni animorum* [. . .] *standi virilitas propria Romanae gentis nota esset.* The lacuna before *standi* is not universally accepted.

59. For the sources and issues, see Rawson 1991: 510 ff.

ing arrangements at the theater a manifestation of the idealized structure of Roman society. His innovations can be read as an attempt to emphasize even more clearly the boundary between the stage and the state that we have been describing, and to use this distinction specifically to differentiate the restored society of Augustan Rome from the disorder of the Late Republic,[60] with which, as we have seen, the excesses and turmoil of the theater were particularly associated. Not only does Augustus prescribe who sits where and make the seating arrangements more visually striking by requiring all those seated in the central stands to wear their white togas;[61] he also forbids anyone from the highest classes to appear on the stage itself.[62] The importance of the radical separation between the stage and the stands in Augustan Rome is also revealed in the fate of the actor Pylades.[63] When hissed at by one of the spectators, Pylades pointed to him from the stage, thus reversing the spectacular order by making the spectator himself an object of attention (*conspicuum*). For this the emperor banished him from Italy.

II. The Dramatic Digression (7.2)

Livy's description of the first attempt to build a permanent theater in Rome was contained in his lost book 48. But the surviving summary preserves the argument used by the consul Nasica to prevent construction: a theater would not be beneficial and would harm the public character (*inutile et nociturum publicis moribus* [*Per.* 48]). Nasica's objection does more than merely reflect the traditional fears about the dangers of the theater; the language in which those fears were expressed also recalls the defining characteristics of history as a literary genre.[64] As we have seen, the usefulness of history, its ability to profit its readers, was fundamental to Polybius's rejection of Phylarchus's attempt to mix history and tragedy, and Livy's preface describes his *History* as healthy (*salubre*), whereas the theater is harmful to public morals. This brief example

60. So Rawson 1991: 509.

61. Rawson 1991: 510–11, points out that Augustus's insistence that no one in the central seats wear dark clothing would have created an especially powerful visual impression.

62. Suet. *Aug.* 43.3.

63. Ibid. 45.4.

64. The point is equally valid even if the abridgment records not the precise phrases of Nasica but the *topoi* of his oration.

shows how for Livy the double status of the theater as both a literary form and a pernicious social phenomenon made it particularly valuable as a vehicle for defining his own text. The Roman construction of the theater as a political space apart, which acquired a special significance in the wake of Augustus's corrections of the transgressions of the Late Republic, meant that when Livy adopted the traditional literary dichotomy between history and drama, he was simultaneously asserting the place of his *History* in the "real" civic life of the Roman state. It is no accident therefore that the rejection of history's rival genre is here backed by the authority of Rome's highest magistrate. The purpose of this section is to show that Livy's longest direct treatment of the theater as an institution, his excursus on the origin of drama in book 7, possesses a similar programmatic function. The opposition between history and drama developed in the excursus also informs Livy's account of the duel between Torquatus and the Gaul, where again two systems of representation are measured against each other in terms of their effect on their audiences.

I shall begin by quoting the passage itself, which occurs in the context of Livy's highly annalistic presentation of the events of the year 364 B.C.E. near the beginning of book 7 (7.2):

During this and the succeeding year, when C. Sulpicius Peticus and C. Licinius Stolo were consuls, there was a pestilence. In the latter year, nothing was done worthy of memory except that, as an attempt to restore the *pax deorum,* a *lectisternium* was held for the third time since the founding of the city; and since the force of the plague was not relieved by human counsels or divine aid, when the minds of all had been overcome by superstition, even theatrical performances [*ludi scaenici*]—an unfamiliar thing for a warlike people; for the circus had until then been their only form of spectacle—are said to have been introduced among the other attempts to placate the wrath of the gods. However the institution was small at first, as almost all things are at the beginning, and essentially foreign [*res peregrina*]. Without any singing, without expressing the content of songs through gestures [*sine imitandorum carminum actu*], the players summoned from Etruria, leaping to the rhythm of the flute, produced not indecorous dances in the Etruscan manner. Then the youth began to imitate these players, while at the same time trading jests among themselves in crude verses; nor were their voices disconnected from their movements. So the institution was taken over and became established by being often performed. To the native actors, the name of *histriones* was given, since *ister* was the Etruscan word for player. These men no longer exchanged rough and impromptu jests like Fescennine verse, but performed *saturae* composed in meter with the song and choreography now written out to flute accompaniment.

After a number of years Livius Andronicus, who in place of *saturae* had first dared to introduce a play with a plot, likewise made another innovation.

As all poets then did, he himself used to perform in his own dramas; when he had worn out his voice through frequent encores, having asked the permission of the audience, he is said to have stationed a slave boy in front of the flute player to sing for him and to have danced the song with a much more vigorous motion since he was not impeded by the use of his voice. From then on, all actors continued this practice, and only the dialogues were performed in their own voices. After the institution of the theater, because of this form of performing plays, grew distant from jokes and casual jesting and a game [*ludus*] had turned into a craft [*ars*], the youth began to exchange jokes stitched into verses in the old manner and left the performance of plays entirely to the *histriones.* Thence are derived the sketches [*exodia*] that are combined especially with Atellan farces. The youth kept to themselves this new type of performance, which they had taken from the Oscans, and did not allow it to be polluted by the *histriones.* And thus the provision remains that the performers of Atellan farces are not removed from their tribe and continue to perform military service on the grounds that they have no share in the craft of the theater [*ars ludicra*]. So the first origins of the drama deserve to be set among the small beginnings of other institutions so that it will be clear how from a healthy beginning, the drama has grown into a madness [*insania*] that would be scarcely tolerable in luxurious kingdoms.

As even a cursory reading will show, Livy's excursus is anything but straightforward. Over two centuries of literary history are packed into slightly over a page of the author's most obscure prose. The general tendency of his account emerges clearly enough: the drama grew from small but respectable beginnings to a form of madness. But almost every detail of the process has raised a host of questions.[65] Nor does Livy's presentation of drama as an institution that has undergone a progressive process of decline accord well with his desire to characterize even the first *ludi scaenici* as a fiasco and a religious failure, although the inconsistency itself reveals the strength of Livy's animus against the theater. Finally, the question of Livy's sources and the degree to which he reworked them is also difficult to resolve, since all earlier accounts of the history of the theater have to be reconstructed from writers who postdate Livy.[66] But even

65. For a discussion of the literary historical problems, with bibliography, see Waszink 1972.

66. The fullest introduction to the problem is to be found in Waszink 1948. Waszink argues strongly that Varro was Livy's exclusive source, but the discussion is somewhat oversimplified because of Waszink's unwillingness to allow that any of the authors through whom he recovers Varro's account could themselves have used a variety of sources. For example, when Augustine writes *neque enim et illa corporum pestilentia ideo conquievit, quia populo bellicoso et solis antea ludis circensibus assueto ludorum scaenicorum delicata subintravit insania* (*Civ. Dei* 1.32), in spite of the many echoes of the language Livy uses, Waszink (1948: 228) does not acknowledge the possibility of any Livian influence, even an indirect one, and assumes therefore that these terms and ideas were present in Varro. Nevertheless,

if the excursus is derived largely from Varro, as J. H. Waszink argues, the very decision to include such a digression, and the clear connection between the history of drama and Livy's larger conception of the decline of Rome sketched in the preface[67] testify to the importance that the theater as an institution held for Livy and invite a closer analysis of the role the digression plays within his text.

Like Varro in the *Antiquitates rerum divinarum,* Livy initially presents drama as a religious institution, here introduced as a response to a crisis in the *pax deorum.* However, despite its religious role, Livy emphasizes the drama's foreign character. It is a *res peregrina,* particularly anomalous in regard to Rome's military traditions. The first performers are Etruscan, and Livy's inclusion of the derivation of the word for actor from that language further reinforces the alien character of the institution. If Waszink is right that in Varro's account the tradition of exchanging jokes in verse predated the importation of Etruscan actors, then Livy seems to have here reworked his material to make the origins of drama appear exclusively foreign.[68] As the excursus goes on, the drama becomes alien in other respects as well. The progressive professionalization of the theater gives the dramatic performances themselves an importance independent of their social and religious context. As Livy says, what had been a *ludus,* a word that recalls both the public festivals that provided the occasion for the drama and the jesting of the indigenous Roman youths,[69] became an *ars,* a craft or profession. Correspondingly, the practitioners of this *ars* are now excluded from a place in the citizen body, and the youth turn to another medium for their jokes that has not been "polluted" by actors. Indeed, the very shape of Livy's excursus contributes to the impression that as the drama becomes increasingly autonomous, it becomes increasingly a distracting and disconnected phenomenon. The account begins with the description of the theater as a religious practice connected to a certain moment in the history of the state but becomes more and more concerned with the technical and formal innovations that give the institution a history in its own right.[70]

---

he does demonstrate the importance of Varro for the substance, and even some of the language, of Livy's excursus.

67. The similarities with the preface were first discussed by Weinreich 1916: 409.

68. Waszink 1948: 234–35.

69. For a discussion of the meaning of *ludus,* see Wagenvoort 1956. Of the various associations of *ludere* and its compounds, the opposition to *seria* forms a consistent feature.

70. Another issue at stake in the contrast between history and drama implicit in Livy's excursus is the role of imitation in each medium. The first dramatic performances in Rome were nonmimetic (*sine imitandorum carminum actu* [7.2.4]); that is to say, they were not representations of a specific plot. Livy, however, draws particular attention to the idea of

The most sweeping rejection of the mature drama comes in the final sentence of the excursus and is couched in the now familiar language of health and healing: the contemporary drama is an *insania,* a madness or disease. Beyond the implicit contrast with the "healthy" genre of history, an allusion made more emphatic by the other references to the themes of Livy's preface that accompany it, the metaphor bears an additional relevance in this context. Since the drama was imported originally to cure a pestilence, the description of drama as an *insania* itself points out the extent to which the practice has failed to fulfill the social and religious function for which it was designed. Again literary polemic merges with the criticism of drama's failure as a civic institution. The unhealthiness of drama is no longer a metaphor, it can be demonstrated by the practical effect the drama has had upon the state.

The antithesis between history and the drama implied in the comparison to an *insania* is heightened by the formal structure through which Livy fits the digression into the fabric of his work. Significantly, this structure also hinges on the word *insania,* which recalls the *morbum* that provides the occasion for the beginning of the digression (7.2.3) and will be the focus of the narrative proper when it resumes in the first sentence of the next chapter (7.3.1). The resulting ring composition strongly demarcates the excursus from the flow of the narrative. What is more, since the digression is set at the beginning of the year, it is directly juxtaposed to the annalistic formulae that link the course of Livy's narrative to the continuity of the Roman state itself (7.2.1 and 7.3.3). This elaborate pattern of framing and contrast may indeed be seen as a narrative equivalent to the contemporary tendency to segregate the space of actual dramatic performances and to contrast them with the hierarchized displays of Roman order in the stands.

---

imitation by repeating the verb *imitari* in a different context at the beginning of the next sentence (7.2.5): the Roman youth began to imitate the actors. This repetition suggests a connection between the use of imitation within the drama and the social effects of dramatic performances. Even in the later dramas that did have plots, and therefore did imitate actions, what the stage offered was emphatically only a representation. Dupont 1985: 49, describes "a correlation between imitation and *déréalisation*" and argues that the unreal nature of theatrical spectacle was crucial to the definition of the *ludus* as a space apart from the conduct of serious business. Therefore as the Roman youths imitate the performance they watch, they are themselves drawn away from their place in the state and into the world of "play." But the kind of imitation that history encourages is a very different one. Not only does the historian represent real events, but his representations in turn provided for the reactualization of the events described within the sphere of "real" public activity (see ch. 1, sec. I).

Similarly, Livy's text frames the institution of drama by shaping its history as an example of the larger pattern of decline that the whole of his narrative elucidates. If this use of drama to reflect the decline of the state itself should seem inconsistent with the aim of constituting drama as alien and distinct from the larger processes of history, it may be that the problem is precisely that Roman history, in the period of its unhealthiness, has become analogous to drama. The degeneration of Rome as a whole can be understood as a failure to maintain the boundaries that exclude the foreignness and luxury associated with the drama from the state. *Avaritia,* it must be remembered, also came to Rome from abroad, as did the conquered spoils that nourished it.[71] By insisting on the distinctions that define the drama as alien, and at the same time linking it with the characteristics of Rome in its decadence, Livy thus reveals how far the Roman state itself has fallen away from its ideal form. He simultaneously exploits the negative connotations of drama to reestablish a set of oppositions between traditional and alien practices through which the causes of Rome's decline can be seen as foreign excrescences to be excised from the state, just as the drama is institutionally contained. We shall see later in this chapter that other historical moments when native traditions have ceased to be operative are also characterized as dramatic intrusions into Roman history.

Even at its "healthy beginning" in 364 B.C.E., drama was clearly not the "appeasement" (*placamen*) that the gods required. Not only does the plague not die down as a result of the performances, but while the first drama is being performed, the Tiber bursts its banks and floods the circus (7.3.2). Indeed, the outcome of this experiment, and the description of drama as an *insania,* suggest that far from the theater being a remedy for pestilence, the pestilence should rather be read as an omen predicting the coming of drama and perhaps of the future *insania* of the state that drama mirrors in turn. Thus it is significant that the practice that finally cures this plague possesses features that point to the social value of history itself and its privileged connection to the public life of the state:

When the quest for *piacula* had worn out their minds as much as the sickness had their bodies, it is said to have been recalled through the memory of the elders that a pestilence was once ended by a nail driven by a dictator. Influenced by this religious scruple the Senate ordered a dictator to be appointed for the purpose of driving this nail. . . . There is an old law, written

71. See ch. 1, sec. III, with bibliography.

in archaic words and letters, requiring the *praetor maximus* to drive a nail on the Ides of September; this law was attached to the right side of the Temple of Jupiter Optimus Maximus where there is a shrine of Minerva. Since letters were rare in those days, they say that this nail served as a record of the number of years and that the law itself was dedicated in the temple of Minerva because numbers were Minerva's invention.—Cincius, an author attentive to such records, confirms that at Volsinii too there are nails fixed in the side of the temple of Nortia, an Etruscan goddess, to mark the passage of years.—The consul M. Horatius dedicated the temple of Jupiter in the year after the expulsion of the kings; the sacred rite of driving the nail was transferred from the consuls to the dictators because their *imperium* was greater. The custom had then been interrupted, but the matter seemed worthy of the appointment of a dictator. [7.3.3–8]

The ritual to which the Romans turn after the failure of drama thus has a double connection with the history of the state. First, historical memory provides the means through which the ritual that cures the plague is recovered. Hence the whole episode provides a simple example of the practical utility of preserving knowledge of the past. But at the same time, the ritual practice itself, as opposed to the *nova res* of drama, constitutes a tradition whose history is coextensive with that of the Republic[72] and has as its ultimate purpose nothing other than the production and display of a historical record that makes such knowledge possible.

The continuity between the nail driving as a ritual act and the "text" that results from it, the nails that in place of letters mark the passage of years, is an important feature of Livy's account. As opposed to drama, whose performers are excluded from participation in the politics of the state, this ritual cannot be separated from the exercise of political authority. It is the responsibility of a magistrate, indeed, of the magistrate who possesses *maius imperium* (7.3.8), and its history as an institution chronicles the transmission of power within the state. Thus the historical tradition in the narrow sense, the preservation of a record of the past, results directly from the continual reenactment of the forms and practices that constitute Roman public life. Here, in fact, the production of such a record becomes the ultimate goal of the magistrate's performance.

This interdependence between written records of the past and the very institutions and practices they record may explain the attention Livy draws to his own use of sources within the passage. In contrast to the ac-

72. Livy reminds his readers, however, that it too may have Etruscan antecedents (7.3.7).

count of the origins of drama, where much controversy has arisen because Livy cites no authorities for the information he presents, this passage places great emphasis on the sources of the historian's knowledge. The primary evidence for the practice of driving nails is preserved through an inscription; the Etruscan parallel derives from Cincius Alimentus. The citations here may partly be explained by Livy's desire to increase his own credibility in what may have been a controversial discussion,[73] but they also make it possible to trace a line of succession linking Livy's own text to the ritual he describes. This is particularly true of the inscription recording the ancient law. The text of the inscription provides Livy's historical source, but the inscription itself, as a monument affixed to the side of the same temple where the dictator drove the nails,[74] seems to have directly taken over the place and function of the record left by the ritual.[75]

The contrast Livy draws in his excursus between the alien *insania* of drama and the practice that eventually cures the plague raises issues that emerge again a few chapters later in the account of the duel between Torquatus and the Gaul. Chapter 3 demonstrated that the victory over the Gaul resulted directly from the Romans' ability to use spectacles to connect their individual champion to the collective power of the state, while the gestures and threats of the Gaul remained an insignificant distraction. We can now see that much of the language used to describe the behavior of the Gaul recalls the description of drama, while the rituals that precede and follow the Romans' victory share the most important characteristics of the nail-driving rite. The first point Livy made about the drama in his excursus was that it was a particularly strange in-

73. There was certainly controversy at the time about the nature of Manlius's office, and the language of 7.3.8–9 suggests that the survival of rival versions might account for Livy's procedure. Both the inscription and the material from Cincius confirm that the practice of driving the nail was of sufficient importance to warrant the creation of a dictator and would thus rebut the assumption that Manlius was appointed primarily to fight the Hernici.

74. The verb *fixa* describing the inscription strengthens the connection with the rite of *clavi figendi* (7.3.5).

75. Livy's double use of the verb *dicere* at the beginning passage similarly points to the link between the transmission of historical data and the transmission of political authority on which the ritual practice depends. As the main verb in 7.3.3, *dicitur* ("it is said") makes clear that Livy is reporting earlier opinions, but the same verb *dicere* is used three times in the next sentence to describe the act by which the *dict*ator himself is appointed and in turn appoints his master of the horse.

stitution for a military people.[76] Since there is no greater proof of the propriety and social utility of any practice than its ability to procure military victory, the association here established between "acting" and the actions of a defeated contestant in single combat provides a particularly powerful confirmation of Livy's rejection of drama and locates it within a larger opposition between effective and ineffective modes of visual contact.

The costume of the Gaul, a colorful cloak and embossed golden armor, exemplifies the same kind of luxurious ostentation as some Late Republican theatrical productions, where the actors were dressed in cloth of gold.[77] The three elements of the Gaul's performance that Livy uses to differentiate his behavior from the Roman's are *cantus* ("song"), *exsultatio* ("dancing up and down"), and *armorum agitatio vana* ("the pointless shaking of weapons" [7.10.8]). The term *cantus* is not strictly appropriate to the Gaul, who has only spoken and stuck out his tongue, but it is a component of dramatic performance and is explicitly mentioned as such by Livy.[78] *Exsultatio* recalls *praesultat,*[79] which is used by Manlius to describe the conduct of the Gaul before the Roman lines. Both words are related to *salto,* applied to the dancing of the first Etruscan performers at Rome.[80] *Agitatio* in this context is perhaps colored by its relationship to *ago* and *actus,* the *voces propriae* for theatrical performance.[81]

The Romans receive their champion with praise and congratulations. "Among those jesting with certain crude jokes in military fashion, almost in the manner of *carmina,* the *cognomen* Torquatus was heard" (7.10.13). The language in which this exchange is described, *inter carminum prope modo incondita quaedam militariter ioculantes,* recalls the amateur performances of the Roman youths, which Livy's account has specifically set apart from the *ars ludicra, inconditis inter se iocularia fundentes versibus.*[82]

76. For more on the antithesis between drama and warfare in Roman culture, see Edwards 1993: 101 ff.

77. Dupont 1985: 75, describes such elaborate theatrical costumes based on Pliny *HN* 36.116.

78. 7.2.7. The related *canticum* and *cantare* are used at 7.2.9.

79. 7.10.3. The word only occurs in Livy.

80. 7.2.4. *Praesultator* is used by Livy to mean a dancer at public spectacles, although not dramatic spectacles, since the reference occurs in bk. 2 (2.36.2).

81. Cf. 7.2.4., 7.2.7, 7.2.8, 7.2.9, and 7.2.11.

82. 7.2.5. Although the youths are not explicitly indicated as the performers here, they are mentioned in connection with Manlius when he dons his armor before the duel (*armant iuvenem aequales* [7.10.5]). For more on the particular connection between the Roman *iuventus* and dramatic performances, see Morel 1969.

This jesting served to reinforce the connection between Manlius and his community that had earlier ensured his victory and now gave it meaning. Moreover, this ritual is the means by which the cognomen Torquatus is established, a historical marker by which the memory of the exploit is preserved. Thus in contrast to the Gaul's decontextualized dance, socially disconnected and militarily useless, the Roman performance, within the tradition specifically associated with the military and cut off from the formal drama, manages both to be socially integrating and to serve as a vehicle for the preservation of Torquatus's deed as an *exemplum*.

III. Tragedy and the Tarquins

Rather than portraying the theater as an essentially "democratic" institution, as some scholars have interpreted it,[83] Livy explicitly connects the excesses of dramatic performances with monarchy. The *insania* that the theater has become would be intolerable even in wealthy and luxurious kingdoms. The association between the drama and kingship makes sense on a number of levels. If dramatic performances can be taken as defining an antithesis to an idealized conception of Roman society, there was no institution more out of place in Rome than kingship. Indeed, the Roman tragic stage was, as we have seen, the representation of a royal palace, and the extravagant stage buildings of the Late Republic themselves became signs of the dangerous and improper pursuit of personal prestige by those who financed them. But for the historian, the *regnum* as archetype of a political system alien to the *res publica* could also be linked to a specific period in Roman history. While the first six kings of Rome receive a generally positive treatment as the originators of the public institutions that still defined the Roman state, the reign of the last king, Tarquinius Superbus, becomes in Livy's text an anomalous interruption in the course of Roman history, a period when all the city's political traditions are overturned, against which the newly founded Republic can be defined.[84] Thus Tarquin's *regnum* occupies a place in

83. E.g., Rumpf 1950; Frézouls 1981: 194; and, to some extent, Nicolet 1980: 363 ff.

84. Livy expresses his views on kingship as an institution most directly in the preface to his second book: *regnum,* especially in its most unpleasant manifestation, the *superbia* of the last king (2.1.2), forms an antithesis to the ideal of *libertas.* However, not only did all of the earlier kings contribute to the growth of the city (ibid.) but the period of monarchy was necessary for the development of *libertas* itself (2.1.3 and 2.1.6; see Phillips 1974: 90–91,

Livy's narrative not unlike that of the theater in the public life of the state, and Livy develops this connection by framing his account of the last king's reign with episodes explicitly described as dramas. The murder of Servius Tullius through which Tarquin gains the throne is a "tragic crime" (*tragicum scelus*), one of only two times the word "tragic" is used by Livy;[85] thc rape of Lucretia, the event that precipitates the founding of the Republic, results from a pastime devised by the king's sons, described as a *iuvenalis ludus* (1.57.11), for which Livy employs both the setting and language of comedy.[86]

But a closer look at Livy's condemnation of the *insania* of the theater suggests that the presentation of these events as dramas has a broader function within his text than to signify the corruption of Tarquin's regime. The *regnum* Livy mentions in the passage from book 7 was not located on the stage; rather, it described the state in which unrestrained theatrical performances took place. The transgression of the restraints that ideally govern the theater means that the inversions that ought to be

---

who discusses the role that fear of the king plays in the creation of a collective identity). Already in his treatment of the debates over Romulus's successor (1.17), Livy characterizes the *regnum* as inferior to *libertas* but necessary for restraining the dangerously competitive impulses of the *nobiles* (which the monarchical constitution itself arouses [1.17.1]). This ambivalent attitude toward the kingship as an institution derives in part from the very ambiguity of the Latin word *rex,* which, as Cicero (*Rep.* 2.49) describes, does double duty as a term for the ideal king, "a pretty good constitution" but inclined toward tyranny (*Rep.* 2.47), and the full-blown tyrant ("than which no creature fouler, more horrible, or more detestable to gods and men can be conceived" [*Rep.* 2.48]). That the last king of Rome belongs emphatically in the latter category appears unmistakeably from his cognomen, *Superbus* (for *superbia* as a political attitude equivalent to *regnum* in its pejorative sense, see Bruno 1966: 237 f., 248 ff.). Tarquin's ascendency is also explicitly distinguished from the reigns of the earlier kings by the hstorian's eulogy for the deposed Servius Tullius, with whom "just and legitimate *regna* also perished" (1.48.8).

For Livy's presentation of the evolution of Roman institutions under the monarchy, see Luce 1977: 234 ff.; for more on the traditional opposition between *libertas* and *regnum* in Roman political thought, see Wirszubski 1950, esp. 5 and 62 ff., and Bruno 1966: 236 ff.; for its other manifestations in Livy, see Bruno 1966. Miles 1995: 152 f., demonstrates that the conflicting interpretations of *regnum* are in play from the very beginning of the reign of Romulus.

85. 1.46.3. The other use of *tragicus* occurs in the description of an actor at 24.24.2.

86. The description in Scafuro 1989 of how Livy uses elements of comedy to shape his presentation of the Bacchanalian conspiracy (38.8–19) provides a complementary treatment of another Livian passage. Scafuro's observation that at the moment when the *scortum* Hispala changes her allegiance from the society of initiates to the nation as a whole by betraying the secrets of the mystery to the consul, the comic paradigm breaks down (Scafuro 1989: 135), is especially interesting. For a similar analysis of how Tacitus depicts the political transgressions of Nero as particularly anomalous by constructing them as dramatic episodes within his narrative, see Woodman 1992.

restricted to the stage have propagated themselves among the audience. So too the "dramas" in book 1 do not simply reflect the anomalies of Tarquin's reign; they engender and perpetuate them. And as in book 7 the drama was contrasted with another ritual that healed "sickness" and put Rome's legitimate political power on display, so here the creation of the Republic results from the production of other forms of visual display that both reveal the failures of the *regnum* and reconstitute Roman society. Finally, it must also be remembered that the *regna* Livy evokes in book 7 are used to characterize not Rome's ancient past but her present. So, too, we shall see that the particular social ills that the end of the *regnum* exemplifies relate directly to the contemporary issues of civic loyalty discussed in the preceding chapter, and the display that provides their remedy can again be connected with the healing ritual of sacrifice, the audience for which is now expanded to include Livy's own readers.

A survey of the events that bring Tarquin to power will make clear both the social tendencies that differentiate this period in history and why drama as a form of spectacle should be particularly associated with them. Tullia, a daughter of Servius Tullius, was originally married to Arruns, a son of the previous king (1.46.4ff.). But when she perceives his ambition for power to be much less than her own, she contrives his death, as well as that of her sister, who was married to her husband's more aggressive brother, L. Tarquinius. Having married Tarquinius herself, she goads her new husband to regain the throne that rightly belongs to him as the son of Tarquinius Priscus until, "inspired by womanly furies,"[87] he initiates a conspiracy to seize power. He summons the Senate, occupies the throne, and delivers an attack against Servius as a slave who has revealed his origins by constantly favoring the lowest classes (1.47.8ff.). When Tullius himself arrives to challenge him, Tarquin grabs the aged king and hurls him down the steps of the *curia*. Tullia, who has just appeared in the forum itself to proclaim her husband king and been hustled away by him, finishes off her aged father as he gropes his way home by running him over with her wagon (1.48.1ff.). Thence "contaminated with the blood of her father," she returns to her *penates,* whose anger ensures "that a similar ending will follow swiftly upon the evil beginning of the reign."[88]

Livy's portrayal of these events focuses especially on the interaction between the family and the state as two social entities. We have seen that

87. 1.47.7: *muliebribus instinctus furiis.*
88. 1.48.7: *malo regni principio similes propediem exitus sequerentur.*

for Cicero, the ability to place the state above the family as the object of loyalty and affection marked a crucial stage in the development of each individual's civic identity. Livy historicizes this process by relating key events in the growth of the Roman state to the increase of patriotic feelings among its individual citizens. Thus his account of the founding of the Republic, for which Tarquin's reign prepares, makes the transformation in Rome's constitution inseparable from a revolution in the loyalties of the Romans themselves. *Libertas* would have been impossible had not "the love of wives and children and the dearness of the land itself," generated a sense of communal loyalty by binding the *animi* of what had been a transitory population.[89]

But if affection within the family paves the way for full participation in the state for the other Romans, for the Tarquins, it has an opposite effect. It is the exhortations of his wife Tullia that lead Tarquin to overthrow the legitimate ruler, a sign both of the inversion of normal hierarchies within the family and of how this in turn leads to the privileging of family interest over public duty. Throughout the narrative, the dynastic ambitions of the Tarquins mean that they constantly overvalue the family against the state. Superbus justifies the deposition of Servius Tullius on the grounds that as the son of Tarquinius Priscus, he himself is the legitimate king: "He has occupied the throne of his father, and much better the king's son be the heir to the kingdom than the king's slave."[90] Not only does he define public status on the basis of domestic status, but in so doing, he reverses one of the great models of inclusion formulated under the monarchy, the adoption of Servius Tullius. The new king is as devoted to the interests of his sons as he was alive to his own prerogatives as *filius*.[91] As a ruse to overcome the town of Gabii, Sextus Tarquinius pretends that his father the king has finally turned against his own family and forced him into exile, a lie that serves to underline the

89. 2.1.5. For further analysis of this process, see Bonjour 1975b: 66 f., Phillips 1979, and Feldherr 1997.

90. 1.48.2: *se patris sui tenere sedem; multo quam servum potiorem filium regis regni heredem.*

91. The importance of this theme in Livy's account of the reign of Tarquinius Superbus is also highlighted by Dumézil 1949, who argues that the indulgence shown by the Tarquins toward their sons contrasts specifically with Roman ideals of fatherhood and thus helps delineate the Etruscan character of their reign. Similarly, the strength of the bond between husband and wife among the Tarquins, as revealed by the influence that Tanaquil possesses over Tarquinius Priscus and Tullia over Tarquinius Superbus, has been interpreted as a deliberately anomalous, un-Roman feature of their dynasty (see Hallett 1984: 70 f. and n. 10).

real closeness between father and son, who communicate with one another through secret signals, *tacitis ambagibus* (1.53.6), impenetrable to any outside observer. Thus the Tarquins, who like the other Romans originally came to the city as immigrants, fail to make the connection to the state that Livy describes as the fundamental prerequisite for the Republic. The contrast emerges most clearly when, after the first consul Brutus has executed his own sons for plotting against the Republic, the former king is described as an exile, wandering again among the cities of Etruria begging his allies "not to allow him to perish before their eyes with his adolescent sons."[92]

The very same inversion in loyalties that keeps the Tarquins essentially foreign is also what give Livy's depiction of the end of the *regnum* its distinctively tragic features. Since the more intimate bonds of family now determine the course of public affairs, Livy's narrative is continually pulled away from the public spaces of the city into the private, unseen realms of the *domus*. Livy links the royal palace (*regia*) itself with the reign's tragic nature: "for the Roman royal palace too brought forth an example of tragic crime" (*tulit enim et Romana regia sceleris tragici exemplum* [1.46.3]). The palace provides a powerful symbol of the family ambitions of the Tarquins, and as such it is especially contrasted to the senate house where the public deposition of Servius takes place. But at the same time, the *regia* also assumes the role of a tragic stage set, through which characters enter and exit. Tullia, contaminated with the blood of her father, returns to her *penates* (1.48.7); she does not emerge again in the narrative until the regime falls, when she is described "fleeing her home" as those who see her invoke the furies of her parents (1.59.13). Similarly, Tullia herself, as the driving force within the royal household, assumes a prominence unusual for women in historical narrative and becomes the center around which tragic imagery clusters. Phrases like *muliebribus instinctus furiis*, "inspired by womanly furies," which make Tarquin seem like a fatally misguided Orestes, also point to the unnatural dominance of his wife within the *familia*.[93]

But not only do these tragic characteristics represent the nature of the *regnum*, the *regnum* itself comes into being as a result of them. The "tragic" scene that Tullia plays for Tarquin within the palace drives him toward his public crime as it converts him too into a tragic character.

92. 2.6.2: *cum liberis adulescentibus*. The same phrase was used to describe Brutus's sons two chapters before, at 2.4.1.

93. See also Hallett 1984: 71.

The bribery and the enticements that secure Tarquin's position prior to his coup (1.47.7) can be read as the extension of this "tragic" influence outward, again through a series of secret meetings, so that the other "fathers of families" (*patres gentium*) become the servants of Tullia's ambition. Thus the actions that Livy described as tragic generate a hidden network of intrigues that successively draw more and more people away from their duty to the state, until the *res publica* itself is subsumed under their influence.

The private ambitions that prompt Tarquin's coup are cloaked behind the appearance of public legitimacy he creates. The final deposition of Tullius is deliberately portrayed as a public act. It takes place in the Senate and is preceded by an address in which Tarquin justifies his action on constitutional and political grounds: Tullius assumed the kingship without any of the customary procedures, as "a woman's gift."[94] As king, he has proved himself an advocate of the lowest classes against the better. According to Tarquin, it is Tullius's reign that has been the anomaly, and he, too, depicts the inversion of power within the state as the result of an overturning of the hierarchy within the family. The kingship of Servius, he suggests, constitutes an extended Saturnalia, when slaves are given the power of insulting their masters.[95] His own usurpation will be the restoration of legitimate order, and by throwing the king physically down the Senate steps, *in inferiorem partem* (1.48.3), he seems to signify that Servius has been returned to his proper place. These are the only actions of Tarquin's that are accessible to public view, and taken on their own terms, they suggest that, if not perfectly justifiable, his attempt at least springs from recognizably political motives.[96]

There is however one publicly visible manifestation of the true nature of the new reign and of Tarquin's display in the senate house. Tullia's sudden appearance in the Forum can be read as a representation of the bursting out of private ambitions into the political centers of the state. Not only does Livy depict her decision to show herself as a result of shamelessness,[97] but a similar direct intervention by women in the public life of the state is again portrayed as a violation of public decorum in the speech Cato delivers against the repeal of the *lex Oppia* (34.1.7ff.). There, too, that women should appear in such a manner in public was taken as evidence of the breakdown of male authority within the

94. 1.47.10: *muliebri dono.*

95. 1.48.2: *satis illum diu per licentiam eludentem insultasse dominis.*

96. Ogilvie 1965: 186, points out the reminiscences of Catiline in Tarquin's speech.

97. 1.48.5: *nec reverita coetum virorum.*

home.[98] Appropriately for the role he is playing, Tarquin now gives the appearance of exercising authority over his wife by ordering her to depart. Yet the very language in which he does so betrays her influence. He employs the verb *facessere,* a rare and archaic word, which occurs most commonly in drama and appears only two other times in Livy, once in the context of the speech Tullia herself had given urging Tarquin to seize the throne.[99]

Tarquin's appropriation of the public forms of legitimate authority in this scene gives a particular point to Livy's explicit characterization of the preceding events as tragic. The mode the historian chooses for representing the preliminaries to the coup introduces a discrepancy between the perceptions of his readers and those of the audience for Tarquin's actions. Tarquin is at pains to conceal the "dramatic" nature of what has happened, and hence when his wife, the inspiring fury, appears in public, he drives her away. For the audiences within the narrative, it is therefore impossible to perceive what is taking place as the intrusion of an anomalous regime, precisely because this "dramatic interlude" has usurped the forms and appearances of real government. It is only when Tarquin's coup is staged as a drama, as Livy stages it for his readers, that it takes on the socially useful function of a negative *exemplum,* defining by contrast the proper conception of the *res publica.* Thus the deployment of allusions to tragedy within Livy's text, far from being simply a problem of style, resembles the use of drama in Roman ritual as a carefully orchestrated antithesis to the civic framework in which it was embedded. Moreover, by so carefully delineating the overthrow of Servius Tullius as tragic, the historian counters precisely the elision of the boundary between the space of the dramatic performances and Roman public life that Tarquin strives to produce, and that also provided a constant source of anxiety in the case of actual theatrical spectacles. Significantly, the strategy that the historian here uses to isolate Tarquin's reign within the course of his history has a close parallel in the new king's own attempt to use the rhythms of religious ritual to depict the reign of his predecessor as a carnivalesque interruption of legitimate authority.

98. 34.2.1: *si in sua quisque nostrum matre familiae, Quirites, ius et maiestatem viri retinere instituisset.* A final link between Tullia's appearance here and Cato's speech involves women's right to use the ceremonial carriage known as a *carpentum.* One of the provisions of the lex Oppia was that women should be forbidden to appear in a *carpentum,* and this is precisely the vehicle Tullia uses to run over her father.

99. 1.47.5: *Facesse hinc Tarquinios aut Corinthum.* For its dramatic use, see Ogilvie 1965: 190.

IV. Sacrifice and the Restoration of the *Res Publica*

When the Tarquins are finally driven from power, it is the result of an analogous process of publicizing the hidden crimes of the monarchy in a manner that makes their improper and profoundly un-Roman nature unmistakable. The exposure of the rape of Lucretia by Brutus, the first consul of the Republic, involves assimilating that crime to another mode of ritualized public spectacle, sacrifice. As drama reflects and reproduces the ethical misalignments that lead to Tarquin's usurpation of power, so, as the preceding chapter illustrated, sacrifice exerts an opposing influence by creating a sense of community among its spectators. Thus Brutus's display of the body of Lucretia, like his later execution of his own sons, forges the new conception of civic identity that Livy makes inseparable from the Roman *res publica*. And the historian, whose role in representing the monarchy had been to resist the king's portrayal of events by exposing the "dramatic" origins of his reign, can again align his narrative with the public displays of an authentic magistrate.

The *penates* of the regia, outraged at Tullia's actions, are said to have ensured that the untimely end of the king's reign will be like its beginnings, and Livy's narrative emphasizes this symmetry by again stressing the transgression of boundaries between public and private space involved in the rape of Lucretia. The regime symbolically began when Tullia shamelessly rode out of the regia into the spaces of public assembly. It will end when a man who ought to be with his fellows on the battlefield enters a private house to violate a truly modest wife.

The events that provide the context for the rape similarly epitomize the regime's failure to distinguish properly between public and private and show how the resulting inversions serve to degrade, both ethically and politically, each individual Roman citizen. The Romans are at war with Ardea, but it is a war that is being fought for the most un-Roman motive of personal gain (1.57.1).[100] The king wishes both to recover the private wealth that he has expended in the adornment of the city and to use the spoils to reconcile the sentiments, or as Livy puts it, to corrupt the *animi*,[101] of the people, who feel that they have been forced to perform the

100. For another analysis of the narrative motifs that link the siege of Ardea with the rape itself, see Philippides 1983: 113–14.

101. 1.57.1: *delenire animos.*

work of slaves in undertaking the king's building projects. The concatenation of bribery, corruption, foreign spoils, and enslavement that results from Tarquin's failure to keep public and private resources separate[102] anticipates the later effects of luxury on the state and has the political consequence of dividing the population into masters and slaves.[103]

As the war with Ardea itself violates Roman military traditions, so the entertainment that precedes the rape takes place during a hiatus in military activity and promotes throughout an improper inversion of the domestic and military spheres: the soldiers' camp becomes a place for diversion and entertainment; competitions are waged and victories won within the *domus*. At a drinking party, where the royal youth "while away their leisure" (*otium*)[104] during the siege of Ardea, a "contest" (*certamen*) arises about whose wife possesses the best character, and as a way of deciding the winner they agree to visit the home of each unexpectedly to see how their wives are occupying themselves. The young men mount their horses and speed off to Rome, where they find the wives of the princes engaged in much the same activities that they themselves had been, extravagant drinking parties.[105] Lucretia, the wife of the king's nephew, Collatinus, by contrast, is discovered unimpeachably spinning wool at their home in Collatia. She therefore receives the "praise of winning the competition,"[106] and her husband is proclaimed *victor*. However, the sight of both her beauty and her chastity "inspires"[107] one of the princes, Sextus Tarquinius, with a desire to rape her. A few days later, he returns to Collatia, and, having been received as a guest, enters Lucretia's bedroom that night with a drawn sword. When he finds her unfrightened by the fear of death, he finally "conquers"[108] her by threatening to kill a male slave as well and place his corpse in her bed as though he had been her lover.

It is appropriate that Livy should again invoke drama when describing the activity that draws the young men away from their duty on the battlefield and into the private spaces of the *domus*. As R. M. Ogilvie has

102. The notable exception to this tendency is the construction of the temple of Jupiter Optimus Maximus, which was financed by the spoils of the Volscian war (1.53.3). Notice, too, that the people are not unwilling to perform manual labor on the construction of the temples of the gods (1.56.1).

103. Contrast the effects of the Servian constitution Tarquin replaced, which ensured a stable class system and gave every class a place within the structure of the state.

104. 1.57.6: *otium . . . terebant.*

105. 1.57.9: *in convivio luxuque.*

106. 1.57.10: *laus certaminis.*

107. Ibid.: *incitat.*

108. 1.58.5: *vicisset.*

pointed out, the conception of a contest of wives has parallels in Roman comedy, and the entire *ludus* is punctuated with a banter that contains many expressions reminiscent of stage dialogue.[109] Like the tragedy with which the reign began, the dramatic allusions here do more than characterize the anomalous nature of the young men's actions; each of the characters is also made into a spectator, and the crime that follows is explicitly portrayed as a result of the act of watching. Rather than observing the kinds of military displays described in chapters 2 and 3 and so being inspired to fight more boldly, Sextus is impelled by the sight of Lucretia to penetrate further into the *domus*. Concomitantly, the paradigm of drama accentuates the social distinctions that also form the background to the youths' actions. Lucretia herself is incorporated into the drama, and, given the Roman contempt for those who appeared on stage, the very fact of being put on display in this contest anticipates the lowering of status with which Sextus threatens her. So too the "praise" she wins and the *castitas* she manifests become, within the inverted world of the drama, an impetus only for her degradation. By contrast, at the scene of her death, Lucretia places herself on display but this time as an *exemplum* that will act to preserve the reputation for chastity, and hence the status, of Roman wives.[110]

It is the suicide of Lucretia that begins the process of publicization that converts her rape from a private outrage, as indeed Sextus's crime would have been regarded prior to Augustus's moral legislation, to the event that provokes a national revolution.[111] Her violated body becomes the center of a new spectacle, whose audience gradually expands to include the entire *res publica*. Having invited her husband and father, each accompanied by one friend, to the house in Collatia, she kills herself in their presence after denouncing her rapist.[112] Her corpse is carried out of

109. See esp. 1.57.8, *age sane*, and 1.58.7, *satin salve*, with the discussion of Ogilvie 1965: 220–24. The closest parallel in Roman comedy to the contest as a whole is the scene described in Ter. *Heaut.* 275 ff. For an analysis of tragic elements in Livy's narrative of Lucretia, see Corsaro 1983: 112, who, however, describes them as products of the intrinsically "tragic" nature of Livian narrative, rather than as part of an attempt overtly to characterize these events as dramatic.

110. Philippides 1983: 115–16, presents a somewhat different view of the function of dramatic allusions in the episode, arguing that Livy establishes an antithesis between the staged or public sections of the narrative and the rape, which occurs in the *cubiculum*. According to this reading, the "dramatic" portions of the narrative allow for the display of virtue, which "cannot fail to be perceived by the community," and so provide a corrective to the harm Lucretia's reputation may have suffered as a result of Sextus's attack.

111. See also Joplin 1990: 64 f.

112. Lucretia's overt, almost scandalous, declaration may be opposed to Sextus's command that she be silent before her rape. *Tace, Lucretia* (1.58.2) are the words with which he

the home and into the forum of the town of Collatia, where those who see it are "astonished by the *indignitas* of the action" (1.59.3). The next step is for Brutus to narrate her violation and death in Rome itself.

The events culminating in the rape had been accompanied by a progressive narrowing of the audience of spectators in a manner that reflects the exclusive and divisive civic structure obtaining under the monarchy. The initial audience for the *certamen* proposed at the banquet was already restricted to the kinsmen of the king,[113] and when Sextus returns to Collatinus's house, even they have been excluded. The first acts of the revolution thus reverse the narrative motion from public to private space that resulted from the *ludus*. What is more, the process of exposure can also be mapped against the concentric levels of social organization whose harmonization within one another is essential for the formation of the Republic. Collatia, the native town, or to use Cicero's term the *patria loci* (*De leg.* 2.5), follows the family group and is succeeded in turn by Rome, center of the *res publica* itself.

The crucial moment in the transformation of the rape from a private to a public crime results from the intervention of a figure who is not a member of Lucretia's immediate family, L. Junius Brutus.[114] After Lucretia has stabbed herself, her relatives are consumed by grief, but Brutus "snatching the knife from the wound and holding it, still dripping with blood, before him, says, 'By this blood, most pure [*castissimum*] before the royal injustice, I swear, and I make you gods my witnesses, to drive out with fire, sword and whatever force I can, Tarquinius Superbus together with his criminal wife and children'" (1.59.1). Both gesture and language begin the redefinition of Lucretia's death by treating it as a sacrifice. An oath sworn by blood is rare in Roman religion,[115] but where blood is used in ritual, it often derives from sacrificial victims or appears in a sacrificial context.[116] And *coniurationes* were often confirmed through sacrifice.[117] The word *castissimum* is also relevant here; al-

initiates his attack and may be viewed as the dynasty's final attempt to prevent the revelation of its crimes. It is also notable that the reign whose beginning depended on the silencing of Tullia should end with the speech of Lucretia. For more on the significance of this phrase within the episode, see Joshel 1992: 126 ff.

113. Livy says that the banquet itself was made possible because of an unequal division of supplies between the *primores* and the *milites* (1.57.4).

114. Brutus is present originally, as *amicus* of Lucretia's husband, in the capacity of an adviser to the family.

115. Ogilvie 1965: 226.

116. For the ritual use of sacrificial blood, see Fowler 1911: 33–34.

117. The strongest evidence that the oath connects the death of Lucretia with sacrificial procedure comes in the description Dionysius of Halicarnassus gives of the oath the first

though Lucretia, as a woman married only to one husband (*univira*), was sexually chaste, the adjective *castus* is also used for ritual purity. In fact, this is its customary meaning in Livy.[118]

In the preceding chapter, sacrifice was discussed in terms of the social bond it created among its spectators. Each sacrifice offers the spectator the double possibility of seeing himself either as part of the group that exacts the death of the victim or of sympathizing with the victim itself. While, as we saw, the two potentials are both inescapably present in every sacrificial scene, when the spectator's identification with the victim becomes too overpowering, the sacrifice serves to alienate its audience from the larger group responsible for the killing. Brutus converts Lucretia's death into just this kind of impure sacrifice. The observation that Lucretia's blood is no longer *castus* introduces the motif of ritual impropriety. Similarly, Lucretia's proclamation of her own innocence, "although I absolve myself from crime, I do not release myself from punishment" (*ego me etsi peccato absolvo, supplicio non libero* [1.58.10]) both increases the reader's sympathy for her unjust suffering, and, from a sacrificial perspective, removes the supposition of the victim's guilt, which, in Greek rituals like the Buphonia, justifies its killing.[119]

The sacrificial interpretation of Lucretia's death thus becomes another means of representing the impropriety of her violation, but now in

---

consuls swear after the expulsion of the Tarquins. This is virtually the same oath that Brutus here indicts over the corpse of Lucretia, and, according to Dionysius, when the consuls take the oath, they do so "standing over the remains of sacrificial victims [στάντες ἐπὶ τῶν τομίων]" (Dion. Hal. *Ant.* 5.1.3). For military *coniurationes* confirmed through sacrifice, see Bleicken 1963: 58 ff.; and for the role of sacrifice in the collective oath of the Samnites (Livy 10.38), see ch. 4, sec. III. The most famous *coniuratio* to be confirmed by blood and/or sacrifice was Catiline's (Sallust *Cat.* 22.1–2; Dio 37.30.3).

118. The only other occasion where a word related to *castus* is used of sexual purity is earlier in the Lucretia episode (1.57.10). Otherwise, cf. 7.20.4; 10.7.5; 10.23.9; 27.37.10, and 39.9.4. See also Moore 1989: 121–22.

119. 1.58.10. For the guilt of the ox at the Buphonia, see Burkert 1983: 138. For the idea of the "comedy of innocence" as a means of justifying sacrifice, see, originally, Meuli 1946, esp. 226 ff., 266 ff. For a very different Girardian reading of the Lucretia episode, which also focuses on Lucretia's role as victim, see Joplin 1990. Joplin argues that Lucretia acts as surrogate victim in the sense that the violence practiced against her is a displacement of the "mimetic rivalry" between powerful males. By making Lucretia's rape the crime that causes the fall the Tarquins, the tradition in which Livy participates establishes a distinction between the "good violence" that expels the Tarquins and the "bad violence" of internal political competition at the expense of the single female victim. This victim is made complicit in the ideology that necessitates her death and, to a degree, responsible for the civic violence that follows it. For another analysis of the narrative logic that requires the death of the violated women in the Lucretia and Verginia episodes, see Joshel 1992: 124 f.

a medium that reveals its implications, not just for the *domus,* but for the state as a whole. It also creates a link between Livy's narrative and actual Roman ritual, for it was an impure sacrifice that motivated the expulsion of the kings as it was reenacted every year at the festival of the *regifugium.* In this ceremony, which took place on February 24, the very date Ovid assigns for the rape of Lucretia, a surrogate for the king, the *rex sacrorum,* performs a sacrifice in the forum and immediately flees the area.[120] H. H. Scullard, using the analogy of the Greek Buphonia, where the sacrificer is also forced to flee, assumes that the *rex* takes on himself the guilt of an impure sacrifice.[121]

The initial response to Brutus's oath by Lucretia's father and husband is to turn "from mourning to anger."[122] At every stage in the journey to Rome the spectacle that Brutus produces or the narrative he delivers becomes an instrument for converting the personal grief of the spectators into an impetus for collective action. Thus the shift in civic identity that is required for the formation of the Republic results directly from Brutus's representation of the Tarquins' crime. The effects of the spectacle appear most clearly in the scene at Collatia. "Each lament for themselves the foul and violent deed of the prince. They are moved not only by the sorrows of her father, but also by Brutus, who chides them for their tears and ineffectual lamentation and recommends that they take up arms against those who have dared such hostile actions; this is what befits men and Romans."[123] Again, the change from an individual to a unified response to the rape parallels the witnesses' shift from identifying primarily with the father to conceiving of themselves as Romans, and concomitantly viewing the Tarquins as public enemies (*hostes*).

If Lucretia's death, as an image of impure sacrifice, alienates its viewers from the regime responsible for her death, the beginning of the Republic by contrast offers other examples of collective action where the

120. Ovid *Fasti* 2.685–852.

121. Scullard 1981: 81. The connection between this procedure and Greek *Fluchtritual* is made by Meuli 1946: 280. On the Buphonia, see Burkert 1983: 136–43. For a discussion of other Roman rituals that may have been connected specifically with the expulsion of the Tarquins, see Mastrocinque 1988: 47–48.

122. 1.59.2: *totique ab luctu versi in iram.*

123. 1.59.4: *pro se quisque scelus regium ac vim queruntur. movet cum patris maestitia tum Brutus castigator lacrimarum atque inertium querellarum auctorque quod viros quod Romanos deceret, arma capiendi adversus hostilia ausos.* See the analysis of this passage by Phillips 1974: 90 ("violation of family ties, by outraging a sense of community based in part on such ties, leads directly to the destruction of established political forms") and the remarks of Burck 1968: 82.

citizens band together to punish or expel transgressors. The expulsion of Collatinus, while not explicitly described as sacrificial, can profitably be understood according to the logic of sacrifice established in the Lucretia episode. Indeed, Livy links Collatinus's banishment directly to Lucretia's death by depicting it as an extension of the oath he swore by Lucretia's blood (2.2.5).[124] The other Tarquins were expelled by violence, but Collatinus is persuaded to go by Brutus. The first words of Brutus's exhortation are "you, by your own will . . . " (*hunc tu tua voluntate* . . . [2.2.7]).[125] Collatinus, rather than be subjected to violence must leave of his own will, in a manner that will absolve the state of any blame, just as the propriety of sacrificial ritual required that the victim meet death willingly.[126]

The moment that reveals most clearly how the social order of the Republic is articulated and propagated through sacrificial spectacle comes when Brutus presides over the execution of his two sons for plotting to restore the Tarquins.[127] Again the crowd's support of the punishment and acknowledgment of the victims' guilt stands in contrast to the sympathy that had been aroused by the sight of Lucretia's corpse. But as a confirmation of the new regime, this scene also answers the dramatic

124. And indeed in his version of events the fulfillment of this oath provides the only motivation for Collatinus's banishment; Plutarch (*Pub.* 7.1–5) and Dionysius (*Ant. Rom.* 5.9.2–12.3), by contrast, present the expulsion of Collatinus as a sequel to and result of the conspiracy on the part of the young *nobiles* to recall the Tarquins: Collatinus's sympathy for the rebels, who include his nephews, both contrasts with Brutus's willingness to execute his own sons and presents Collatinus himself as distinctly out of place in the moral climate of the Republic. Cicero, too, would seem to have located this episode after the conspiracy (*Rep.* 2.53), although like Livy he also links Collatinus's banishment explicitly to his *nomen*. For more on the background of the story and other surviving versions, see Ogilvie 1965: 238 f.

125. In Cicero's treatments of Collatinus (*Rep.* 2.53; *Brut.* 53; *Off.* 3.40), his departure is involuntary. A precedent for Livy's emphasis on Collatinus's acquiescence is however to be found in Piso fr. 19 Peter: *L. Tarquinium, collegam suam, quia Tarquinio nomine esset, metuere eumque orat uti sua voluntate Roma concedat.*

126. Other legends too connect the figure of Brutus with transformations in Roman sacrifice, and one in particular presents him as effecting a shift away from the alienating sacrifices instituted by Tarquinius Superbus. Macrobius, *Sat.* 1.7.34–35, tells that Tarquin originally instituted the practice of sacrificing young boys during the festival of the Compitalia in response to the injunction of the Delphic oracle that *pro capitibus capitibus supplicaretur.* Brutus cunningly reinterpreted the oracle by substituting the "heads" of poppies for those of boys. For an analysis of this and other religious reforms connected with Brutus, see Mastrocinque 1988: 37–65.

127. For bibliography on the much discussed problem of the relationship between execution and sacrifice, with a special emphasis on Roman material, see Burkert 1983: 46, n. 46.

episode that began the reign of the last king. There, the supremacy of family connections over public institutions was revealed when the son deposed the slave who had become king. Here, Brutus complements the execution of his sons by granting *libertas* to the slave who alerted the consuls to their conspiracy. More important, if Tarquin concealed private ambitions behind the public role he was playing, the culmination of Livy's account of the execution comes when Brutus's feelings as a father are revealed through the performance of his duties, "with a father's spirit shining forth amid the performance of his public duty" (*eminente animo patrio inter publicae poenae ministerium* [2.5.8]).

It is the balance revealed in the last sentence between the personal experience of Brutus and the civic role he performs that structures Livy's account of the scene:

> The traitors were condemned and the punishment exacted, a punishment more remarkable [*conspectius*] because the consulate imposed on a father the duty of taking retribution from his sons and fortune made the executor of the penalty the very man who would have been removed had he been a spectator. The youths stood bound at the stake but the children of the consul drew the eyes of all away from the other conspirators as if they were unknown.[128] Men did not pity the punishment more than the crime by which it had been earned: that they, in that very year, should have taken it into their heads to betray to a once proud king and now dangerous exile the newly liberated *patria*, the *pater* who had liberated it, the office of the consulate, which originated from their own family, the patricians, the people, and the gods and men who composed the Roman state. The consuls took their places; the lictors were sent to exact the penalty. They strip the youths, lash them with rods, and strike them with the ax. During all this time the father, his face and countenance, were a spectacle for the crowd, as a father's spirit shone forth amid the performance of his public duty. [2.5.5–8]

Throughout the passage, brief, objective descriptions of the execution give rise to longer analyses of the responses of the spectators, which in turn seem to alternate between the anger they feel as citizens toward the traitors and the sympathy with which they regard the consul. As in the trial of Horatius, the tensions that arise in the feelings of the spectators produce a doubling of the spectacle itself, so that by the end of the passage the audience's gaze has moved from the condemned to the face of their father. Livy's description of the figure of Brutus generates a corresponding problem in perspective. Brutus is imagined at the beginning of

128. In fact, they were *nobiles*.

the passage as a spectator, yet his presence makes the scene more "worthy of attention," and by the end he has become the *spectaculum*. This shift between a subjective and objective role means that Brutus is at once the focus of attention and occupies the position of the other spectators. And it is by identifying themselves with the consul that his fellow citizens can perceive the tension between civic duty and private loss as their own.

Within the context of the narrative, the execution of Brutus's sons, like the spectacles that surrounded the fall of Alba, takes on an initiatory function. The conflicts experienced by the spectators articulate precisely the shift in loyalties required for the formation of the Republic, where the new sense of national identity that is the prerequisite for *libertas* both depends on and supersedes natural affection for the family. So the spectacle in which the new civic order is confirmed does not mask or conceal these conflicts; on the contrary, it exposes them in a manner that requires every member of the audience to experience the duties of citizen and *pater* simultaneously. To signal the importance of the spectacle for the formation of citizens, the scene ends when the slave Vindicius is given both *libertas* and *civitas*.[129]

In conclusion, throughout this charged sequence of episodes, Livy contrasts drama and sacrifice as two media of political communication that activate antithetical processes within the Roman state. The covert ascendancy of the private and domestic ambitions of the Tarquins, which Livy associates with drama, continually results in the enslavement of Roman citizens both collectively and individually. The sacrificial rituals of the Republic bring about *libertas* by doubly publicizing personal experience: the private sufferings of Lucretia's family and of Brutus himself are exposed to the public gaze and thus generate within each of their spectators the shared emotions that, as the preface to book 2 implies, become the basis of a new sense of national identity. Correspondingly, the shift from *regnum* to *res publica* brings about a different relationship between the historian's own representation of events and the public displays through which each regime exercises its power. By directly depicting Tarquin's reign as a series of dramatic episodes, Livy at once signals its discontinuity with the rest of Roman history and counters the king's own pretenses of legitimacy. But even as the model of theatrical spectacle encourages readers to distance themselves from events that are designated as drama, the sacrifices that bring about the revolution require

129. For other interpretations of this episode, see Tränkle 1965: 327–29, Thomas 1984: 516 ff., and Feldherr 1998.

their audiences to identify with the objects of their gaze. So Livy's account of Brutus's execution of his sons enables his own readers to reconstruct precisely the experiences of the actual spectators and to end, as they do, with their attention focused on the *animus patrius* of Brutus, which the spectacle of the execution renders visible (2.5.8). Under the Republic, history becomes the medium through which the public displays that create *libertas* can be communicated to the reader.[130]

This congruence between Livy's narrative and the public representations of the first consul receives confirmation when, as a culmination of the process of exposure that leads to the revolution, Livy depicts Brutus acting as a historian. After having displayed the body of Lucretia in the forum at Collatia, Brutus moves on to the Roman forum, where he delivers an oration that not only describes the rape of Lucretia but also refers to the murder of Servius Tullius, and even to the digging of the Cloaca Maxima (1.59.7–11). In other words, he recapitulates much of Livy's own narrative. In fact, Livy says that Brutus recalled even more horrible deeds, which are difficult for the historian to relate.[131] However, this difference in content, even the necessary distancing created by such an authorial aside, is less significant than Livy's implication that at this moment Brutus's action and his own are comparable.

V. Verginia

The general similarity between the episodes of Verginia and Lucretia needs no emphasis: once again, a tyrannical regime that has illegally taken power in Rome is brought down when one of its leaders, Appius Claudius, attempts the sexual violation of a freeborn woman, whose death becomes the act that mobilizes political resistance.[132] But the thematic connections Livy's treatment creates between the two

130. Correspondingly, Frier 1979: 204 ff., shows that the language with which the historian begins his second book, with its reference to *res pace belloque gestas, annuos magistratus,* is explicitly annalistic. Thus the distinctive literary form of Livy's historical narrative comes into being precisely as the distinctive political form of the Roman Republic replaces the monarchy.

131. 1.59.11: *his atrocioribusque, credo, aliis quae praesens rerum indignitas haudquaquam relatu scriptoribus facilia subiecit, memoratis.*

132. Livy makes the comparison explicit from the beginning of his account of Verginia (3.44.1).

events go beyond the similarity of their plots. Here, too, the issue of the illegitimate use of the forms of public authority for the pursuit of private ends structures the entire narrative and manifests itself in the spatial opposition between *domus* and *forum*. The political enslavement of the entire state to the *regnum* of Appius again reveals itself in an attack on the freeborn status of one individual Roman woman. Indeed, the procedure most directly involved in the attempts of Verginia's father and betrothed to protect her is the *vindicatio in libertatem*, the origins of which go back to the execution of the sons of Brutus, where the new *libertas* of the nation was symbolized by the freeing of the loyal slave Vindicius. But for our purposes the most significant similarity is that once again Livy employs allusions to drama to characterize Appius's attempt to use the façade of public authority against Verginia, while the liberation of the state is effected by the creation of a spectacle that here, even more explicitly than in the case of Lucretia, is depicted as an improper sacrifice. Thus this episode confirms the importance within Livy's text of the opposition between drama, as the mechanism for usurpation and enslavement, and sacrifice, through which the traditional order is restored.

The episode begins when Appius Claudius, the most important of the *decemviri*, who have illegally remained in office by failing to hold the promised consular elections, is seized with desire for the plebeian maid Verginia.[133] While her father is serving in the army, he instructs his *cliens*, M. Claudius, to lay public claim to the girl as his slave. Claudius seizes the girl on her way to school (*ludus*) and brings her to court, which is presided over by Appius himself (3.44.6ff.). In two separate scenes, Appius resists the appeals of Verginia's betrothed, Icilius (3.45.4–11), and of her father (3.47), who has been hastily summoned from the camp. When Appius rejects his plea and awards Verginia to his client, Verginius pretends to acquiesce and with the decemvir's permission withdraws for a moment with his daughter, whom he suddenly kills as the only way of securing her *libertas* (3.48.4–6). The horror of this event provokes a rebellion against the decemvirs, which is further enflamed when Verginius, still bearing his bloody dagger, tells his story to the army (3.50.2–10).

Explicit reference to the drama is made during the first trial scene when Appius's client, by claiming that Verginia is his slave, is said to "act

133. 3.44.1: *Ap. Claudium . . . stuprandae libido cepit.* Cf. the description of Sextus Tarquinius at 1.57.10: *Ibi Sex. Tarquinium mala libido . . . stuprandae capit.* The political leaders are taken captive by their desire.

out a play that was known to the judge, since he himself was the author of its plot" (*notam iudici fabulam petitor, quippe apud ipsum auctorem argumenti, peragit* [3.44.9]). Terms suggesting dramatic performance permeate the language of the sentence. *Fabula* is the correct term for play, especially when it is "acted" (*peragit*), and *argumentum,* which can also suggest the legal "argument" M. Claudius is about to put forth, here designates primarily the "plot" of the drama Appius has composed.[134] This designation of the trial as a drama has the further effect of accentuating how closely the events Livy describes resemble situations typical of the stage, particularly of Roman Comedy:[135] Many of the central characters of the episode can be readily assimilated to standard comic roles. Verginia becomes the silent beloved, Icilius the *adulescens amator,* and Appius, described with the dramatic phrase *amore amens,*[136] acts as the powerful rival. So, too, one of the central issues of comic plots, the connection between civic status and marriageability, also governs the action here.[137] Icilius's ability to make Verginia his wife depends on establishing that she is in fact freeborn, while the rival's desire to make her his concubine requires that she be a slave.

Once again, however, the dramatic shaping of this episode cannot be explained simply as a stylistic choice, much less as an attempt to elide the differences between history and drama. Because this "drama" is being played out not on stage but in the law court, and the rival is himself the judge, the comic model breaks down. No means exist for the would-be husband to restore Verginia to her rightful status and bring about the resolution of conflicts between desire, family expectations, and social norms that the comic paradigm demands. Thus the allusions to comedy here introduce a set of expectations whose disastrous reversal ultimately reinforces the distinction between the spheres of drama and of the public actions that properly constitute the subject of history. If this were only a comedy, Verginia would undoubtedly be reunited with her family. But what is taking place here, as the "heroine's" hideous death makes inescapably plain, is no *ludus;* this is not a fictive event distanced from its

134. *OLD,* s.v. *argumentum,* § 1a and 5a.

135. The act of abduction with which Appius's plot begins also, however, has analogies in tragedy. Cf., e.g., Aesch. *Suppl.* and Soph. *OC* 818 f.

136. 3.44.4. The two terms recur at 3.47.4, where Ogilvie 1965: 486, compares Plautus *Merc.* 82 and Terence *Andria* 218. However, this language is not restricted to the comic stage; the similar expression *animo aegro amore saevo saucia* is used of Medea in the Nurse's introductory monologue in Ennius's *Medea* (= fr. 254 Vahlen).

137. For the relationship between marriage and civic status in New Comedy, see esp. Konstan 1983: 15–32.

audience by the conventions of the stage, but a trial taking place in a real Roman courtroom and as such recorded in Livy's text.

The imagery of role-playing and acting had previously been used to indicate Appius's essential duplicity,[138] but it also points to a central characteristic of Livy's portrayal of the decemvirate, the discrepancy between appearance and reality created by the decemvirs' illegal usurpation of the forms of public office. The decemvirs rule as if they were magistrates; they preside at trials and have the outward trappings of power. But once they have failed to hold consular elections and have exceeded the limits of their office, they cease to have any legitimate authority. Thus Livy describes them on the Ides of May, 449 B.C.E., the date when the new magistrates should have taken office, as "private citizens acting like decemvirs, yet with their courage for wielding power undiminished, and still wearing the insignia that gave the appearance of honor."[139] They are again designated as *privati* who have unjustly taken possession of the *fasces* by their opponent, M. Horatius Barbatus, who equates this situation with the end of *libertas* itself and the return of *regium imperium* (3.39.8). The real vacuum at the heart of the state is perhaps most chillingly revealed in a slightly earlier scene. After an invasion by the Sabines and Aequi, the decemvirs attempt to summon the Senate. But since they lack the constitutional authority to do this, the senators do not appear. "The people looked around for a senator in all parts of the Forum, but rarely recognized one; then they gazed upon the *curia* and the emptiness surrounding the decemvirs" (3.38.9).

But the precedent of the Tarquins suggests a further significance to the intrusion of dramatic elements in Livy's account of the trial: not only have the appearances of power been deprived of their substance, they have been taken over to serve private ends. Just as Tarquin adopted the outward forms of political action to conceal the "tragic" impetus that inspired his coup, so here an event that appears to be a trial turns out to be a *fabula*. The inseparability between the processes of the trial and the dramatic "plot" concocted by Appius appears most clearly in Livy's handling of the legal details of the case. Those who speak on behalf of Verginia demand that Appius not hand her over to the man who claims to be her master, "Lest her reputation be imperiled before the question

138. Thus when Appius has secured his reelection as *decemvir,* Livy says that "was the end for Appius of wearing the mask of another" (*ille finis Appio alienae personae ferendae fuit* [3.36.1]).

139. 3.38.1: *privati pro decemviris, neque animis ad imperium inhibendum imminutis neque ad speciem honoris insignibus, prodeunt.*

of her status is decided" (3.44.12). Ogilvie points out that this plea for *vindiciae secundum libertatem* was impossible since, according to Roman law, minors in such a situation could only legally be handed over to their fathers, and Verginia's father was away with the army. He assumes therefore that Livy has fallen into error through a misunderstanding of legal practice.[140] However, precisely this legal issue is raised within the text by Appius Claudius himself. In fact, as the decemvir makes clear, the very law that forbids him to hand Verginia over to anyone except her father was one of the provisions that he himself had made in defense of the Romans' *libertas* (3.45.1). Appius's pursuit of Verginia therefore requires not that he disregard the laws of the state but that he scrupulously obey them. As a result, the furtherance of his own private aims becomes indistinguishable from the proper conduct of public business. He has, to paraphrase Livy's words, "written the script for this performance" not only because he has cooked up the plot itself, but also because he has written the very laws that ensure its success.

The issues involved in the trial scene also activate the same larger conflict in ethical alignments as the events surrounding the creation of the Republic itself. In the crudest terms, Appius subordinates the *res publica* to the needs of his own body, but, as we saw in the preceding chapter, the civic bond requires not just a reversal of these priorities but an ability to think of the state in the same terms as one thinks of the family and even the body.[141] The way Livy has portrayed Appius's attempt on Verginia makes the sympathetic relationship between all these entities as clear as the episode of Latinius's dream. Appius's actions are at once an attack on collective *libertas,* the structure of the *gens,* and the integrity of his victim's body. His "plot" requires that she lose her citizenship and her place in the family together with her chastity: M. Claudius is to claim that Verginia is a slave, not a freeborn citizen, and that she is in fact not her father's daughter. The very name of the heroine makes the connection between sexual integrity and membership in the family inevitable. Ogilvie suggests that the name Verginia itself "was simply a hypostatization of *virgo,*"[142] and Livy himself seems to reinforce this connection when he introduces Verginius as "father of the virgin" (*pater virginis, L. Verginius* [3.44.2]). Whatever this wordplay tells us about the

140. Ogilvie 1965: 483. Cf. his earlier comment, "L. preserved the legal fustian but betrays his ignorance of the procedure of the law . . . by confusions" (1965: 478).

141. For another analysis of the motif of bodily control in these episodes, see Joshel 1992: 117–21.

142. Ogilvie 1965: 477.

historical tradition behind Livy's account, it has the more immediate thematic significance of clarifying that once the maiden ceases to be a *virgo,* she ceases to be Verginia.[143]

The first attempt within the narrative to counter Appius's plan relies on converting the "drama" of the trial into a different spectacle that will at once reveal the transgressive nature of Appius's regime and make even more explicit how the overthrow of order within the state has a direct consequence for each individual citizen. The first trial scene ends when Icilius emerges into the Forum to challenge Appius's decision. When the lictors attempt to drive him away, he delivers a speech that begins with the threat of revelation: "I shall have to be removed by the sword for you to keep in silence what you wish to be concealed." The promised revelation takes two forms. First Icilius portrays the attack on Verginia in a way that makes clear how the outrage to the family is the inevitable consequence of the loss of political *libertas.* "Even if you have taken away the protection of the tribunate and the right of *provocatio,* still your lust has no power [literally, "kingship"] against our children and wives."[144] (Verginius himself in the second trial scene will go even further. Not only the Roman social structure is at risk but even the distinction that separates men from animals. "Is it your will to rush into mating in the manner of sheep and wild beasts?" he asks the decemvir.)[145] At the same time, Icilius provokes a direct manifestation of Appius's tyranny by forcing the decemvir to use the traditional emblems of magisterial power against him: "Call all of your colleagues and lictors; order the rods and axes to be prepared. . . . Vent your rage on our backs and necks, but let chastity at least be preserved."[146] The imagined scene of the symbols of

143. A reminder that the connection between sexual integrity and free status was much more than just a literary construct can be found in an anecdote about a latter-day Verginius told by Valerius Maximus (6.1.6). Atius Philiscus was a freedman who as a slave had performed sexual services for his master. When he discovered that his own daughter had been sexually promiscuous, however, he promptly killed her. Valerius adopts a perspective unsympathetic to Philiscus and tells the story as an example of hypocrisy; having been a prostitute himself, Philiscus becomes an "avenger of purity" (*vindex pudicitiae*). But surely Philiscus's motivation was not merely a newfound prudishness. Even though there is no question of rape here, the girl's lack of sexual purity symbolically marks a return to the slavery that her father has escaped.

144. 3.45.8: *Non si tribuniciam auxilium et provocationem plebi Romanae, duas arces libertatis tuendae, ademistis, ideo in liberos quoque nostros coniugesque regnum vestrae libidini datum est.*

145. 3.47.7: *placet pecudum ferarumque ritu promisce in concubitus ruere?* Notice again how political terminology again reinforces the link between lust and the abuse of power. *Placet* is the word used to describe an official decree.

146. See also Joshel 1992: 123–24.

Roman *libertas* being directed against the bodies of individual Roman citizens fighting for their wives and daughters is made all the more striking by the implied contrast with the actions of Brutus himself, the "fierce avenger of violated purity" (*pudicitia*),[147] who unbound the fasces to punish his own sons. Livy points out the effectiveness of Icilius's strategy by commenting on the crowd's response. "The multitude was aroused, and a confrontation seemed inevitable." Appius, however, is able to defuse the danger in a characteristic manner. He tries to portray Icilius's complaint as a danger to public order, again maintaining the fiction that he is only behaving as a magistrate should. "Appius said that it was not a case of Icilius defending Verginia, but rather that a disorderly man, in pursuit of a tribunate, was looking for an opportunity to make trouble" (3.46.2).

The crisis, when it comes, will take the form of a scene very much like the spectacle that Icilius imagines. Appius, having ruled in favor of his *cliens,* does indeed employ his lictor to part the crowd with words that seem to echo Icilius's challenge: "Go, lictor, remove the crowd and clear a path for a master to take possession of his property" (*I, lictor submove turbam et da viam domino ad prehendendum mancipium* [3.48.3]).[148] Indeed, Livy says that he "thunders forth" this command, as though he were now taking on the role of Jupiter himself.[149] But at the same time that Appius assumes the mantle of public authority most directly, the object against which this force is directed appears at her most powerless. The crowd moves apart to reveal Verginia "deserted, a prey [*praeda*] to injustice [*iniuria*]."[150] As the pretense of legitimacy is denounced as *iniuria,* the description of Verginia as *praeda* recalls her father's denunciation of the decemvir's actions as reducing human beings to the level of beasts. The instant that she loses her *libertas,* she is at once reduced to the status of a foreign captive, or indeed, of an animal.

The sequel to Appius's action, Verginius's killing of his daughter while formally cursing the decemvir and proclaiming her *libertas,* marks the point where the spectacle of impure sacrifice explicitly takes the place of the false trial. The knife with which the deed is performed has been

147. 2.7.4: *acer ultor violatae pudicitiae,* so he is mourned at his funeral by the Roman *matronae.*

148. The imperatives recall Icilius's own *iube.* Also Appius begins his speech in the previous sentence with *proinde,* the same initial conjunction that Icilius had used in the same sentence.

149. 3.48.3: *intonuisset*

150. 3.48.3: *desertaque praeda iniuriae puella stabat.*

snatched from a butcher shop and thus implies the mixing of human and animal blood that, as in the scene of the Samnite initiation ritual, serves as the most obvious sign of corrupted sacrifice.[151] At a deeper level, it is the failure to maintain the boundaries that distinguish the victim from the sacrificer and the other participants that results in the breakdown of legitimate sacrifice. Such transgressions are doubly apparent here. The victim not only belongs to the same species as her killer; she is even a member of the same family. Thus the violations of sacrificial practice here replicate precisely the violations of the social order that resulted from the decemvir's actions. The *gens* disintegrates, and the distinction between man and beast breaks down. What is more, the ritual corruption of Verginia's death complements exactly the dynamics of the relationship between Verginia and the crowd of spectators when Appius first sends the lictor against her. There, too, the crowd identified closely with the victim; indeed, she was physically placed among them so that the violence threatened by the lictor was quite literally directed against them.[152] This is just the kind of sympathy that the substitution of a nonhuman sacrificial victim was designed to moderate.

Livy is unique among ancient sources in describing the exact location where the death of Verginia took place: "near the temple of Venus Cloacina by the shops that are now called new" (3.48.5). The presence of a shrine is one of the details that contributes to the sacralization of the scene, but the cult associations of Venus Cloacina have a special relevance for the Verginia episode. Pliny derives the title Cloacina, not from

151. 3.48.5: *ab lanio cultro arrepto.* The sacrificial nature of the act is also suggested by the proximity of a temple and confirmed by the use of Verginia's blood specifically to "consecrate" Appius (3.48.5). Cf. Ogilvie 1965: 488, on the connotations of this phrase: "Verginius was neither a priest nor a magistrate with sanction of official ceremony to conduct a *consecratio capitis.* Yet L. means evidently to convey something more potent than a curse. By writing *consecro* he hints at magic, where a mere curse or *exsecratio* would be dramatically too mild. There is nothing resembling it in the narrative of Dionysius."

152. Throughout his narrative, Livy has described the crowd as quite literally enveloping Verginia. A crowd forms immediately when M. Claudius claims Verginia (3.44.7). A way must must be made through it for Icilius (3.45.5). Before the second trial, the entire *civitas* is said to have gathered in the Forum, and Verginius goes about within it seeking support for his cause (3.47.1 ff.). Finally, after the decree has been issued, M. Claudius's first attempt to take possession of Verginia is repelled by the "globe" of women and supporters who encompass her (3.47.8). This imagery, as in the account of the old soldier's complaints discussed in ch. 4, provides a visual corollary for the idea that the sufferings of the individual victim in this case are directly connected to the ills of the state as a whole; that she represents the state in microcosm. As the *civitas* gathers around her in these scenes, so the restored Republic will soon be reconstituted when the sight and story of her death are transmitted to an everlarger circle of spectators.

sewer (*cloaca*), but from the ancient word for purification (*cluere*),[153] and purification, under two seemingly contradictory circumstances, seems to have been this Venus's particular function.[154] The myrtle branch, one of the two cult symbols the goddess holds, is connected both with marriage and with the purification of a warrior stained with the blood of the battlefield. The link between the transition from an unmarried to a married state and the motion from war to peace was made in the aetiological legend that Pliny gives for the temple. This was said to be the place where the Romans and the Sabines, who had been preparing to do battle after the rape of the Sabine women, laid down their arms and purified themselves with myrtle. Thus the cultic associations of the shrine provide an ideal setting to reveal all of the transgressions involved in the Verginia story. Verginia is not a bride being prepared for marriage, but a maiden being killed to prevent her enslavement. Her father is not purified from the blood of the battlefield on his return to the city. On the contrary, he flees the city for the battlefield stained with the blood of his daughter. Even more important, the aetiological legend of the temple links the shrine to an episode in Roman history where marriage led directly to the formation of the larger social bonds through which the Roman state grew. As such, the rape of the Sabine women perfectly exemplifies the importance of "the love of wives and children," which Livy in the preface to book 2 had claimed as one of the forces that ensured harmony within the newly liberated *res publica*. In this case, however, it is the violation of the marriage bond that reveals the disintegration of social order within the state and correspondingly leads to an armed rebellion.

Ogilvie suggests that the story of Verginia might itself be regarded as the aetiological legend behind the cult.[155] But as we have seen another, and far more appropriate, story already existed to account for its origins.[156] What is more, Livy is the only author who explicitly mentions Verginia in connection with the shrine. Dionysius by contrast, whose account is in every way much more detailed than Livy's, mentions only the Forum and the butcher's shop.[157] Thus, rather than simply reflecting an

153. Plin. *HN* 15.119.

154. The following description of the cult represents the synthesis of Coarelli 1986: 84–89, with further bibliography.

155. Ogilvie 1965: 487, with bibliography.

156. Although, of course, there is no reason that there could not have been conflicting legends.

157. Dion. Hal. 12.37.5. See also Diod. 12.24, where again only the butcher shop is mentioned.

essential element in the story, the reference to the shrine of Venus Cloacina can be regarded as part of Livy's use of Roman religious traditions as a context that throws into relief the anomalous and transgressive nature of the episode.

• • •

At the same time that Livy sets the episode against the background of ritual practice, he contextualizes it in another sense as well. The reference to the shops "that are now called new" allows his audience to locate the scene precisely within the landscape of the contemporary city. I suggest that both the allusions to cult and sacrifice and the geographic specificity of his description serve the same ends. Although the Forum has changed its aspect over the centuries since the decemvirate, the historian's text overcomes temporal distance and makes the event he describes visible in the present. At the same time, the city itself, although it no longer preserves the exact configurations of its past, nevertheless gains a new series of historical associations. So the religious rituals that Livy uses as models for the construction of scenes like the death Verginia themselves create a visual link to the past. Each sacrifice or ritualized performance ideally reproduces an endless series of identical rituals extending backwards through time. The *rex sacrorum* who flees the Forum every year continually reenacts the exile of the Tarquins, at least for those who, like Livy's audience, know the story. Indeed, Livy's text incorporates both the synchronic and diachronic aspects of such occasions, at once providing the historical background that gives each performance meaning and, in the case of the sacrificial scenes examined in the preceding two chapters, shaping his record of the past to convey the immediate experience of ritual. By contrast, the decemvir Appius, by superimposing a *fabula* on the public procedures of the trial, disguises his actions as magistrate, making them inaccessible to the viewer, at the same time as he inverts the moral precedents that should govern them.

Appendix: Tanaquil and the Accession of Servius Tullius

If Tarquinius Superbus's reign has an "end like its beginnings," the same can also be said for the reign of Servius Tullius himself since the circumstances of his deposition also recall the events that brought him to the throne. Then, too, it was within the *domus* of the previous king, Tarquinius Priscus, a region closed to public view, that the decisive actions occurred, and again it was a woman, Tanaquil, the king's wife, who assumed an active role both in ensuring Servius's succession and in mediating between the *domus* and the *populus*. In this appendix, I argue that the similarities between the situations of Servius and Superbus can be subject to two antithetical interpretations, which correspond to the profoundly ambivalent nature of Livy's portrait of the kingship itself. On the one hand, it is possible to read the actions of Tanaquil, as indeed Superbus himself will do, as calling into question the legitimacy of Servius's position: he received the throne through a "woman's gift" (*muliebre donum*).[158] In this case, Tullia's actions will appear only as a more extreme and heinous version of what the earlier queen had done, and the entire reign of Servius, although infinitely more "constitutional" than Tarquin's own *regnum,* will nevertheless form part of a larger pattern of degeneration, within which each reign appears to violate the proprieties of succession to a greater degree than its predecessor. On the other hand, the similarities between the conduct of Tanaquil and Tullia also throw into relief the important differences between their actions in a manner that reconfirms the impression that the reign of Tarquin, with its overprivileging of family concerns over public legitimacy, does indeed constitute an anomaly within the course of Roman history.

Livy's narrative offers two possibilities for Servius's origins. Initially he is presented as the son of a slave, as Tarquin himself will later claim, but Livy almost immediately presents an alternate account of the king's ancestry, to which, he says, he himself inclines: Servius's mother was the wife of the chief (*princeps*) of the Latin town of Corniculum (1.39.5).[159]

158. 1.47.10: *non interregno, ut antea, inito, non comitiis habitis, non per suffragium populi, non auctoribus patribus, muliebri dono regnum occupasse.*

159. In supporting this version, Livy complements Tanaquil's own interpretation of the oracle by removing Servius from the ranks of *servi* and recording him within his history as "regal." So, too, Livy's narrative appears determined by Tanaquil's interpretation of the miraculous flame in much the same way that Papirius Cursor's interpretations of divine signs shape the historian's treatment of the battle of Aquilonia (ch. 2, sec I): Tanaquil's claim that the flame signifies Servius's future greatness receives explicit affirmation neither from any character within the narrative nor from the historian himself. Yet Livy seems to construct his account in accordance with her statement that Tullius has been singled out by the gods. Thus he begins his description of Tullius's rise to prominence with the phrase *evenit facile quod dis cordi esset* (1.39.4).

When the town was captured by the Romans, she was recognized among the captives, and saved from slavery, by the Roman queen Tanaquil and gave birth to a son. Later, when this child was asleep within the palace, a miraculous fire burst out around his head, and only went out when he woke up. Again Tanaquil intervenes. Leading her husband to a secluded place, she interprets the omen of the flame for him: Servius is destined to be a "light" in doubtful times and to provide the "fuel" (*materies*) for great glory.[160] As a result, Servius is raised as a *liber* and eventually becomes the king's son-in-law.

Later, when Tarquinius Priscus has been mortally wounded by the jealous sons of Ancus Marcius, the king whom he himself succeeded, Tanaquil takes action again. She closes off the king's house from the people who have been attracted by the disturbance and, although the king is in fact near death, proceeds to treat him, "as though there were some hope" (1.41.1) Meanwhile, Servius Tullius is summoned. Taking him by the right hand, Tanaquil begs him to avenge the king's murder and delivers the following exhortation:

The kingdom belongs to you, Servius, if you are a man, and not to those who with alien hands have done this foul deed. Rouse yourself and take as leaders the gods who portended that this head would be famous by surrounding it with a divine fire. Now let that celestial flame rouse you: now wake up indeed. We, too, reigned, though only immigrants. Think of who you are, not whence you were born. If your wits are dazed by the suddenness of the event, then follow my advice. [1.41.3]

With these deeply ambiguous words, Tanaquil can be seen as offering a precedent for Tullia's later incitement of Tarquinius Superbus to overthrow her father. Tanaquil too seems motivated by dynastic considerations, the fear that her husband's murderers will take the throne. And the phrase with which the speech ends, "follow my advice" (*mea consilia sequere* [1.41.3]) claims an unseemly degree of personal influence over Servius and contrasts with her earlier wish that Servius "follow the gods as leaders" (*deosque duces sequere* [ibid.]). Indeed, in the control she exerts over Tarquinius Superbus Tullia sees herself as emulating the example of Tanaquil, who, "though only a foreign woman, bestowed two kingships in succession, first upon her husband then upon her son-in-law" (1.47.6).

But Tullia's reference to Tanaquil as a model for her own attempt to usurp public authority in the service of personal and dynastic motives

160. 1.39.3: *lumen . . . rebus nostris dubiis, . . . proinde materiam ingentis publice privatimque decoris.*

also serves to remind the reader of the crucial differences between Tanaquil's speech and the one she has just delivered. Tullia argues that Tarquin should reign precisely by virtue of his birth and heritage: "Your paternal *penates,* the *imago* of your father . . . and the *nomen* Tarquinius create and proclaim you king" (1.47.4). Tanaquil had made exactly the opposite point when she exhorted Tullius not to think of his origins but of "who he was." So, too, while Tullia's speech leads to the violent overthrow of the reigning king in favor of the heir of the previous dynasty, Tanaquil's speech is aimed at foiling just such a plot. For Tanaquil, the demands of the *domus* are the same as those of the state, rather than opposed, as they are in Tullia's promotion of her husband.

The gestures with which Tanaquil accompanies her address to Servius also suggest that Tanaquil acts not to disrupt but to preserve the continuity of legitimate public authority. The queen begins by taking Servius's right hand, a gesture appropriate to the act of supplication, but one that also recalls the emphasis on hands and on physical contact that accompany the official inauguration of a new king, as Livy described it at the accession of Numa. During that procedure, the augur first holds the *lituus* in his right hand (1.18.7). Then, after marking out the grid of *regiones* for the taking of omens, he moves the *lituus* to his left hand and touches the king's head with his right.[161] The act of touching the head of the new king is further emphasized in the accompanying prayer to Jupiter, when the augur uses the phrase "Numa Pompilius whose head I hold."[162] Similarly, Tanaquil herself refers to the head of Servius Tullius, and the demonstrative pronoun *hoc* with which she describes his *caput* can suggest that she either points to his head or perhaps touches it.[163] What is more, this mention of Servius Tullius's head recalls the sign from the gods confirming Tullius's accession, which Tanaquil herself had interpreted. Thus Tanaquil's actions fulfill precisely the same functions as an *inauguratio:* she affirms through the interpretation of signs that the gods approve Servius and consequently proclaims him king.[164]

These recollections of the official ceremony by which a new king was inaugurated again allow two antithetical interpretations: Obviously,

161. 1.18.8: *lituo in laevam manum translato, dextra in caput Numae posita.*

162. 1.18.9: *Numam Pompilium cuius ego caput teneo.* For the ritual significance of this gesture as part of an augmentative rite, see Linderski 1986: 2289–91.

163. Ogilvie 1965: 162, describes the phrase as a "striking circumlocution" and suggests that its purpose here is to give particular emphasis to the head of Servius, as the locus of the omen that Tanaquil interpreted.

164. 1.41.3: *Tuum . . . est regnum;* cf. 1.18.9 of Numa: *quibus* [sc. *auspiciis*] *missis declaratus rex.* Of course, the flame around Servius Tullius's head was not comparable to the

Tanaquil has no authority to act as augur, and so her performance can be read as an illegitimate substitute for the actual *inauguratio,* which Servius lacks. So too, in what can only be seen as a perversion of legitimate procedure, Tullia herself will attempt to "proclaim" Tarquinius Superbus king.[165] Alternatively, Tanaquil's actions, which prevent the usurpation of the throne by the king's murderers, provide the only mechanism by which the will of the gods, as revealed in the omen of the sacred fire about Tullius's head, can be revealed and actualized. Thus her private gesture of supplication takes on the form and function of a public *inauguratio* just as the oath Brutus exacts after the death of Lucretia converts a private misfortune into a public event and provides the basis for the oath with which each Roman consul would take office.

The same function of mediating between the public and the private that Tanaquil assumed when she noticed and interpreted the miraculous fire playing about the head of the *servus* Servius, emerges again in the most controversial of all Tanaquil's actions: Although Tarquinius Priscus is already *moribundus,* Tanaquil gives an address before the people "from the window of the upper part of the house" in which she not only deceives them by claiming that the king is recovering but also pretends that he has empowered Servius to act as his representative. It is only after the authority of Servius is well established that the king's death is revealed. Again Tanaquil's presentation of herself to the *populus* offers both a precedent and a foil for the spectacle of Tullia before the senate house. Tanaquil's claim to be acting as a representative of the king serves as a reminder that her deception of the people results only from her own initiative. Thus her public appearance here can be read, in the same way as the spectacle of Tullia before the senate house, as a sign of a woman's usurpation of authority both within the state and within the home, figured by Tanaquil's position in the "upper part" (*superior pars*) of the house.[166] Correspondingly, the authority of Servius Tullius himself takes a form that initially resembles a tyranny; like Tarquinius Superbus later, Servius has to surround himself with an armed guard.[167] Conversely, we

---

precise *auspicia impetrativa* required in the ceremony of *inauguratio* (see Linderski 1986: 2293 ff.); it was a *prodigium* (1.39.1), needing active interpretation rather than simple acknowledgment.

165. 1.48.5: *regemque prima appellavit.*

166. Ogilvie 1965: 162–63, views the description of the *domus,* with its uncharacteristic second story, as an anachronistic addition that betrays the use of motifs drawn from Hellenistic history to elaborate the account of regal Rome.

167. 1.41.6; cf. 1.49.2 of Tarquin.

have seen many examples where the construction of deceptive appearances resulted in the salvation of the state, and where the false impression given by an *imperator* or king was ultimately validated as true. So here the *species* put forward by Tanaquil, like the deceptive speech of Tullus Hostilius in the battle against the Albans, functions to encourage the Romans and to dishearten their enemies; the sons of Ancus, who are also fooled by her words and alarmed by the resulting authority of Servius Tullius, consequently go into exile (1.41.9). If Tanaquil herself lacks the *imperium* possessed by the king, nevertheless her claims are not only based on the omens sent by the gods but later affirmed in Servius Tullius's first military campaign, where his "strength and fortune gleam" (*enituit* [1.42.3], a recollection of the literal gleam produced by the magic flame), and from which he returns to Rome proven to be king (*haud dubius rex* [ibid.]) by the destruction of the enemy.

The geographical specificity with which Livy describes the scene also provides a historical context within which Tanaquil's actions appear in accord with Roman traditions. Curiously, Tarquinius Priscus is imagined as living not in the *regia* but in a house on the Palatine "by the temple of Jupiter Stator," which was built by Romulus as a result of a vow Livy himself records (1.12.6).[168] The associations of this divinity, who "stayed" the Roman's flight after the Sabines had gained control of the citadel, make clear that Tanaquil's speech similarly has the effect both of calming the crowd's fears and defeating the conspiratorial sons of Ancus. But the circumstances in which the temple was vowed have a further relevance for Tanaquil's situation. The Roman victory that followed after their halt on the Palatine marked the end of the conflict with the Sabines that began with the rape of the Sabine women. In the sequel to the victory, it is the Sabine women themselves who act as mediators between their fathers and husbands and bring about the unification of the two peoples and the beginning of the joint kingship of Romulus and Titus Tatius. Thus the events this *monumentum* records establish a precedent for the crucial intervention of women in public crises and for the incorporation of outsiders, like Servius Tullius, not only as members of the Roman state but even as rulers of it.[169]

168. Ogilvie 1965: 162–63.

169. For a similar interpretation of the significance of the temple of Jupiter Stator and the use Cicero made of it in the First Catilinarian oration, see Vasaly 1993: 41–48. In his own invocation of the temple as the setting for Tanaquil's speech, Livy may not only be following a Ciceronian precedent but also relying on his audience's awareness of the events of the Catilinarian conspiracy itself to provide yet another example of an instance where the revelations of a woman, Cicero's informant Fulvia, were crucial in preserving the state.

Epilogue

I began with Livy's reference to the *exempla* his history would offer its readers; I shall end with the *exempla* promised by another historian over one hundred years later. "But still the age was not so destitute of virtues that it did not also produce good *exempla:* there are mothers who accompanied their banished children, wives who followed their husbands into exile, daring friends, faithful sons-in-law, slaves whose loyalty remained bold in the face of torture, great men who endured their fates bravely, and deaths equal to the lauded demises of the ancients."[1] These words from the preface of Tacitus's *Histories* serve as an illuminating contrast to the aspect of Livy's narrative that has been at the core of this book: the idea that the historian's representation of the past brings his readers into contact with a *res publica* whose continual ability to reproduce itself transcends the calamities of time. The *exempla* to which Livy directs attention cannot apply to individuals outside the context of the state; they are for "you and your *res publica.*" So the *exempla* and public spectacles we have examined, like the duels in book 7 or Brutus's execution of his sons, focus on the moment when an individual's own bonds to the state are established. Tacitus's *exempla,* however, have nothing to do with state-building. On the contrary, good examples are now those that illustrate how the smaller social units that define each Roman individual, the family and personal freedom of will that enables disasters to be boldly faced, can preserve their integrity even when chal-

1. Tac. *Hist.* 1.3.

lenged by the hostility of the state. The motion of the Tacitean sentence through exile to death and from the loyalty of wives and friends to individual endurance traces a trajectory of disintegration that precisely reverses the progression from the *domus* to the forum which marked Livy's account of Lucretia's funeral.

Tacitus's redefinition of what constitutes a "good *exemplum*" springs in turn from a more fundamental transformation in the relationship between the historian's construction of the past and the authority structure of the state itself. Scenes like Brutus's execution of his sons not only put on display the moral alignment that makes patriotism possible, but enable those who watch such spectacles to experience a similar redefinition of loyalties. Livy's history becomes an extension of this system of representations, and the depiction of public spectacle as a performative process supplies the model that allows his own text to become an agent of civic regeneration. But the interdependence between public *imperium* and the historian's text that underlies the Livian conception has already been ruled out by Tacitus. Earlier in the preface to the *Histories,* Tacitus establishes a connection between the way history is written and the political system it describes or under which it is produced. Many historians, he claims, have written about the period before Actium, and the *libertas* and eloquence with which they write mirrors the *libertas* of the Republic. However, after power passed into the hands of Augustus alone, the multitude of historians correspondingly diminished, and their own freedom of expression was broken.[2] Not only, therefore, does the integrity with which earlier historians wrote provide an index of the degree of *libertas* within the state itself, but at a more fundamental level the communicative power of their works depends upon public *libertas.* Under the Empire, "*veritas* has been broken in many ways."[3] The ability of a historian's text to provide a valid and accurate representation of the state, of the kind that allows Livy's construction of his history as an unmediated image of the Republic itself, thus becomes impossible.[4] Nor

2. Ibid. 1.1: *nam post conditam urbem octingentos et viginti prioris aevi annos multi auctores rettulerunt, dum res populi Romani memorabantur pari eloquentia ac libertate: postquam bellatum apud Actium atque omnem potentiam ad unum conferri pacis interfuit, magna illa ingenia cessere.*

3. Ibid.: *veritas pluribus modis infracta.* Cf. Raaflaub and Samons 1990: 437, for a different explanation of why "a change in the form of government and the emergence of a new center of power would necessarily create tensions in historiography," one that focuses on the political status of the historians themselves.

4. Where Tacitus positions Livy within his schema of decline is nicely ambiguous. The phrase *post conditam urbem* seems to recall Livy's title and thus to situate him with the prac-

should the decay of historiography under the Empire described by Tacitus be understood simply as a result of repression and flattery. As we saw in chapter 5, Livy himself stresses the link between *libertas* and history as a genre by connecting lapses in *libertas* within the state, like the reign of Tarquinius Superbus or the decemvirate, with disruptions in the course of his narrative.

Tacitus's introduction conveys an idea of Livian history not only as the product of a vanished era,[5] but indeed as a text written in a different language; the forms and expressions that Livy uses to convey the political structure of the *res publica* and to situate his narrative within it have lost or radically changed their meanings. Thus the divine prodigies that, in the context of Livy's *History,* provide manifestations of the gods' role as *auctores* of Roman *imperium* and draw attention to the historian's own preservation of tradition, will acquire an antithetical meaning in Tacitus. No longer signs of the gods' engagement in public affairs, prodigies pro-

---

titioners of Republican *libertas* and *eloquentia.* Indeed, *eloquentia* is a quality for which Livy is praised in the speech Tacitus places in the mouth of Cremutius Cordus (*Ann.* 4.34). However, chronologically, of course, Livy's work dates from after Actium. Similarly, in *Annales* 1.1, Livy's work would seem to mark the cusp of the transition. Is he one of the *clari scriptores* who narrate the events of the "old Roman people"? As we have seen (ch. 1, sec. I), *clarus* is an adjective commonly applied to Livy, but, on the other hand, Livy's own preface explicitly sets his work apart from that of noble and socially distinguished writers (*praef.* 3), which is another meaning of *clarus.* Or should he be classed among those writers who described the reign of Augustus? And if so, was he among the *decora ingenia,* or was his narrative marred by *gliscens adulatio* (see Badian 1993: 19–29)? On the demise of Republican history under Augustus, see also the comments of Raaflaub and Samons 1990: 437 f.

5. Many turns of phrase in the first chapters of Tacitus's *Histories* can be read as invocations of Livy's preface. Livy begins by depicting himself as one of a crowd of writers; Tacitus writes in a solitude, after "those great talents have ceased." Whereas Livy insists that no republic has been "richer in good examples" (*ditior bonis exemplis*) than Rome, Tacitus sets forth an *opus* "abounding in disasters" (*opimum casibus*). When he concedes that the period he treats is "not sterile in *virtutes,*" the phrase again recalls the language of fertility that marks Livy's treatment of *exempla* (cf. *frugiferum, praef.* 10). Tacitus's subject matter, too, described in a form and style recalling the summaries of events that in annalistic histories mark the beginning of a new year, can be read as the undoing of "the growth of empire" that Livy takes as the theme of the beginning of his work (see Ginsburg 1984: 100). Livy's first pentad ends with the salvation of the Capitoline from the Gauls and the preservation of the religious traditions upon which the state depends. By contrast, Tacitus promises to describe the "Capitol itself burnt by the hands of citizens." Another passage in which Tacitus seems to contrast his own work explicitly with Livy's, or at least Livian, history is *Ann.* 4.32, where the historian describes the contents of his *annales* as trivial things to recall (*levia memoratu*) in comparison with the huge wars, sieges, falls of kings, and internal strife that form the subject matter of those who wrote of earlier periods. As Ginsburg 1984: 7, points out, "these are the very subjects of *Ab urbe condita.*"

vide evidence only of their hostility. "For by no more terrible slaughters of the Roman people or by more just signs has it been demonstrated that the gods care not about our safety, but about our punishment."[6]

But taken on its own terms, Livy's preface itself presents a picture of the place of the historian's work in the sociopolitical realities of his age that is fully as complex as Tacitus's. One of the more paradoxical points of comparison between Livy's work and the *Histories* of Tacitus involves the two historians' allusions to their own times. While Livy offers a model of history as socially beneficial, he depicts the period in which he writes as the product of unchecked, and uncheckable, decline. Tacitus, by contrast, promises nothing but disasters, yet the events he narrates bring his reader to the verge of the "rare happiness of the era"[7] of Nerva and Trajan. Livy in his preface presents himself as profoundly out of sympathy with the decadent society of his own time. The reader is constantly struck by the contrast Livy draws between the current condition of the Roman state and the image of its development he presents. We are told that the description of early Roman history will be less appealing to those hastening on to their own time, but that Livy himself is delighted to be able "to remove himself from the sight of the misfortunes that the present age has seen" (*praef.* 5). Although the narrative will eventually end in these times, "when we can endure neither our vices nor their remedies," Livy insists on beginning his project with a prayer for a "fortunate outcome."

The inconsistencies of Livy's preface open up possibilities for many conflicting interpretations of the historian's own political views. Livy can be seen as a naive escapist, longing for the days of Numa and Cato, a conventional moralist, who has simply adopted a mind-set appropriate to his genre, or even an arch-pessimist, whose view of the ailments of the present as incurable deliberately undercuts all his promises of regeneration and calls into question the whole idea of the utility of his history. Problems of dating also play a role in the discussion.[8] If the preface was composed before Actium, it can be taken as the product of a longing for order soon to be satisfied by Augustus's own restoration of the Repub-

6. Tac. *Hist.* 1.3: *non enim umquam atrocioribus populi Romani cladibus magisve iustis indiciis adprobatum est non esse curae deis securitatem nostram, esse ultionem.*

7. Tac. *Hist.* 1.1: *rara temporum felicitate.*

8. For evidence on the date of Livy's work, see ch. 1, n. 149. For surveys of scholarly opinions on Livy's attitudes toward the Augustan regime, see ch. 1, n. 51. For a discussion of how the question of date affects the interpretation of Livy's political stance, see Moles 1993: 150 ff.

lic. A later date, by contrast, might make it a lament for the lost Republic and an indictment of the new regime.

But rather than simply reflecting the historian's personal political opinions, the very incongruities of the preface play a crucial role in shaping the reader's response to the text that follows. By positing a vast gulf separating Rome as it is from Rome as it was, Livy raises precisely the question that his narrative sets out to answer: How did we get from there to here? Or rather, what connections are possible between Rome's past and its present? The preface seems to suggest that there can be none, but as the reader proceeds through the first decade, he will discover a Rome much more recognizable than he initially thought. Far from being unstained by the evils of the present, even the earliest periods of Roman history are animated by disputes and dangers that closely resemble the problems of the immediate past.[9] Nor, I suggest, should this phenomenon be regarded only as a legacy of the preoccupations of the Late Republican annalists who were Livy's "sources." So, too, as near as we can tell from what remains of his work, Livy deliberately avoids marking any specific date as the point that separates growth from decline.[10] Indeed, on occasions when the continuities of Roman history seem decisively broken by some cataclysmic event, like the Gallic invasion, Livy is at pains to reveal the traces of the earlier city that survive the change.[11] In this case, it is the sewer lines that both preserve the contours of archaic Rome in the contemporary city and form a pattern of meaning for the reader to "excavate" within the fabric of the text itself.[12] Sewers are mentioned three times in the first pentad, once when the Tarquins are deposed, once, implicit in the name Venus Cloacina, at the overthrow of the decemvirate, and finally at the conclusion of the fifth book when, as a result of Camillus's speech, the Romans have decided not to abandon the site of their devastated city. All three references therefore come at a moment when Rome has been restored from a period during which her native traditions have been usurped or concealed, and the sewers themselves become a sign of both continuity and "recovery."

9. Cf. also the comments of Moles 1993: 150, on how the relationship between past and present is constructed in the preface: "the past will be a mirror for the present, the present for the past—Livy will not in fact be shying away from full engagement with contemporary history. The escapism of section 5 has turned out to be a feint."

10. See Luce 1977: 270 ff. Miles 1986, esp. 2–13, demonstrates that decline itself is a recurrent phenomenon in Roman history.

11. Again, contrast the tendency of the prefaces to both of Tacitus's historical works to divide Roman history into discrete periods separated by particular watershed events.

12. See the final sentence of the first pentad, 5.55.5: *nunc.*

The problem posed by the preface concerning the continuity between the past and the present has a further dimension as well, for it also raises the question of how a literary representation, such as Livy's history, interacts with the real Rome within which his readers lived. At first it seems as though the Rome to which Livy turns to avoid the sight of the present can be regarded simply as an image. The *opus* that rises with prayers for a "fortunate outcome" is Livy's literary *opus,* and appears incompatible with the *opus* that is the state itself. But just as the narrative will show that the past is not in fact discontinuous with the present, so the distinctions between Livy's Rome and the real Rome become blurred. To recognize aspects of present experience in Livy's account of distant events is to overcome at once the temporal separation between past and present and the gap between literary representation and reality. Nor does the process operate only in one direction: at the same time that Livy's incorporation of elements familiar from the present makes his narrative more immediately apprehensible, a reading of his history transforms the way in which his readers respond to the city around them. We have seen, for example, how the topographical references included in the account of the death of Verginia both allow Livy's audience to visualize this event taking place in the Forum as they knew it and inscribes the historian's narrative upon the landscape of the real city.

Of the various strategies Livy uses to define his representation of the Roman past as something more than a literary construct, we have particularly examined his tendency to depict crucial actions, like Brutus's execution of his sons, in the form of public spectacles. By this device, Livy allows his readers to share the perspective of an audience within the narrative who experience such events directly, and are correspondingly subjected to the kinds of political influences that could be conveyed through the medium of vision. At the same time, in taking over the language of public spectacle as the means by which he represents the past, Livy sets his texts among the many forms of public display that were becoming an increasingly important locus for political discourse in Augustan Rome.

While I initially focused on the role of spectacle as a way of placing Livy's work in a nonliterary context, this approach can also provide the basis for a new way of connecting Livy's history to a whole range of other texts produced during the same period. Many contemporary writers, in a variety of genres, were using depictions of spectacle to articulate the relationship between their literary productions and the centers of political power. The boat race in book 5 of the *Aeneid* (5.114–285), for example, combines allusions to the chariot race in Homer's *Iliad* (23.287–650) with features of contemporary circus spectacle. Vergil thus raises the issue of the place of the literary text among other forms of social communication and opens the possibility that his poem could exercise a civic function analogous to the displays orchestrated in the actual circus.[13] The elegists offer an even richer field for this kind of investigation. When Propertius pictures himself reading the placards carried in Augustus's triumph while reclining in his mistress' arms, he claims for his poetry a complex place in the civic life of the state (Prop. 3.4.11–18). At first his position seems scandalous, and we might be tempted to read the poem as another assertion of the antithesis between the values of the elegist lover and the militarism enshrined in official public ceremonies. However, many of the Livian episodes analyzed earlier have made it clear that even the act of watching such a spectacle as a triumph constitutes a form of public participation. Ovid, though, takes the Propertian scene much further: the lover should impress his girlfriend by interpreting the placards for her, and, if he doesn't know what they represent, he can make something up (*AA* 1.219ff.). Here the elegist usurps the right to decide what counts as history and thus breaks the link between *imperium* and representation on which Livy's text depends.

The most dramatic reversal of the Livian paradigm comes when the systems of public communication themselves break down, when spectacle ceases to provide a viable means of contact between the spectator and the *res publica*. The first book of Tacitus's *Histories* again furnishes an example. The utter dissolution of the structures of public authority that marks the "Year of Four Emperors," the starting point of Tacitus's narrative, shows itself in the ineffectiveness of the modes of communication that proved so powerful in the early books of Livy. The figure of Galba himself, gnarled and impotent scion of a noble house, a Late Republican portrait bust come to life, epitomizes the worthlessness of once-honored appearances. His speeches in public have a noble simplicity, but leave the venal soldiery unimpressed. He manifests an *antiquus rigor,* which, Tacitus makes clear, accomplishes less than a little bribery would have done (*Hist.* 1.18). While the rebellion that will lead to his overthrow is being prepared, Galba is in fact conducting sacrifice in the Roman Forum. But no one pays much attention to him, and even Tacitus leaves him behind, turning to the far more significant events taking place in the soldiers' camp with the remark that "Galba, unaware, was troubling the gods of

13. See Feldherr 1995.

an empire that was now another's."[14] As the spectacle of sacrifice is here shown to be an irrelevant diversion, Galba's fall is accompanied by other indications of the impotence of traditional symbols of authority. Otho's rebellion is not to be quelled by the sights that Valerius Corvus used to prevent mutineers from entering the city in Livy's book 7.[15] Galba finally meets his end with gestures that seem a parody of several of the glorious deeds of the Republic, and perhaps even recall Livy's narrative of them. Right beside the *lacus Curtius,* where M. Curtius bravely plunged to his death, the emperor is cast from his litter (*Hist.* 1.41). Surrounded by soldiers, like Cicero at Formiae, he offers his neck to the hostile soldiers with edifying resolve.[16] Or, at least, that's what most people say. Here are plenty of reminiscences of the Roman past, but, like Tacitus's treatment of signs from the gods, they serve only to show how distant that past has become.[17]

14. Tac. *Hist.* 1.29: *ignarus interim Galba et sacris intentus fatigabat alieni iam imperii deos.*

15. Tac. *Hist.* 1.40: *nec illos Capitolii aspectus et imminentium templorum religio et priores et futuri principes terruere.* Cf. Corvus's reference to his *profectio* at Liv. 7.40.4–6.

16. Another Ciceronian touch is the cuirass Galba wears (*Hist.* 1.18.), an allusion perhaps to the one Cicero ostentatiously wore when presiding over the consular elections of 63 B.C.E. (Plut. *Cic.* 14.7).

17. For another interpretation of this scene, in the context of a discussion of Tacitus's own use of *monumenta,* see Rouveret 1991: 3070–72.

Bibliography

Alföldi, A. "Die Penaten, Aeneas und Latinus." *MDAI (R)* 78 (1971): 1–58.

Astin, A. E. *Cato the Censor.* Oxford, 1978.

Badian, E. "The Early Historians." In T. A. Dorey, ed., *The Latin Historians,* 1–37. London, 1966.

———. "Livy and Augustus." In W. Schuller, ed., *Livius: Aspekte seines Werkes. Xenia* 31 (1993): 9–38.

Balsdon, J. P. V. D. *Romans and Aliens.* London, 1979.

Barton, C. *The Sorrows of the Ancient Romans: The Gladiator and the Monster.* Princeton, N.J., 1993.

Bayet, J. *Tite-Live: Histoire Romaine I.* Paris, 1940.

Bayet, J., and Bloch, R. *Tite-Live: Histoire Romaine VII.* Paris, 1968.

Beard, M. "The Sexual Status of the Vestal Virgins." *JRS* 70 (1980): 12–27.

Beard, M., and Crawford, M. *Rome in the Late Republic.* Ithaca, N.Y., 1985.

Benveniste, E. *Vocabulaire des institutions indo-européennes.* Paris, 1969.

Bleicken, J. "*Coniuratio:* Die Schwurszene auf den Münzen und Gemmen der römischen Republik." *Jahrbuch für Numismatik und Geldgeschichte* 13 (1963): 51–70.

Bonjour, M. "Les personnages féminins et la terre natale dans l'épisode de Coriolan (Liv., 2.40)." *REL* 53 (1975a): 157–81.

———. *Terre natale.* Paris, 1975b.

Borzsák, I. "Spectaculum: Ein Motiv der tragischen Geschichtsschreibung bei Livius und Tacitus." *Acta Classica Debrecenensis* 9 (1973): 57–67.

Bowersock, G. W. "The Pontificate of Augustus." In K. Raaflaub and M. Toher, eds., *Between Republic and Empire,* 380–94. Berkeley and Los Angeles, 1990.

Briscoe, J. *A Commentary on Livy Books XXXIV–XXXVII.* Oxford, 1981.

Bruno, L. "'Crimen regni' e 'superbia' in Tito Livio." *GIF* 19 (1966): 236–59.

Brunt, P. A. *Italian Manpower, 225* B.C.–A.D. *14.* Oxford, 1971.

Burck, E. "Livius als augusteischer Historiker." In *Die Welt als Geschichte* 1 (Stuttgart, 1935), 448–87 (= *Wege zu Livius* [Darmstadt, 1967], 96–143).

———. "Aktuelle Probleme der Livius-Interpretationen." *Gymnasium,* suppl. 4 (1964a): 21–46.
———. *Die Erzählungskunst des T. Livius.* 2nd ed. Berlin, 1964b.
———, ed. *Wege zu Livius.* Darmstadt, 1967.
———. "Die Frühgeschichte Roms bei Livius im Lichte der Denkmäler." *Gymnasium* 75 (1968): 74–110.
———. "Livius und Augustus." *ICS* 16 (1991): 269–81.
Burkert, W. "Greek Tragedy and Sacrificial Ritual." *GRBS* 7 (1966): 87–121.
———. *Structure and History in Greek Mythology and Ritual.* Berkeley and Los Angeles, 1979.
———. *Homo Necans.* Translated by P. Bing. Berkeley and Los Angeles, 1983.
Cardauns, B. *Varro logistoricus über die Götterverehrung: Curio de cultu deorum.* Würzburg, 1960.
———. *M. Terentius Varro: Antiquitates Rerum Divinarum.* Wiesbaden, 1976.
———. "Varro und die römische Religion: Zur Theologie, Wirkungsgeschichte und Leistung der *Antiquitates Rerum Divinarum.*" *ANRW* II.16.1 (1978): 80–103.
Cichorius, C. *Römische Studien.* Leipzig, 1922.
Cizek, E. "À propos de la poétique de l'histoire chez Tite-Live." *Latomus* 51 (1992): 355–64.
Coarelli, F. "Architettura sacra e architettura privata nella tarda Repubblica. In *Architecture et société de la avchaïsme grec à la fin de la république romaine: Actes du colloque international organisé par le centre national de la recherche scientifique et l'École française de Rome,* 191–217. Rome, 1983.
———. *Il foro romano I.* 2d ed. Rome, 1986.
Cohen, D. "The Augustan Law on Adultery: The Social and Cultural Context." In D. I. Kertzer and R. P. Saller, eds., *The Family in Italy from Antiquity to the Present,* 109–26.New Haven, Conn., 1991.
Coleman, K. M. "Fatal Charades: Roman Executions Staged as Mythological Enactments." *JRS* 80 (1990): 44–73.
Combès, R. *Imperator: Recherches sur l'emploi et la signification du titre d'imperator dans la Rome republicaine.* Paris, 1966.
Cornell, T. J. "The *Annales* of Quintus Ennius." *JRS* 76 (1986a): 244–51.
———. "The Formation of the Historical Tradition of Early Rome." In I. S. Moxon, J. D. Smart, and A. J. Woodman, eds., *Past Perspectives: Studies in Greek and Roman Historical Writing,* 67–86.Cambridge, 1986b.
———. "The Value of the Literary Tradition Concerning Archaic Rome." In K. A. Raaflaub, ed., *Social Struggles in Archaic Rome,* 52–76.Berkeley and Los Angeles, 1986c.
Cornford, F. M. *Thucydides Mythistoricus.* London, 1907.
Corsaro, F. "La leggenda di Lucrezia e il regifugium in Livio e in Ovidio." In E. Lefèvre and E. Olshausen, eds., *Livius: Werk und Rezeption: Festschrift für Erich Burck zum 80. Geburtstag,* 107–23. Munich, 1983.
Crawford, M. H. *Roman Republican Coinage.* London, 1974.
Davidson, J. "The Gaze in Polybius." *JRS* 81 (1991): 10–24.
Deininger, J. "Livius und der Prinzipat." *Klio* 67 (1985): 265–72.
Deubner, L. "Die Devotion der Decier." *ARW* 8, suppl. (1905): 66–81.

——. "*Lustrum*." *ARW* 16 (1913): 127–136.

Dipersia, G. "Le polemiche sulla guerra sociale nell'ambasceria latina di Livio VIII, 4–6." *CISA* 3 (1975): 111–21.

Dumézil, G. *Horace et les Curiaces*. Paris, 1942.

——. "*Pères* et *fils* dans la légende de Tarquin le Superbe." In *Hommages à Joseph Bidez et à Franz Cumont*, 77–84. *Collection Latomus*, 2. Brussels, 1949.

——. *Archaic Roman Religion*. Chicago, 1970.

Dupont, F. *L'Acteur-roi*. Paris, 1985.

——. *Le Théâtre latin*. Paris, 1988.

——. "The Emperor-God's Other Body." In M. Feher, R. Naddaff, and N. Tazi, eds., *Fragments for a History of the Human Body*, 3: 396–420. New York, 1989.

Earl, D. C. *The Political Thought of Sallust*. Cambridge, 1961.

Eder, W. "Augustus and the Power of Tradition: The Augustan Principate as a Binding Link between Republic and Empire." In K. Raaflaub and M. Toher, eds., *Between Republic and Empire*, 71–122.Berkeley and Los Angeles, 1990.

Edwards, C. *The Politics of Immorality in Ancient Rome*. Cambridge, 1993.

Elsner, J. "Cult and Sculpture: Sacrifice in the Ara Pacis Augustae." *JRS* 81 (1991): 50–61.

Ernout, A., and Meillet, A. *Dictionnaire etymologique de la langue latine: Histoire des mots*. 3d ed. Paris, 1951.

Feichtinger, B. "*Ad Maiorem Gloriam Romae:* Ideologie und Fiktion in der Historiographie des Livius." *Latomus* 51 (1992): 3–33.

Feldherr, A. "Ships of State: *Aeneid V* and Augustan Circus Spectacle." *CA* (1995): 245–65.

——. "Livy's Revolution: Representation and Civic Identity in Livy's Brutus Narrative." In T. N. Habinek and A. Schiesaro, eds., *The Roman Cultural Revolution*. Cambridge, 1997.

Flobert, P. "La *patavinitas* de Tite-Live d'après les moeurs litteraires du temps." *REL* 60 (1981): 193–206.

Flower, H. I. "*Fabulae Praetextae* in Context: When Were Plays on Contemporary Subjects Performed in Republican Rome?" *CQ* 45.9 (1995): 170–90.

Fornara, C. *The Nature of History in Ancient Greece and Rome*. Berkeley and Los Angeles, 1983.

Fowler, W. W. *The Religious Experience of the Roman People*. London, 1911.

Fraenkel, E. *Horace*. Oxford, 1957.

Frézouls, E. "La Construction du *theatrum lapideum* et son contexte politique." In *Théâtre et spectacles dans l'antiquité*, 193–214.Leiden, 1981.

Frier, B. W. *Libri Annales Pontificum Maximorum: The Origins of the Annalistic Tradition. Papers and Monographs of the American Academy in Rome* 27 (1979).

Fries, J.. *Der Zweikampf: Historische und literarische Aspekte seiner Darstellung bei T. Livius. Beiträge zur Klassischen Philologie*, 169. Königstein, 1985.

Gabba, E. *Appiani: Bellorum Civilium Liber Quintus*. Florence, 1970.

Gantz, T. "The Tarquin Dynasty." *Historia* 24 (1975): 539–54.

Geertz, C. "Centers, Kings, and Charisma: Reflections on the Symbolics of Power." In *Local Knowledge: Further Essays in Interpretive Anthropology*, 121–46. New York, 1983. (= J. Ben-David and T. N. Clark, eds., *Culture and Its Creators: Essays in Honor of Edward Shils*. [Chicago, 1977],150–71.)

Gernet, L. "The Concept of Time in the Earliest Forms of Law." In *The Anthropology of Ancient Greece*, 216–39. Translated by J. Hamilton and B. Nagy. Baltimore, 1981. (=*Journal de Psychologie* 53 (1956): 379–406.)

Ginsburg, J. *Tradition and Theme in the Annals of Tacitus*. New York, 1981.

Girard, R. *Violence and the Sacred*. Translated by P. Gregory. Baltimore, 1977.

Goldhill, S. "The Great Dionysia and Civic Ideology." In J. J. Winkler and F. I. Zeitlin, eds., *Nothing to Do with Dionysus*, 97–129. Princeton, N.J., 1990.

Gordon, R. "The Veil of Power: Emperors, Sacrificers, and Benefactors." In M. Beard and J. North, eds., *Pagan Priests: Religion and Power in the Ancient World*, 201–31.London, 1990.

Greenblatt, S. J. *Shakespearean Negotiations*. Berkeley and Los Angeles, 1988.

Gries, K. "Livy's Use of Dramatic Speech." *AJP* 70 (1949): 118–41.

Gros, P. "La Fonction symbolique des édifices théâtraux dans le paysage urbain de la Rome augustéenne." In *L'Urbs: Espace urbain et histoire (1er siècle av. J.-C.–IIIe siècle ap. J.-C.)*, 319–43. *Actes du colloque international organisé par le Centre national de la recherche scientifique et l'École française de Rome* (Rome, 8–12 mai 1985). *Collection de l'École française de Rome*, 98 (1985).

Gruen, E. S. *Studies in Greek Culture and Roman Policy*. Leiden, 1990.

———. *Culture and National Identity in Republican Rome*. Ithaca, N.Y., 1992.

Habinek, T. N. "Sacrifice, Society, and Vergil's Ox-Born Bees." In M. Griffith and D. J. Mastronarde, eds., *Cabinet of the Muses: Essays on Classical and Comparative Literature in Honor of Thomas G. Rosenmeyer*, 209–23.Atlanta, 1990.

Haffter, H. "Rom und römische Ideologie bei Livius." *Gymnasium* 71 (1964): 236–50.

Hallett, J. P. *Fathers and Daughters in Roman Society: Women and the Elite Family*. Princeton, N.J.1984.

Hanson, J. A. *Roman Theater-Temples*. Princeton, N.J., 1959.

Hardie, P. *The Epic Successors of Virgil: A Study in the Dynamism of a Tradition*. Cambridge, 1993.

Harmon, D. P. "The Family Festivals of Rome." *ANRW* II.16.2 (1978): 1592–1603.

Harris, W. V. *War and Imperialism in the Roman Republic, 320–70* B.C. Oxford, 1979.

———. "The Roman Father's Power of Life and Death." In R. S. Bagnall and W. V. Harris, eds., *Studies in Roman Law in Memory of A. Arthur Schiller*, 81–95. Leiden, 1986.

Hartog, F. *The Mirror of Herodotus: The Representation of the Other in the Writing of History*. Translated by J. Lloyd. Berkeley and Los Angeles, 1988.

Heinze, R. *Die augusteische Kultur*. Leipzig, 1933.

Hellegouarc'h, J. *Le Vocabulaire latin des relations et des partis politiques sous la république*. Paris, 1972.

Henderson, J. "Livy and the Invention of History." In A. Cameron, ed., *History as Text: The Writing of Ancient History*. Chapel Hill, N.C.1989: 64–85.

Herrmann, P. *Der römische Kaisereid. Hypomnemata*, 20. Göttingen, 1968.

Heurgon, J. *Trois études sur le 'ver sacrum'. Collection Latomus*, 26. Brussels, 1957.

Hoffmann, W. "Livius und die römische Geschichtsschreibung." *Antike und Abendland* 4 (1954): 170–86.

Holford-Strevens, L. "More Notes on Aulus Gellius." *LCM* 9 (1984): 146–51.
——. *Aulus Gellius.* London, 1990.
Hölscher, T. "Römische Siegesdenkmäler der späten Republik." In H. A. Cahn and E. Simon, eds., *Tainia.* Mainz, 1980: 351–71.
Hopkins, K. *Death and Renewal.* Cambridge, 1983.
Instinsky, H. U. "Schwurszene und *Coniuratio.*" *Jahrbuch für Numismatik und Geldgeschichte* 14 (1964): 83–88.
Jaeger, M. "Custodia Fidelis Memoriae: Livy's Story of M. Manlius Capitolinus." *Latomus* 52 (1993): 350–63.
Jal, P. "Tite-Live et le métier d'historien dans la Rome d'Auguste." *Bull. de l'Assoc. Guillame Budé* 1990: 32–47.
Joplin, P. K. "Ritual Work on Human Flesh: Livy's Lucretia and the Rape of the Body Politic." *Helios* 17 (1990): 51–70.
Joshel, S. R. "The Body Female and the Body Politic: Livy's Lucretia and Verginia." In A. Richlin, ed., *Pornography and Representation in Greece and Rome,* 112–30. Oxford, 1992.
Kajanto, I. *God and Fate in Livy.* (=*Annales Universitatis Turkuensis* 64). Turku, Finland, 1957.
Kellum, B. A. "The City Adorned: Programmatic Display at the *Aedes Concordiae Augustae.*" In K. Raaflaub and M. Toher, eds., *Between Republic and Empire,* 276–307. Berkeley and Los Angeles, 1990.
Kidd, I. G. *Posidonius.* Cambridge, 1988.
Kissel, W. "Livius, 1933–78: Eine Gesamtbibliographie." *ANRW* II.30.2 (1982): 899–977.
Konstan, D. *Roman Comedy.* Ithaca, N.Y., 1983.
——. "Narrative and Ideology in Livy: Book I." *CA* 5 (1986): 198–216.
Köves-Zulauf, Th. "Zweikampfdarstellungen in der römischen Annalistik." In *Actes du Congrés de la FIAC I,* 447–51. Budapest, 1984.
Kraus, C. S. *Livy: Ab Urbe Condita, Book VI.* Cambridge, 1994a.
——. "'No Second Troy': Topoi and Refoundation in Livy, Book V." *TAPA* 124 (1994b): 267–90.
Latte, K. *Römische Religionsgeschichte.* Munich, 1960.
Leach, E. W. *The Rhetoric of Space: Literary and Artistic Representations of Landscape in Republican and Augustan Rome.* Princeton, N.J., 1988.
Leeman, A. D. "Le Genre et le style historique à Rome: Théorie et pratique." *REL* 33 (1955): 183–208.
——. "Are We Fair to Livy? Some Thoughts on Livy's Prologue." *Helikon* 1 (1961): 28–39.
——. *Orationis Ratio.* Amsterdam, 1963.
Lefèvre, E. "Argumentation und Struktur der moralischen Geschichtsschreibung der Römer am Beispiel von Livius' Darstellung des Beginns des römischen Freistaats (2.1–2.15)." In E. Lefèvre and E. Olshausen, eds., *Livius: Werk und Rezeption: Festschrift für Erich Burck zum 80. Geburtstag,* 31–57. Munich, 1983.
Leo, F. "Varro und die Satire." *Hermes* 24 (1889): 67–84.
Levene, D. S. *Religion in Livy.* Leiden, 1993.
Liebeschuetz, J. H. W. G. "The Religious Position of Livy's History." *JRS* 57 (1967): 45–55.

———. *Continuity and Change in Roman Religion.* Oxford, 1979.
Lincoln, B. *Discourse and the Construction of Society.* New York and Oxford, 1989.
Linderski, J. "The Augural Law." *ANRW* II.16.3 (1986): 2146–2312.
———. "Roman Religion in Livy." In W. Schuller, ed., *Livius: Aspekte seines Werkes. Xenia* 31 (1993): 53–70.
Lipovsky, J. *A Historiographical Study of Livy Books VI–X.* New York, 1981.
Luce, T. J. "The Dating of Livy's First Decade." *TAPA* 96 (1965): 209–40.
———. "Design and Structure in Livy, 5.32–55." *TAPA* 102 (1971): 265–302.
———. *Livy: The Composition of His History.* Princeton, N.J., 1977.
———. "Livy Augustus, and the *Forum Augustum.*" In K. Raaflaub and M. Toher, eds., *Between Republic and Empire,* 123–38. Berkeley and Los Angeles, 1990.
Lundström, V. "Kring Livius' liv och verk." *Eranos* 27 (1929): 1ff.
MacBain, B.. *Prodigy and Expiation: A Study in Religion and Politics in Republican Rome. Collection Latomus,* 177. Brussels, 1982.
MacCormack, S. G. *Art and Ceremony in Late Antiquity.* Berkeley and Los Angeles, 1981.
Magdelain, A. *Recherches sur l'imperium: La Loi curiate et les auspices d'investiture. Travaux et recherches de la faculté de droit et des sciences économiques de Paris: Serie Sciences historiques,* 12. Paris, 1968.
Mastrocinque, A. *Lucio Giunio Bruto: Ricerche di storia, religione e diritto sulle origini della repubblica romana.* Trento, 1988.
Mazza, M. *Storia e ideologia in Tito Livio.* Catania, 1966.
Mazzarino, S. *Il pensiero storico classico.* Vol. 2. Bari, 1966.
Mensching, E. "Zur Entstehung und Beurteilung von *Ab urbe condita.*" *Latomus* 45 (1986): 572–89.
Meuli, K. "Griechische Opferbräuche. In *Phyllobolia: Festschrift für P. von der Mühll,* 185–288. Basel, 1946.
Michel, J.-H. "La Folie avant Foucault: *Furor* et *Ferocia.*" *AC* 50 (1981): 517–25.
Miles, G. B. "The Cycle of Roman History in Livy's First Pentad." *AJP* 107 (1986): 1–33.
———. "*Maiores, Conditores,* and Livy's Perspective on the Past." *TAPA* 118 (1988): 185–208.
———. *Livy: Reconstructing Early Rome.* Ithaca, N.Y., 1995.
Moles, J. L. "Livy's Preface." *PCPS* 39 (1993): 141–68.
Momigliano, A. *Alien Wisdom: The Limits of Hellenization.* Cambridge, 1971.
———. "The Historians of the Classical World and Their Audiences: Some Suggestions." *ASNP* 8 (1978): 59–75. (=*Sesto contributo alla storia degli studi classici e del mondo antico,* I, *Storia e letteratura,* 149 [Rome, 1980]: 361–76.)
———. "The Theological Efforts of the Roman Upper Classes in the First Century B.C." *CP* 79 (1984): 199–211. (= *Ottavo contributo alla storia degli studi classici e del mondo antico, Storia e letteratura,* 169 [Rome, 1987]: 261–77.)
Mommsen, T. *Römisches Staatsrecht.* 3 vols. 3d ed. Leipzig, 1887.
———. *Römisches Strafrecht.* Leipzig, 1889.

Moore, T. J. *Artistry and Ideology: Livy's Vocabulary of Virtue.* Frankfurt a/M, 1989.
Morel, J.-P. "La *iuventus* et les origines du théâtre romain." *REL* 47 (1969): 208–52.
Münzer, F. "Opimius (5)." *PW* I.18.1 (1931): 677.
——. "Sulpicius (66)." *PW* II.4A.1 (1939): 811.
Neraudeau, J.-P. *La Jeunesse dans la literature et les institutions de la Rome républicaine.* Paris, 1979.
Nicolet, C. *The World of the Citizen in Republican Rome.* Translated by P. S. Falla. Berkeley and Los Angeles, 1980.
——. "Augustus, Government, and the Propertied Classes." In F. Millar and E. Segal, eds., *Caesar Augustus: Seven Aspects,* 89–128.Oxford, 1984.
——. *Space, Geography, and Politics in the Early Roman Empire.* Ann Arbor, Mich., 1991.
North, J. "Religion and Politics from Republic to Principate." *JRS* 76 (1986): 251–58.
——. "Diviners and Divination at Rome." In M. Beard and J. North, eds., *Pagan Priests: Religion and Power in the Ancient World,* 51–71.London, 1990.
Oakley, S. P. "Single Combat in the Roman Republic." *CQ* 35 (1985): 392–410.
Ogilvie, R. M. "*Lustrum condere.*" *JRS* 51 (1961): 31–39.
——. *A Commentary on Livy, Books 1–5.* Oxford, 1965.
Onians, R. B. *The Origins of European Thought about the Body, the Mind, the Soul, the World, Time, and Fate.* Cambridge, 1951.
Orr, D. G. "Roman Domestic Religion." *ANRW* II.16.2 (1978): 1557–91.
Packard, D. W. *A Concordance to Livy.* Cambridge, Mass., 1968.
Pauw, O. "The Dramatic Element in Livy's History." *Acta Classica* 34 (1991): 33–49.
Penella, R. J. "*Vires/Robur/Opes* and *Ferocia* in Livy's Account of Romulus and Tullus Hostilius." *CQ* 40 (1990): 207–13.
Peter, H. *Historicorum Romanorum Reliquiae.* 2d ed. Stuttgart, 1914.
Petersen, H. "Livy and Augustus" *TAPA* 92 (1961): 440–52.
Philippides, S. N. "Narrative Strategies and Ideology in Livy's 'Rape of Lucretia.'" *Helios* 10 (1983): 113–19.
Phillips, J. E. "Form and Language in Livy's Triumph Notices." *CP* 69 (1974): 265–73.
——. "Livy and the Beginning of a New Society." *CB* 55 (1979): 87–92.
——. "Current Research in Livy's First Decade." *ANRW* II.30.2 (1982): 998–1057.
Porte, D. *Les Donneurs du sacré.* Paris, 1989.
Poucet, J. "Temps mythiques et temps historiques: Les Origines et les premieres siècles de Rome." *Gerion* 5 (1987): 69–85.
Price, S. R. F. *Rituals and Power.* Cambridge, 1984.
Raaflaub, K. A., and Samons, L. J., II. "Opposition to Augustus." In K. A. Raaflaub and M. Toher, eds., *Between Republic and Empire,* 417–54.Berkeley and Los Angeles, 1990.
Rambaud, M. *Cicéron et l'histoire romaine.* Paris, 1953.
——. "Une Dèfaillance du rationalisme chez Tite-Live?" *L'Information littéraire* 7 (1955): 21–30.

Rawson, E. "Cicero the Historian and Cicero the Antiquarian." *JRS* 62 (1972): 33–45. (=*Roman Culture and Society* [Oxford, 1991]: 58–79.)
——. "The First Latin Annalists." *Latomus* 35 (1976): 689–717. (=*Roman Culture and Society* [Oxford, 1991]: 245–271.)
——. *Intellectual Life in the Late Roman Republic.* London, 1985.
——. "*Discrimina ordinum:* The *Lex Julia theatralis.*" *PBSR* 55 (1987): 83–114. (=*Roman Culture and Society* [Oxford, 1991]: 508–45.)
——. "The Antiquarian Tradition: Spoils and the Representation of Foreign Armour." In *Staat und Staatlichkeit in der fruhen römischen Republik.* Stuttgart, 1990: 157–73. (=*Roman Culture and Society* [Oxford, 1991]: 582–98.)
Robbins, M. A. S. "Livy's Brutus." *SPh* 69 (1972): 1–20.
Rosenstein, N. *Imperatores Victi.* Berkeley and Los Angeles, 1990.
Rouland, N. *Pouvoir politique et dépendance personnelle dans l'antiquité romaine: Genése et ròle des rapports de clientèle. Collection Latomus,* 166. Brussels, 1979.
Rouveret, A. "Les Lieux de la mémoire publique: Quelques remarques sur la fonction des tableaux dans la citè." *Opus* 6–8 (1987–89): 101–24.
——. "Tacite et les monuments." *ANRW* II.33.4 (1991): 3051–99.
Ruch, M. "Le Thème de la croissance organique dans la livre I de Tite-Live." *Studii Clasice* (Bucharest)10 (1968): 123–31.
——. "Le Thème de la croissance organique dans la pensée historique des Romains, de Caton à Florus." *ANRW* 1.2 (1972): 827–41.
Rumpf, A. "Die Entstehung des römischen Theaters." *MDAI (R)* 3 (1950): 40–50.
Ryberg, I. S. *Rites of the State Religion in Roman Art. MAAR,* 22. Rome, 1955.
Sacks, K. *Polybius on the Writing of History.* Berkeley and Los Angeles, 1981.
Saller, R. P. "*Familia, Domus,* and the Roman Conception of the Family." *Phoenix* 38 (1984): 336–55.
——. "*Pietas,* Obligation, and Authority in the Roman Family. In *Alte Geschichte und Wissenschaftgeschichte: Festschrift für Karl Christ zum 65. Geburtstag,* 393–410.Darmstadt, 1988.
Scafuro, A. "Livy's Comic Narrative of the Bacchanalia." *Helios* 16 (1989): 119–42.
Scheid, J. "Le Délit religieux dans la Rome tardo-républicaine." In *Le Délit religieux dans la cité antique,* 117–71.Rome, 1981.
——. "La spartizione a Roma." *Studi Storici* 4 (1984): 945–56.
——. *Religion et piété à Rome.* Paris, 1985.
Scullard, H. H. *Festivals and Ceremonies of the Roman Republic.* London, 1981.
Sherwin-White, A. N. *The Roman Citizenship.* 2d ed. Oxford, 1973.
Skutsch, O. *The Annales of Q. Ennius.* Oxford, 1985.
Solodow, J. B. "Livy and the Story of Horatius, 1.24–6." *TAPA* 109 (1979): 251–68.
Stadter, P. A. "The Structure of Livy's History." *Historia* 21 (1972): 287–307.
Strong, E. *Art in Ancient Rome.* New York, 1928.
Stübler, G. *Die Religiosität des Livius.* Stuttgart, 1941.
Sydenham, E. A. *The Coinage of the Roman Republic.* London, 1952.
Syme, R. *The Roman Revolution.* Oxford, 1939.

———. "Review of *Livius und der zweite punische Krieg*," by W. Hoffmann. *JRS* 35 (1945): 106–8.
———. "Livy and Augustus." *HSCP* 64 (1959): 27–87.
———. *Sallust.* Berkeley and Los Angeles, 1964.
———. *The Augustan Aristocracy.* Oxford, 1986.
Thomas, Y. "*Vitae necisque potestas:* Le Père, la cité, la mort." In *Du châtiment dans la cité*, 499–548. *Collection de l'école française de Rome,* 79. Rome, 1984.
Toher, M. "Augustus and the Evolution of Roman Historiography." In K. A. Raaflaub and M. Toher, eds., *Between Republic and Empire,* 139–54. Berkeley and Los Angeles, 1990.
Torelli, M. *Typology and Structure of Roman Historical Reliefs.* Ann Arbor, Mich., 1982.
Tränkle, H. "Der Anfang des römischen Freistaats in der Darstellung des Livius." *Hermes* 93 (1965): 311–37.
———. *Livius und Polybios.* Stuttgart, 1977.
Treggiari, S. *Roman Marriage:* Iusti coniuges *from the Time of Cicero to the Time of Ulpian.* Oxford, 1991.
Turner, V. *Dramas, Fields, and Metaphors.* Ithaca, N.Y., 1974.
———. "Social Dramas and Stories about Them." In W. J. T. Mitchell, ed., *On Narrative,* 137–64.Chicago, 1981.
———. *The Anthropology of Performance.* New York, 1986.
Ullmann, R. *La Technique des discours dans Salluste, Tite-Live et Tacite.* Oslo, 1927.
Van Rooy, C. A. "Livy VII.2 and Valerius Maximus 2.4.4: Two Notes." *Mnemosyne* IV.5 (1952): 236–42.
Vasaly, A. "Personality and Power: Livy's Depiction of the Appii Claudii in the First Pentad." *TAPA* 117 (1987): 203–26.
———. *Representations: Images of the World in Ciceronian Oratory.* Berkeley and Los Angeles, 1993.
Verbrugghe, G. P. "On the Meaning of *Annales,* On the Meaning of Annalist." *Philologus* 133 (1989): 192–230.
Versnel, H. P. *Triumphus: An Inquiry into the Origin, Development, and Meaning of the Roman Triumph.* Leiden, 1970.
———. "*Sacrificium lustrale:* The Death of Mettius Fufetius (Livy I, 28). Studies in Roman Lustration-Ritual, I." *MNIR* 37 (1975): 97–115.
———. "Two Types of Roman *devotio*." *Mnemosyne*, 4th ser., 29 (1976): 365–410.
———. "Self-Sacrifice, Compensation, and the Anonymous Gods." *Entretiens Fondation Hardt* 27 (1981): 135–85.
Veyne, P. "'Titulus praelatus': Offrande, solennisation et publicité dans les ex-voto gréco-romains." *RA* (1983): 2.281–300.
von Albrecht, M. *Masters of Roman Prose.* Translated by N. Adkin. Leeds, 1989.
von Haehling, R. *Zeitbezüge des T. Livius in der Ersten Dekade Seines Geschichtswerkes: Nec Vitia Nostra nec Remedia Pati Possumus. Historia Einzelschriften,* 61. Stuttgart, 1989.
Wagenvoort, H. *Roman Dynamism: Studies in Ancient Roman Thought, Language, and Custom.* Oxford, 1947.

——. "*Ludus poeticus*." In *Studies in Roman Literature, Culture, and Religion,* 30–42. Leiden, 1956. (=*LEC* 4 (1935): 108–20.)

Walbank, F. W. *A Historical Commentary on Polybius.* Oxford, 1957 (I), 1967 (II), 1979 (III).

——. "History and Tragedy." *Historia* 9 (1960): 216–34.

——. "Polemic in Polybius." *JRS* 52 (1962): 1–12.

——. *Polybius.* Berkeley and Los Angeles, 1972.

Walde, A. *Lateinisches etymologisches Wörterbuch.* 3d ed. Revised by J. B. Hofman. Heidelberg, 1938.

Walker, A. D. "*Enargeia* and the Spectator in Greek Historiography." *TAPA* 123 (1993): 353–77.

Wallace-Hadrill, A. *Houses and Society in Pompeii and Herculaneum.* Princeton, N.J., 1994.

Walsh, P. G. "The Literary Techniques of Livy." *RhM* 97 (1954): 97–114.

——. "Livy and Stoicism." *AJP* 79 (1958a): 355–75.

——. "The Negligent Historian: Howlers in Livy." *G&R,* n.s., 5 (1958b): 83–88.

——. *Livy: His Historical Aims and Methods.* Cambridge, 1961a.

——. "Livy and Augustus." *PACA* 4 (1961b): 26–37.

——. *Livy. Greece and Rome: New Surveys in the Classics,* 8. Oxford, 1974.

Waszink, J. H. "Varro, Livy, and Tertullian on the History of the Roman Dramatic Art." *Vigiliae Christianae* 2 (1948): 224–42.

——. "Zum Anfangsstadium der Römischen Literatur." *ANRW* I.2 (1972): 869–927.

Weinreich, O. "Zur römischen Satire." *Hermes* 51 (1916): 386–414.

Weinstock, S. *Divus Julius.* Oxford, 1971.

Weissenborn, W., and Müller, H. J. *Titi Livi Ab Urbe Condita Libri: Erklärende Ausgabe.* 7th ed. Berlin, 1962.

Wheeldon, M. J. "True Stories: The Reception of Historiography in Antiquity." In A. Cameron, ed., *History as Text: The Writing of Ancient History.* Chapel Hill, N.C. 1989: 36–63.

White, Hayden, *Metahistory: The Historical Imagination in Nineteenth-Century Europe.* Baltimore, 1973.

——. *Tropics of Discourse: Essays in Cultural Criticism.* Baltimore, 1978.

Wiedemann, T. "The *Fetiales:* A Reconsideration." *CQ* 36 (1986): 478–90.

Wilhelm, H. E. "Symbolisches Denken in Livius' Bericht über den Kampf der Horatier und Curiatier." *ARW* 33 (1936): 75–83.

Wirszubski, C. *Libertas as a Political Idea at Rome during the Late Republic and Early Principate.* Cambridge, 1950.

Wiseman, T. P. *Clio's Cosmetics: Three Studies in Greco-Roman Literature.* Leicester, 1979.

——. "Monuments and the Roman Annalists." In I. S. Moxon, J. D. Smart, and A. J. Woodman, eds., *Past Perspectives: Studies in Greek and Roman Historical Writing,* 87–100.Cambridge, 1986.

——. "The Origins of Roman Historiography." In *Historiography and Imagination: Eight Essays on Roman Culture,* 1–22. Exeter, 1994.

Wissowa, G. *Religion und Kultus der Römer.* Munich, 1902.

Woodman, A. J. *Rhetoric in Classical Historiography.* London, 1988.
———. "Vergil the Historian." In J. Diggle, J. B. Hall, and H. D. Jocelyn, eds., *Studies in Latin Literature and Its Tradition in Honour of C. O. Brink,* 132–45. *PCPS,* suppl. 15. Cambridge, 1989.
———. "Nero's Alien Capital." In T. Woodman and J. Powell, eds., *Author and Audience in Latin Literature,* 173–88. Cambridge, 1992.
Yavetz, Z. "The *Res Gestae* and Augustus' Public Image." In F. Millar and E. Segal, eds., *Caesar Augustus: Seven Aspects,* 1–36.Oxford, 1984.
Zanker, G. "*Enargeia* in the Ancient Criticism of Poetry." *RhM* 124 (1981): 297–311.
Zanker, Paul *The Power of Images in the Age of Augustus.* Translated by Alan Shapiro. Ann Arbor, Mich., 1988 .
Zehnacker, H. "Tragédie prétexte et spectacle romain." In *Théâtre et spectacles dans l'antiquité,* 31–48. Leiden, 1981.
Zetzel, J. E. G. "*Romane memento:* Justice and Judgment in *Aeneid* 6." *TAPA* 119 (1989): 263–84.
———. "Looking Backward: Past and Present in the Late Roman Republic." *Pegasus* 37 (1994): 20–32.
———. *Cicero:* De re publica, *Selections.* Cambridge, 1995.
Zinserling, G. "Studien zu den Historiendarstellungen der römischen Republik." *Wissenschaftliche Zeitschrift der Friedrich-Schiller Universität Jena* 9 (1960); *Gesellschafts- und sprachwissenschaftliche Reihe,* 4–5: 403–48.

General Index

Index Locorum

Designer:	Ina Clausen
Compositor:	Impressions Book and Journal Services, Inc.
Text:	10/13 Galliard
Display:	Galliard
Printing and binding:	Thomson-Shore, Inc.